P9-BAT-847

PRAISE FOR STEVE OSBORNE'S

The Job

"An enjoyable read. It's real life, and it's told by a gifted storyteller who also happened to be a gifted cop. . . . Osborne writes with passion about his work. . . . For a job that usually deals with the dregs of society, an unlikely strain creeps into Osborne's tales—compassion. Osborne balanced toughness with empathy as he sought to ferret out wrongdoing while on duty." —*The Buffalo News*

"Nobody tells a cop story better than a cop, and Osborne tells them as well as I've ever heard (and I've heard a lot of them). . . . For every bad cop there are twenty heroic ones— and Steve Osborne was one of them. —Brian McDonald, author of *My Father's Gun: One Family, Three Badges, One Hundred Years in the NYPD*

"Wonderful. . . . Not only was Osborne an excellent policeman (he retired as a lieutenant and the commanding officer of the Manhattan Gang Squad), he's a fabulous storyteller, crafting his memories into well-honed tales filled with drama, humor and heart." —*BookPage*

"[An] engaging memoir. . . . [Osborne's] frank and intimate voice . . . suffuses his prose." —*Publishers Weekly*

"Raucous recollections. . . . [Osborne] comes off as an avuncular, world-weary tough guy. . . . Yet he elevates his perspective by displaying empathy for the civilians, victims and even criminals he has encountered." —*Kirkus Reviews*

"Cops are innately good storytellers, and Osborne must be one of the best." —*Booklist*

"Often funny, occasionally sobering and always entertaining."
—*Shelf Awareness*

Steve Osborne

The *Job*

Steve Osborne was a New York City police officer for twenty years before retiring as a lieutenant and commanding officer of the Manhattan Gang Squad, with numerous citations for his police work. He has told his stories before packed audiences at The Moth storytelling venues across the United States. He has written for *The New York Times* and *USA Today.* Now a consultant for television and film productions, Osborne lives in upstate New York with his wife and their two dogs, Jingles and Duke.

The Job

The *Job*

TRUE TALES FROM THE LIFE
OF A NEW YORK CITY COP

Steve Osborne

ANCHOR BOOKS
A Division of Penguin Random House LLC
New York

FIRST ANCHOR BOOKS EDITION, MARCH 2016

Copyright © 2015 by Steve Osborne

All rights reserved. Published in the United States by Anchor Books, a division of Penguin Random House LLC, New York, and distributed in Canada by Random House of Canada, a division of Penguin Random House Canada Ltd., Toronto. Originally published in hardcover in the United States by Doubleday, a division of Penguin Random House LLC, New York, in 2015.

Anchor Books and colophon are registered trademarks of Penguin Random House LLC.

The Library of Congress has cataloged the Doubleday edition as follows:
Osborne, Steve (Stephen T).
The job : true tales from the life of a New York City cop / by Steve Osborne.
pages   cm
1. Osborne, Steve (Stephen T).   2. New York (N.Y.) Police Department—Officials and employees—Biography.   3. Police—New York (State)—New York—Biography.   I. Title.
HV7911.O78A3 2015   363.2092—dc23   [B]   2014032375

Anchor Books Trade Paperback ISBN: 978-1-101-87214-7
eBook ISBN: 978-0-385-53963-0

Author photograph © Michael Everett

www.anchorbooks.com

Printed in the United States of America
10 9 8 7 6 5 4 3

Whenever my wife and I would watch the Oscars or some other big awards show, she would always have the same comment. She would say that if I ever won an award, I would remember to thank everybody else in the world who contributed and forget to thank her. I would try to convince her otherwise—how could I forget her?—but she never believed me. Now, chances are I won't be winning an Oscar anytime soon, so I would like to take this opportunity to thank my wife, because without her my life would be empty, and none of this would have been possible.

To my mother, who, even if I had written this thing in crayon, would think it was the best book since the Bible. And to my father, who taught me how to be a man and that police work is a noble profession.

To The Moth, thank you for sharing your stage and for the warm, loving environment you provided. Truly, without you guys none of this would have been possible.

Contents

Author's Note

Some of these stories happened many years ago when I was a very young cop, and some were viewed through adrenaline-fueled tunnel vision. My memory is no better or worse than anyone else's, and I kept to the facts as best as I could remember them. Whenever possible, I consulted with the individuals involved and/or went back to the scene of the incident to help my recollection. Many of the names, locations, and details of the cases were changed or intentionally left out to protect the privacy of the innocent.

The Job

Introduction

I'm not quite sure how it happened, or even why, but a few months after retiring from the New York City Police Department, I picked up a pad and pen and started writing. Like most cops, I had stories to tell, and for some reason I can't explain, I felt the need to put them on paper. I had no training in writing, other than police reports, but that little voice in the back of my head—the one that kept me safe all those years—was now nagging at me to tell my stories.

For twenty years my family and friends really didn't understand what I did for a living. It was like I was living a double life, and they only knew half of it. I would go to work early in the evening, and most times I didn't return till early in the morning. Of course they knew I was a cop—but what did that mean? Most civilians get their information about police work from the newspapers, which barely get half the story right, or they get it from television shows that are ninety-nine percent pure, out-of-this-world fantasy.

Sometimes I would share some of the funny stuff about the job, but the blood and gore, and especially the danger, I needed to keep to myself. When my wife would call me at work and ask how things were going, I would always tell her I was having a nice quiet night. Even if I was sitting on some dark street, armed with two guns strapped to my hip, waiting for some perp wanted on a homicide to show up so we could jump him. My answer was always the same. I'm having a nice quiet night.

Once I was sitting in my office talking to her on the phone and there was a shooting right on the station house block. The sound of gunshots boomed and echoed through my office window, causing me to duck. This might sound unusual, a drive-by shooting right next to the station house, but at the time I was working in the Bronx, and in the Bronx, shit happens. I had to put my hand over the receiver so she wouldn't hear the gunfire and go nuts worrying. When I tried to hang up so I could run outside, she got mad at me. She was busy telling me that the bills were killing us this month and we had to watch the spending. I wanted to tell her that I had to go, because I thought something else just got killed down the block, but I couldn't do that. Instead I think I told her my stomach was upset because I ate some bad rice and beans, and I had to go to the bathroom—now! A few seconds later I was charging down the block, gun in hand, running into who knows what. The credit card bills and the mortgage were going to have to wait.

I wanted to write some of my stories down just in case I dropped dead or I crossed the street one day and got run over by a bus. I didn't want them to die with me. I don't claim to be anything special, and my experience is no different than any other cop out there. I just took the time to write some of it down. When I would get together with my buddies, mostly other retired cops, it wouldn't take long before the tales started flying, and each story was just as incredible as the last.

When I entered the police academy an old-time instructor told me, "Kid, you just bought yourself a front-row seat to the greatest show on earth." What he was telling me wasn't anything new. I think every old cop has used that line on every new cop in every city and every small town in every corner of the country. And the reason it's used so much is because it's true—every word of it. I don't care if you work in Manhattan or in some tiny village out in the middle of nowhere with just one lawman in it, we all have stories. I wish all of us would put them on paper, because there's nothing funnier or more terrifying than a good cop story.

Like most active cops, I've forgotten much more than I remembered. When I was in uniform it wasn't unusual to handle twenty jobs a night. And when I was in plainclothes, my team and I would make several felony collars a week, mostly robberies, assaults, and gun arrests. I wish I would have kept a diary or taken more pictures, then maybe I could recall more, but some stories stay with you forever. Some you never forget, no matter how hard you try.

When I was a kid my father was a cop. Not the easiest childhood in the world, but it was interesting. Whenever I would do something bad, and tried lying about it, he was always one step ahead of me. He was used to interrogating murderers, so getting the truth out of me wasn't that difficult. I usually cracked under the pressure in about ten seconds.

I grew up in a no-nonsense blue-collar neighborhood where toughness was valued as much as, or more than, anything else. And in that neighborhood, the old man reigned as king. You either loved him or feared him, and he really didn't care which it was. He was also the neighborhood problem solver. Once some pervert had flashed one of the neighborhood teenage girls and it was brought to his attention. This was the old days, so not everything was adjudicated with an arrest. When I asked him how he handled it, the only thing he said was "He'll never do that again." I'm not quite sure what that meant, but the guy was never seen or heard from in my neighborhood again.

He was also a great storyteller, as were his friends. I loved it when his cop buddies would come by the house, swaggering in with all that hardware hanging off their belts and talking about what happened out on patrol the night before. To me these were the coolest guys in the world, real men, and I wanted to be one of them. I never wanted to be a doctor or a lawyer or even an astronaut. I wanted to be the one standing over the dead guy in the middle of the street, trying to figure out who killed him. It's not that I'm a dummy or an underachiever, it's just that none of those other professions called me as much as police work did. I think that's why I was a solid C student in school. Algebra, physics, and geometry were useless to me. I was never going to do brain surgery or travel to the moon. I was going to be a cop. Deep down inside I knew I was put on this earth to catch bad guys. I just wish it paid as much as some of those other professions.

When I first started writing, I didn't know where it was going or what it would lead to. I just kept listening to that little voice in my head that told me to shut up and keep writing. After I wrote my first story, "Growing Pains," I took a chance and handed it out to a few trusted friends and relatives to get some input. If the writing sucked, and I was wasting my time, I figured I could always start a vegetable garden or maybe make beer in a home brewery to help fill up my free time. But what happened next surprised me. Almost everybody said they had a tear in their eye by the time they finished reading the story. It wasn't the reaction I was expecting, but I figured having the ability to make people cry (without whacking them over the head with a nightstick and dragging them off to jail) was a good start, so I kept at it. The next story was "Hot Dogs," and my same trusted advisers said it made them laugh. Then came "Mug Shot," and they were getting misty again.

Being a cop for twenty years makes you very cynical, and skeptical. Every day when you're on patrol people lie to you, or at least tell you what you want to hear, so when I heard those first couple of compliments I didn't know whether to believe them or not. I'm more of a meat eater than a vegetarian, so the vegetable garden wasn't really calling me, and the more I thought about making beer the less it appealed to me. It seemed like a lot of unnecessary work. Going to the store and buying a nice cold six-pack was more to my liking, so I kept at the writing.

When I was writing my next story I kept wondering if my circle of advisers was just telling me what I wanted to hear and trying not to hurt my feelings, so I reached out to a friend of mine, Liz Tuccillo, a professional writer. She had written books, television shows, and movies, so I figured she must know what she's talking about. One of her books was a bestseller and made a boatload of money, and a television show she wrote for will be in syndication forever, so I showed her my stuff. She was a little more critical, going through the finer points of sentence structure, but the bottom line was, she thought it was good stuff. A little rough around the edges concerning grammar, but the stories were great. I implored her not to be nice to me because I could get plenty of that at home. I needed an honest answer from a pro on whether I was wasting my time or not. And just like a no-nonsense Italian chick from New York would put it, she also told me to shut up and keep writing.

About a year later, totally out of the blue, she calls me up and says that she is doing this storytelling show called The Moth. She explained to me that regular people get up onstage and tell a true story about something that happened in their life. I figured what the hell, it sounded easy enough. She said the producers were in a jam because it was the night before the show and some cop who was supposed to perform caught a homicide. They needed somebody who could jump in at the last minute, and they asked her if she knew anybody—maybe another cop. The universe works in mysterious ways!

I went off to a quiet corner by myself, called the Moth office, and pitched two stories over the phone. I'm not sure if the pitch went that great or they were just really desperate, but they asked me to come in right away. I went to the office and met the artistic director, Catherine Burns, who was very patient and caring. She was kind and sweet, almost motherly, as she got me ready for the next night. She was apparently used to dealing with novices like me who have never performed onstage in front of a live audience before. We had less than twenty-four hours before the show and there wasn't much time to rehearse, so we just did a couple of run-throughs, and hoped for the best.

It all seemed simple enough, but when I got there things changed. The show was at the Players Club in Gramercy Park, and there were three hundred frigging people in the audience. I was expecting a few hippies in the basement of a church snapping their fingers for applause instead of clapping. I never thought to ask Catherine how many people would be there, and I think she intentionally left that part out. When I looked at the crowd panic set in. I would rather have chased a guy with a gun down a dark alley than get up on that stage. This was the most terrifying experience of my life, and that includes being involved in a few thousand arrests.

When I told Catherine I didn't think I could do this, she got up into my face like a cranky old desk lieutenant, pointed her finger at me, and growled, "You just get up there and do it." She went from Mother Teresa to Knute Rockne in about two seconds.

There were five storytellers going on that night, and I was going to be number four. To use a baseball analogy, that's like batting ninth in the lineup. I was a last-minute fill-in, and the expectations for me were pretty low, but that didn't help my nerves. As I sat in my seat waiting to go onstage, things only got worse. The theme of the show was "Crimes and Misdemeanors," so one guy told a story about doing twenty years in prison for a murder he didn't commit. He told the audience how the police were corrupt and incompetent. It got a huge round of applause. Another storyteller was a defense attorney, and his tale was also about how screwed up the criminal justice system is. Then Liz got up and told a story about getting arrested at a demonstration outside the Republican National Convention by a group of less-than-friendly riot cops. She also explained how a baloney sandwich can be used as a pillow while sleeping on the dirty floor in a severely overcrowded Central Booking.

This was bad, bad, bad. The audience seemed to be a Manhattan artsy, liberal bunch, and I was sure they were going to hate me. When I had rehearsed at home in front of my wife she got worried, because in the middle of my story I made a crack about liberals. She got scared and warned me I better take it out. My own expectations for the night were pretty low as well. I figured it had all the makings for the most embarrassing night of my life, so I thought, fuck it, I might as well go down in flames. I left the line about the liberals in.

When I walked up onstage, shaking like a guy going to the electric chair, my mind was scrambling. After the last three stories about corrupt cops and an incompetent criminal justice system, I figured I was dead meat. I had to think of something fast. As I shuffled up the steps, then bounced across the stage full of nervous energy, something happened. I don't know where it came from, maybe it was some kind of divine intervention, but the first words to pop out of my mouth assured the audience that the guy in my story was "one hundred percent guilty." I told them, "Please don't have any doubts about that." It was the last thing they expected to hear, and the next thing I know, the whole room erupts in laughter and applause. I was off and running, and there was no stopping me now.

I was up onstage for about fifteen minutes telling the "Hot Dogs" story, but I don't remember much of it, other than the microphone in my face, and the blinding white lights shining in my eyes. But what I do remember most was that out of the entire night my liberal crack got the most laughs and applause. All of a sudden I loved liberals, and they loved me. They were my people, and I was theirs. My story was the biggest hit of the night. It was like I was a minor league ballplayer brought up to the majors at the last minute and I hit a grand slam to win the game.

After the show people were lining up to shake my hand and tell me how much they liked my story. I'm not a very good-looking guy. I'm not exactly the type girls fight over when I walk into a room, so when several very nice-looking ladies came up to meet me, I got a big kick out of it. I was only in showbiz for a few minutes, but I was digging it already.

When I left the Players Club I was walking on air. It was a great experience and I met a lot of very nice people, but figured it was a one-time thing, so I went back to my regular life—and to writing. About two weeks later I got a call from The Moth, and they asked me if I was interested in doing a nationwide tour. To me it was a free vacation, and maybe a few more hot girls to hang out with (luckily my wife thought I was exaggerating), so I said yes. The next thing I know, I'm in L.A. telling a story in front of about two thousand people. After that it was Seattle, San Francisco, Denver, and more. I even went to Scotland to perform at the Edinburgh Fringe Festival. The UK crowd almost fell out of their chairs when they heard my New York accent. Some of them must have thought I was making this shit up.

Getting up onstage in front of a live audience isn't easy, and I'm not that crazy about it. To this day it would be a hell of a lot easier, and a lot more fun for me, to chase down some guy with a gun rather than to get up onstage and tell a story. The satisfaction comes after the show, when people come up and tell me how much they enjoyed it. And, I hope, learned something from it. After retiring from the police department I thought my days of helping people were over. I figured I would drink beer, go fishing, grow old, then drop dead. I just assumed, like most cops, my memories and experiences would die with me. But maybe not.

I was lucky enough to have National Public Radio feature a couple of my stories. Afterward I would get fan letters from young people from across the country who were thinking about a career in law enforcement, and they would tell me how my story made them realize they were making the right choice. Dog lovers told me how much they enjoyed the story about my dog Griffin, and how much it made them cry. One guy told me after listening to the story about the deathbed experience I had with my father, it made him rethink, and appreciate, the relationship he had with his dad. It seemed my stories were affecting people on a much deeper level than I ever thought possible.

One day, after he heard one of my stories on *The Moth Radio Hour* on NPR, I got an e-mail from an editor at Doubleday publishing. He thought it was imperative that I put my stories in a book. I have to admit that, for a solid C student, it seemed like a daunting task. My eighth-grade English teacher, Sister Kathleen, used to beat the crap out of me on a regular basis and remind me that I was never going to amount to anything in life. Her wicked left hook to the side of the head and her humiliating and dire predictions still haunt me to this day. But it didn't stop me from being a wiseass in class.

For a guy who started out in life with a high school diploma and a driver's license, I wasn't sure I could pull this off. But my editor, another person who reminded me of a cranky old desk lieutenant, gave me the same advice my trusted circle of friends and relatives did: Shut up and write. And as usual, it was good advice, so I shut up and continued writing.

I went on the job—that's what we cops call it, "the job," because for guys like us, it's the only job in the world—in the early eighties when the crack epidemic hit like one of Sister Kathleen's left hooks, so looking back at them, the bad old days gave me plenty to write about. At the time crime was going through the roof in New York City and nobody was safe—even the cops. There were over two thousand homicides a year, and even in the good neighborhoods, you took your life in your hands walking down the street late at night. I was recently at a cop Christmas party at my old precinct. A good way to check the barometer of a neighborhood is how many street robberies are occurring. I asked one of the cops how many they were doing a month these days, and with a seriousness I found amusing, she said, "Oh, about twelve."

Twelve! You gotta be shitting me! That blew my mind. When I was there we were doing a minimum of 120 a month. And those were only the ones that were reported. Back then people figured it was useless to make a report, so half the time they took their lumps and just went home. If they weren't shot, or stabbed, or didn't have the shit beat out of them, they chalked it up to a bad New York experience. One night we had eight robberies on a four-to-twelve tour—and that was during a blizzard!

I'm proud to say that I and the cops I worked with played a part in turning the city around. Now when I walk around in some of the neighborhoods I used to work in, I hardly recognize the place. Those same streets where I would only walk around with a gun clutched in my hand inside my coat pocket are now trendy little enclaves. People sit around at outdoor cafés sipping their lattes, without a care in the world. Some of my new liberal friends might think we were a little aggressive enforcing the law—and maybe we were sometimes—but at least now you can go out at night without getting robbed or caught in the cross fire of two assholes shooting it out. Parks that were only inhabited by junkies, drug dealers, and any other type of savage criminal you could think of are now filled with moms pushing baby strollers and kids enjoying the play-grounds. New York is quite a different place from when I walked my first foot post.

The stories you are about to read take place over a twenty-year career—from my first day on patrol as a rookie in uniform to my last, as commanding officer of the Manhattan Gang Squad. Not too many cops can say they made a collar on their first day on patrol, and their last. The first one I was happy about, but the last one I definitely could have done without.

If you've ever looked at a cop standing on a corner and wondered what goes on behind that tough-guy persona, I want to take you there. I definitely don't speak for all police officers, because these are my stories, and my experiences. I also realize that I'm nothing special. I'm just an average guy who decided to pin on a shield and strap on a gun and do one of the most difficult, dangerous, and interesting jobs you could think of.

1

Think Fast

I stopped the car under the giant arch at the Fifth Avenue entrance of Washington Square Park. I took the lid off my coffee and nestled in. When I was in the police academy, an old-time instructor once told me, "Congratulations kid, you just bought yourself a front-row seat to the greatest show on earth."

At the time I wasn't exactly sure what he meant, but sitting here was the perfect example. The park on a sunny Saturday summer afternoon is packed with all kinds of people: drug dealers, NYU students, hippies, street performers, tourists, and the ever-present cop-hating liberals.

The park is only about two square blocks, but today there had to be a few thousand people hanging around watching or participating in the show. And if you're a people watcher like me, there's no better place to sit and have your coffee.

I was a rookie at the time and didn't get a chance to see the inside of a radio car too much. But today was such a nice day I guess a few of the senior cops had "banged in" (taken off). The desk lieutenant was a cranky old bastard who had no use for rookies. He didn't trust them and didn't like them. The only way to get on his good side was to stay out of trouble and buy him a cappuccino once in a while. But today he was shorthanded, so he grabbed me and another rookie and assigned us as Sector Adam-Boy.

I was excited, this was starting out to be a great day. Unlike most normal people, I didn't want to be home on a beautiful summer weekend barbecuing or swimming at the beach. I wanted to be working. The radio was jumping. There was excitement in the air and I wanted to be a part of it. This was cops and robbers time!

After roll call my new partner and I decided I would drive first. I hustled over to the desk, grabbed the car keys, and went out to the parking lot to find my home and office for the next eight hours. Much to my surprise the car was practically new. RMP 2297 only had a few hundred miles on it.

Most of the cars in the precinct were beat-up pieces of shit with dents, missing hubcaps, and worn-out seats. The last car I had was so bad I had to wedge a milk crate between the front and back just to hold the seat upright. On the dashboard, scribbled in ink, somebody wrote, "This job sucks!" Obviously the last cop to use the car was a fat-ass, disgruntled individual who didn't like the job very much. I didn't feel that way just yet and hoped I never would.

This car obviously belonged to one of the senior cops, so I had better be careful with it. I reminded myself to bring it back at the end of the tour clean and with a full tank of gas or I wouldn't see the inside of a car again for a very long time.

The cop I was working with today wasn't exactly a go-getter. He seemed content to do as little as possible in life. Not a bad guy, but some cops are like that. Do as little as possible and just get through the next eight hours. I had only worked with him a few times in the past, so we were still feeling each other out.

I took a sip of my coffee, settled back in my nice new firm seat, and watched the world go by. A Japanese tourist with a map in his hand stopped and asked for directions. I took the map, pointed to the little arch, and informed him, "You are here." He looked at the map, then at the fifty-foot arch over his head, and in machine-gun broken English said, "Thank you, thank you, thank you very much. Thank, thank you." He kept on smiling and waving as he walked away.

I liked helping tourists because they were always so polite and grateful. I just wished the people of New York whom I protected every day were a little more grateful, then maybe I would not have become so cynical at such an early age.

Everybody loves a fireman. When the fire department comes to your house they're coming to save you. But when the police come that usually means somebody's leaving in handcuffs. Somebody they care about, usually a husband, boyfriend, son, or baby's daddy is going to jail. So most of the time people aren't too happy to see you.

Sitting in the park is like watching a nonstop parade. People are constantly coming and going. And some never seem to go anywhere. They're always walking, but they never seem to get anyplace. Those are the drug dealers. If they did all that walking in a straight line, they would probably end up in Philadelphia before the night was over—but they don't. They walk in circles from one end of the park to the other, looking for buyers, watching out for the cops, and keeping an eye on their stash.

Occasionally I would stare them down. Even when we were in plainclothes, they knew who we were, and we knew who they were. Nobody was fooling anyone. The same forty or fifty dealers were working the park every day, and the same handful of cops were breaking their balls and locking them up.

The obvious question is, why didn't I just go and slap handcuffs on them, haul them off to jail, and end this silly game of cat and mouse we always seem to be playing? It's not that simple. I wish it was. First, you need probable cause to arrest someone. You need to see him do a "hand-to-hand" with some buyer or you need to see him with the drugs on him. The hand-to-hands happen very fast and the stash is never on their person, it's always hidden somewhere close by until they need it.

They usually hide it in the bushes or in a garbage can, or under the bumper of a car. I've seen a pregnant girl pushing a toddler in a baby carriage holding the stash. She kept it in the baby's diaper.

They need to keep it someplace where they can keep an eye on it because dealers and junkies will steal from each other. There really is no honor among thieves. Especially when it comes to drugs.

Making a collar is not as easy as you think, and if you don't have all your ducks in a row the district attorney's office will downgrade your charges and let the perp plead out to almost nothing. Or worse, throw you and your case out the door, leaving you and the city open to a lawsuit. It's kind of a game, but the game has rules and the consequences are serious, so we play by the rules. Criminals have rights whether we like it or not. No cop likes getting sued or having to face charges at the Civilian Complaint Review Board for excessive force. Unfortunately the people who suffer the consequences are the parents and their kids who want to enjoy the park.

Another obvious question is why we don't just throw all the dealers out of the park. A handful of cops could clean this park up in five minutes, but you can't do that either. Some liberal lawyer would be all too willing to sue the city and us on their behalf for violating their rights.

But sometimes we do throw guys out of the park when they do something stupid—like fighting or mouthing off to us. It's a good way to enforce some discipline without having to make an arrest. They hate losing their "park privileges" for the day because they can't hang out with their buddies. But especially because they can't make money.

At any given time there are ten times more drug dealers out on the street than there are cops. We could all collar up the first five minutes of the tour, but then there wouldn't be any cops left out on the street. Couple that with the fact these guys get very little jail time, and you have another reason why cops become cynical. Sometimes I can't blame my partner for wanting to do as little as possible and just go home after eight hours, safe and in one piece.

As I was watching the parade a small commotion caught my attention. A couple of Jersey guys with brown paper bags in their hands were walking into the park whooping and howling. Watching them through my rearview mirror, I could just tell they were from New Jersey. They were white muscle-head jock types and had the look that said "instant asshole; just add alcohol."

As they passed I called them over to the car, pointed to the brown paper bags, and said, "Dump it out." One of them, the alpha male of the group, thought about protesting but then thought better of it.

I don't do it to be mean. I like a beer or two myself. I do it to keep them from getting drunk, then stupid, then arrested. I had better things to do than deal with a couple of drunk morons.

As I sat making small talk with my partner, sipping my coffee and watching the world go by, a woman in her early fifties walked past my half-open window and said in an excited whisper, "Officer, you better get over there, they're fighting."

And as discreetly as she could she pointed over her shoulder to the other side of the park. It was obvious she did not want to be seen talking to the cops and labeled a rat, but she obviously thought it was important enough to tell me.

The park was thick with bodies. People were walking, biking, and roller blading in every direction. I could hardly see fifty feet in front of me. Looking at the crowd, I debated driving around the outside of the park but decided it would take too long, so I put the car in drive and began to nudge my way through the crowd.

I drove past a guy sitting on the grass playing a guitar surrounded by four good-looking girls. They sat staring at him, enchanted by his half-assed musical ability. The guy sucked but the girls seemed mesmerized. I wanted to kick myself for not learning to play the guitar.

As I pushed through the crowd some people had this annoyed look on their faces like I was bothering them. I put the flashing red lights on to let everybody know I had somewhere to go and maybe something important to do. It just seemed to annoy them even more.

I made my way around the fountain which is the focal point of the park and scanned the crowd looking for the fight, but there was no yelling, no screaming, and no bottles breaking. Nobody seemed to be alarmed, which is a good thing. How bad could the fight be if nobody was watching or seemed to even notice?

As I finally reached the other side of the fountain I spotted them. Two black guys were in a heated dispute. I recognized both of them. They were park regulars and weren't virgins when it came to being arrested or to the criminal justice system.

From a distance I could tell one of them was in a crazed, wild rage. He was yelling and pointing his finger at the other. I couldn't hear what he was saying, but he seemed to be accusing the other guy of something. The second guy was backing up, with his hands out in front of him in the surrender position. He had a very scared look on his face and seemed to be trying to say something, but the first guy was hearing none of it. It was easy to tell which one was the aggressor.

As I drove closer I was getting a little pissed because both were ignoring me and the flashing red lights on the roof of my car. The lights should have been warning enough to stop their silly bullshit and start walking. I decided that if they didn't start walking in about two seconds they would be losing their "park privileges" for the day.

New York can be an emotionless city sometimes. Not many people seemed to be paying any attention to these guys. Were they all too busy doing their own thing? Or was it the "don't get involved" survival instinct most New Yorkers have? I don't know, but no one seemed to give a rat's ass that these guys were at each other's throat.

Maybe they didn't see my lights because it was such a sunny day, so I tapped the siren to get their attention. I was hoping to break this up without having to get out of the car. But I got nothing! They didn't even look in my direction.

I was surprised and slightly annoyed that they were still ignoring me and the one-hundred-decibel siren I was blaring in their direction. But as I inched closer I could see why: the aggressor was in an all-consuming rage. His eyes were bulging and his nostrils were flared. The veins in his neck were popping, and spit flew out of his mouth as he screamed and threatened his intended victim. There was literally murder in his eyes.

The second guy was obviously scared to death and totally focused on the maniac in front of him. It was early in my tour and I had most of the night in front of me, so I wasn't happy about making a collar just yet, but I could tell calmer heads might not prevail here.

As I moved in closer it happened! Right in front of me, and a thousand uninterested park revelers, suddenly the aggressor lifted up his shirt, reached into his back pocket, and pulled out what looked like a ten-inch steak knife. It literally took a split second to turn from a yelling match to a knife fight.

I was shocked! I couldn't believe this was happening right in front of me. And both of them were so focused on each other neither one noticed I was even there.

As the aggressor whipped out the knife, he took two steps forward and cocked his arm. There was no doubt he was preparing to stab his victim right in the chest. I could tell he didn't pull this thing out just for show. He intended to use it.

As the perp stepped forward, the soon-to-be-dead victim tried to backpedal a few steps, but he wasn't fast enough. He was a bit too clumsy and stumbled. He was dead and he knew it.

My police academy instructor was right, I had a front-row seat to the greatest show on earth and today's show was "Murder in the Park."

I couldn't believe what I was looking at. Now I was totally and completely focused. The sights and sounds of a thousand people were gone. My partner was saying something, but I couldn't hear him either. I was riveted by these two guys. All I could see was a hand holding a ten-inch steak knife. I had tunnel vision!

I had to do something, but what? I would have been completely justified in jumping out of the car and shooting this guy, but there was no time. In about a half a second he was going to plunge that knife into this guy's chest.

In police work there is an old saying about how we have a split second to make a life-and-death decision. And it's absolutely true. I'm not an accountant with an eraser on my pencil or an actor who films the same scene twenty times until he gets it right. I have one chance to make a life-and-death decision and a half a second to do it in.

I couldn't scare the guy off with the lights and siren, and there was no time to jump out and get a shot off. What was I going to do? I had to think fast! What happened next was more of a reaction rather than a decision. I hit on the gas pedal and nailed him with the car. I didn't think I hit him that hard, but he bounced off and went flying, and luckily so did the knife. I just wanted to nudge the car in between them, but I guess my adrenaline was really pumping and I nudged a little harder than I wanted to. It looked much worse than it was.

At the same time my victim, who was scrambling backward in circles trying to get away from his attacker, ran into the side of the car and bounced off with a thud. I had nudged both of them. In fact I think the victim got it a little worse than the guy with the knife but who cares, it worked and he didn't get stabbed. After the little thuds I hit the brakes. The car came to a screeching halt with the aggressor and my victim a little stunned. The victim was staring at me with this half-smiling and half-shocked look on his face. He seemed relieved. He probably had thought he was a dead man and obviously hadn't expected anything like this was going to happen. The perp was staring at me because I just snapped him out of his rage and back into reality.

I jumped out of the car and ran over to the perp and slapped handcuffs on his wrists. Just because I stunned him doesn't mean he's not dangerous anymore. Always cuff your perp!

I then pointed to the perp's intended victim and growled, "Don't move, you're not going nowhere." The last thing I needed was for the victim to disappear on me—because they often do. He was the reason I just ran the other guy over, and without him it would be my word against the guy with the Chrysler emblem now stamped on his ass. So before he had a chance to even think about taking off, my partner grabbed him and held on tight.

With the victim secured and my perp in handcuffs, the excitement started to settle down and my tunnel vision faded. Everything seemed to slow back down to normal speed and I had a chance to take it all in. The sights and sounds of thousands of people having a nice day in the park started to come back into focus.

To me it seemed like a job well done. I had just saved someone's life. It's not every day you get to do that. But just as I was feeling a little bit proud of myself for preventing a murder, I heard a voice from the crowd yell, "FUCK THE POLICE!"

That was quickly followed by "The police ran the brother over!" Another voice from the other side of the crowd seemed to agree. "Yeah, he wasn't doing nothing. They just ran the brother over!"

The crowd outnumbered us by several hundred to one and they were getting ballsier by the second. The next thing I knew, bottles were crashing all around us. The crowd was grabbing anything they could to throw at us.

The previously emotionless and uninterested crowd was now an angry mob. They could ignore an attempted murder but not a little police activity. And all their anger seemed to be directed at me. Plus I couldn't believe my bad luck. A short distance away the Parks Department was doing some cement work, and there was a nice pile of bricks for the crowd to arm themselves. One of them sailed through the air and landed on the roof of my car, leaving a big dent.

I felt the need to explain myself, but nobody wanted to listen. I wanted to tell them to relax, I just saved this guy's life, but no one seemed interested in my side of the story. Or even a spirited debate. They were out for blood—in particular mine.

My victim shrugged and gave me a sympathetic look that said, "I would like to help but they are not going to listen to me either." The look also said, "Besides, it's against my principles to help the police."

This was turning ugly real fast. Several hundred people who didn't even see what actually happened believed I ran this guy over for no reason, just because one cop-hating, and probably drug-dealing, asshole said so. I was pissed. I couldn't understand how quickly everyone wanted to believe it.

I think what annoyed me more than anything was that so-called normal people were getting in on the action. Regular people were whipping themselves up into a misguided, self-righteous frenzy and joining in on the chants. I spent every day of my work life protecting these people and they turned on me. I expected it from the drug dealers and crackheads but not the "normal" people.

As the chants of "FUCK THE POLICE!" became louder and more rhythmic I picked up my perp and threw him into the back of the car. He was hobbling a little but nothing seemed to be broken. I was relieved because if his legs were all fucked up and pointing in different directions it would have made matters worse.

Plan A was to look for other witnesses to help corroborate my story, but that plan was out the window fast. Plan B was to grab my perp and victim and get out of Dodge before one of these flying bottles caved my skull in.

As I shoved my perp into the backseat of the car, a beer bottle came crashing through the rear windshield, showering me and the perp with broken glass and stale beer. That was followed by several more crashes as bottles and bricks and anything else the crowd could find came raining down on me and my new car.

The glass was in my hair, my ears, and even in my mouth. As I wiped beer from my face and spit out little pieces of what used to be the back window, my perp came up with a bright idea. He looked up at me and with a big grin on his face said, "Maybe you should let me go."

The grin on his face really pissed me off, so I told him, "Maybe you should shut the fuck up before I knock your teeth out." And I reminded him, "This is all your fault, asshole."

I was a little relieved that he found it all amusing. That meant the little trip I sent him on, flying through the air, probably didn't cause too much damage.

Out of the corner of my eye I saw this guy running at us holding a garbage can over his head. He throws the can and it lands on the hood of the car, leaving a big dent and garbage all over the car. He was smiling and laughing and jumping up and down. You could tell he was real proud of himself as the crowd cheered. I made a promise to myself I was going to find him someday and do something to him with a garbage can that he wouldn't like very much.

I snatched the radio off my belt and transmitted a signal "10-85 FORTHWITH"—a request for backup, *now*. The great thing about working in Manhattan is help is never too far away. Right away I could hear the sirens starting up in the distance. They could tell by the sound of my voice that I was in some deep shit and needed help.

Yee-haa, motherfucker, the cavalry is coming.

Another great thing about being a New York City cop is that there are almost forty thousand of us. If I need help, there will be cops coming from all directions. And they'll keep coming! The hard part is trying to get them to stop coming once you call for help. They'll be running up out of the ground—Transit. They'll be swooping in from the air—Aviation. They'll even be coming from the sea—Harbor—and on horses—Mounted. Whatever I need to bail me out of a bad situation, the NYPD has it.

Another old-time instructor at the police academy told us that if you ever get shot or stabbed and need blood, instantly there will be forty thousand cops sticking out their arms and saying, "Take mine." It's a good feeling knowing that you belong to a family. And that family is also the biggest and baddest gang in the city.

I yelled over to my partner to get the victim into the car. The vic didn't want to come with us but he had no choice. I needed him to be my complainant because without him and his version of the events, it would look like I really did run the brother over for no reason. Then I really would be in some deep shit.

As we put the victim in the car a bottle flew past my ear and bounced off the roof, leaving another dent. I couldn't help but think about how much shit I was going to be in with the lieutenant over this one. Taking it to the car wash and filling it up with gas was not going to smooth this over. I was going to have to buy him cappuccinos from now till doomsday.

As the mob was getting dangerously close, the first of several police cars plowed through the crowd. The flashing lights and blaring sirens caused them to calm down a bit and back off. Several cops jumped out, nightsticks in hand, yelling at the crowd, and immediately the bottles and bricks stopped flying. The brave hearts in the crowd throwing the stuff weren't stupid. They knew that if we caught one of them in the act of throwing something, they would end up getting a wood shampoo—a nightstick over the head.

Some older cop I didn't know sauntered over to me like Robert Duvall in that famous scene from *Apocalypse Now* where the bombs were bursting all around him, and very matter-of-factly said, "What do you have, kid?" I pointed to my perp and said, "I got a collar." I started to tell him what happened, how I saved this guy's life, but he wasn't interested either! I couldn't believe it. Nobody wanted to hear my side of the story. Not even the other cops!

He cut me off and said, "Are you okay? You hurt?" I told him no. Then he cut me off again. "All right, get the hell out of here. We'll take care of this."

I jumped into the driver's seat and slammed the car into drive, but at the last second I realized I forgot something. The *knife!* I needed that knife as evidence. When I hit the brakes my partner yelled, "What are you waiting for? Let's *go!*"

I was already anticipating a couple of neighborhood liberals showing up at the precinct to make a complaint against me, so I needed all my ducks in a row and the knife was going to be important. I scrambled back out of the car trying to look for it as fast as I could. There was broken glass and garbage all over the place, and I couldn't find the knife. Somebody must have picked it up in all the confusion. I wasn't surprised, it happens all the time.

I jumped back into the driver's seat and hit the gas. I leaned on the siren and not so gently plowed my way through the crowd toward the street, and safety. I glanced over my shoulder at my partner, who was sitting in the backseat between my perp and complainant. He was making sure they didn't try to kill each other again. He gave me a look that said, "You should have let the perp stab the guy."

And he was right. If I'd let the perp stab the guy I would have had a nice collar for murder, and no aggravation. The lieutenant might have even put me in for a medal.

I parked the car in the lot behind the station house and walked this caper into the precinct. By now my perp was walking fine. There was absolutely nothing wrong with him. Him flying through the air looked worse than it really was. The funny thing about these guys is their resiliency. Ask any cop. It's like they're made out of rubber. They get shot, stabbed, thrown off a roof, even run over with a car and they bounce right back. It's an amazing phenomenon. A cop can get shot in the pinkie, and somehow the bullet will travel up his arm, through his armpit, into his heart, and he'll die. These guys, the next day they're back on the street doing the same stupidity they were doing before.

When I marched my perp and complainant up to the desk, the lieutenant was waiting for me. Having heard the commotion on the radio he asked me what happened, and if we were okay.

I was touched. The grumpy old guy seemed genuinely concerned about me and my partner. I was hoping he would still be that concerned when I told him about the car. I started to tell him the story about how I saved this guy's life, but he was even less interested than the crowd was. To him it was just another war story, and he must have heard a million of them.

My partner threw the perp in a cell and I found a chair for the victim. I actually thought about cuffing him to the chair so he wouldn't walk out when I wasn't looking, but you can't do that. So I warned him that he better not do a Houdini on me.

Now it was time to tell the lieutenant what I was dreading most, about the car. He obviously knew we had a bit of a melee on our hands, but what he didn't know was that the crowd had been using our car for target practice.

We walked out to the lot and I showed him what used to be a nice, shiny, new police car. I brushed some broken glass out of my hair, just so he would know what a close call I had and maybe he would feel sorry for me.

He didn't say a word as he eyeballed the broken back window and the dozen or so dents. I still felt the need to explain to him how I was completely justified doing what I did, but I didn't. I decided to lighten things up a little and said, "Hey Lou . . . can I get you a cappuccino?" He didn't think it was funny. He just gave me a look that said, "Fucking rookie, hope you like walking."

The lieutenant turned out to be a really good guy. It took a little while, about three years, to be exact, but one day he started being nice to me. He actually smiled at me once. Desk lieutenants are like that, it takes some time before they warm up to you. Before they will trust you. But after three years of me working my ass off, and bringing in some good collars, he finally decided I was an okay guy. Rookies can be a pain in the ass, and who was I to argue the point?

I walked back into the precinct and found my complainant. He hadn't tried to leave yet, but he looked antsy. I could tell I was going to have to keep an eye on him so he didn't slip out the front door. I was going to have to work fast to get what I needed out of him.

When I walked up to him I gave him a look that said, "You owe me." I handed him a pen and a legal pad and told him to write out a statement about what happened. I knew I couldn't count on this guy showing up to court or the Civilian Complaint Review Board, so I needed a good written statement out of him.

When I first asked him to do this, he gave me this wiseass look and tried telling me he couldn't write. That he wasn't a good speller. Obviously he didn't like being in the station house or helping the police, but tough shit. I helped him so he's going to help me now.

I was a little pissed thinking that I was going to be walking a foot post for a while, so I got up into his face and explained the facts of life to him. I said, "Look, motherfucker, if it wasn't for me you'd be dead right now. You'd be laying in the park with a steak knife stuck in your heart and a sheet over your face. So don't break my fucking balls!"

I pointed to a desk and a chair and said, "Now sit down and write!"

I guess the image I painted for him of the knife and the sheet worked. He sat down and put pen to paper.

As he was writing I made myself busy. I grabbed an arrest report, fingerprint cards, and a stack of other forms. Processing an arrest is definitely time consuming.

When he handed me back the pad he had this proud "job well done" look on his face, sort of like a kid handing in his homework. When I sat on the edge of the desk and looked it over I felt like a teacher grading a paper. I didn't know what to expect but I was pleasantly surprised. My drug-dealing pupil could write! His penmanship wasn't that great, but he was fairly articulate. He wrote a great statement covering my ass. He even described the knife as being twelve inches!

I took the pad and stuffed it safely into my folder with all my other paperwork. Then I walked him out the front door of the precinct. It was time to cut him loose. I thanked him for the statement and told him he was free to go.

But before he turned to leave I stopped him. There was one more thing I forgot. There was one last piece of the puzzle I needed. It wasn't important but I just wanted to know. I wanted to know what the fight was about. He shrugged his shoulders and said it was no big deal. I countered and told him it must have been a little bit of a big deal because he almost got killed over it.

Whatever it was, he seemed ashamed of it. By the look on his face I could tell he was guilty of something. Something that even the lowest of the low out on the street look down upon. He didn't want to say it at first, but then he finally, in a very roundabout way, hinted at it. The perp had suspected him of stealing his stash and was now demanding money!

We both knew that out in the street a crime like that is a "stabbable" offense. When one dealer steals another dealer's stash there's no calling the cops. There's no suing the guy to get your shit back. You just kill him. That's it, problem solved. It will never happen again. Plus, you make an example out of the guy. The next time somebody eyeballs your stash he'll think twice about it.

If my perp had been tried by a jury of his peers—drug dealers—he would have walked on this one. He would have been found "not guilty."

After baring his soul about his misdeeds he turned and started walking. He was walking fine now. I had gotten him checked out by EMS, and there was nothing wrong with him either. He had a spring in his step, and I could tell he was glad to be back on the street and out of the station house. As he took a few pain-free steps toward freedom and back to drug dealing he slowed down. His feet shuffled for a moment as he seemed to be thinking about something. It was like he forgot something. Something important.

He turned and looked back over his shoulder at me. I could tell he had something on his mind. Did he have something else to get off his chest? I didn't know. For a second I thought he was going to ask me for a dollar or to get him onto the subway for free. But suddenly he turned, took a few steps toward me, and stuck out his hand. He was getting ready to say something to a cop that he was not used to saying. He mumbled, "Thank you."

I looked at his hand for a moment. It caught me by surprise. The average cop gets more "Fuck you"s than "Thank you"s in his career, and I didn't expect this.

After all the crap I had been through that day it was nice that someone said thank you. At least someone appreciated what I did. When we shook hands I felt really good about myself. I felt like I accomplished something. Even if only the two of us knew what I did. I felt like being a cop in this world actually means something.

It's not like I did the world any big favor by saving this guy. I was sure he wasn't going to go to medical school and discover the cure for cancer. He was most likely going to continue dealing drugs until he did some real jail time or somebody did kill him. But who am I to judge? (Well, I do it all the time.)

When I walked back to check on my prisoner I was feeling good. I had a spring in my step, but as I passed through the heavy steel door to the cell area I slowed. There was that ever-present, sweet, spicy, pungent smell that smacked me in the face. It hung in the air like a thick cloud.

The cop assigned as the cell attendant today was burning incense.

I hated the smell, but it wasn't as bad as the stink of body odor it was covering up. Most of the perps don't put personal hygiene on top of their daily list of things to do, so the cells have this constant stink that never goes away. It hangs in the air and clings to the cement walls and iron bars. It smells like the inside of a dirty gym bag.

I looked into the holding cell to make sure my prisoner was okay. You need to check on them frequently because once they are in your custody they are *your responsibility*. If they escape or somehow manage to hang themselves or just drop dead—it's *your* fault. And prisoners can be ingenious. If my guy figured out a way to tie his Calvin Klein boxer shorts around his neck and end it all, the police department would be looking to hang me also.

There was a desk and a chair nearby so I plopped myself down and started banging out the paperwork. As I was sitting there making my way through form after form, I could hear my prisoner starting to bitch about his leg. He knew I was out there and was whining loud enough to get my attention.

Prisoners also love to complain. Once incarcerated they have nothing better to do than be a pain in the ass. And if they have a choice they would rather spend time in the emergency room than Central Booking. Almost all of them know the routine. If they complain about being sick or injured the sergeant down at Central Booking won't take custody of them until they are medically cleared.

And it's not like they have to pay any medical bills. The city pays for everything. So they go to the hospital, get checked out, and if they're lucky, have the nurse get them something to eat. Then after a couple of hours spent killing time and a few thousand dollars of taxpayer money wasted, it's time to go see the judge. To these guys getting locked up is no big deal. It's a way of life.

So I cut him off and said, "What's your problem? What are you crying about?" He laid there on the wooden bench looking at me with a wiseass grin and said, "You fucked up my leg. I got to go to the hospital."

I wasn't sure if I believed him or not. I knew I had nudged him a good shot, but he seemed to be walking fine a few minutes ago. So I told him to lay back down and stop the bitching. I told him that if he shut the fuck up and let me finish my paperwork, I'd buy him a soda and a bag of potato chips before going to jail. Maybe if he was real good I'd get him a cigarette.

But he was on a roll. He was determined to be a ball breaker. Somehow, my sending him flying through the air made him feel like he was in the right. Like *he* was the victim. He was peeking through the bars and taunting me. He said, "I'm gonna sue your ass. I'm gonna sue the city. I'm gonna sue all you motherfuckers. You fucked up my leg."

So far this had been "one of those days," and I was in no mood for any crap out of him. If he was really hurt I'd take him to the hospital, it was no big deal. I'd probably get some overtime out of it. But if he wasn't I had better things to do than listen to his nonsense.

Prisoners are like really bad kids. They will try to test you and see how much they can get away with, and the best way to deal with them is to put your foot down. You have to be firm but fair. Never abuse a prisoner, but you have to let him know who's in charge. Normally you can bribe them to be quiet with a cigarette and a bag of chips, but this guy was determined to be a pain in the ass. He knew I was a rookie and probably figured he was going to have some fun with me.

He kept going on about the leg and how he was going to sue the city. How he was going to get rich over this. Finally after a few minutes I had enough of his bullshit. I dropped my pen and grabbed the keys to the cell.

You should have seen the look on his face when I stormed over to the cell and flung the door open. He knew he pushed things a little too far.

I stepped in and got right up into his face. I grabbed him by the shirt and pulled him in close. He and I were nose to nose. I wanted to have his full attention. I told him, "Look, jerkoff, if your leg is messed up and you need to go to the hospital, I'll take you to the hospital. It's no big deal. If not—shut the fuck up!"

He tried looking away. He was like a kid being scolded. The eye contact was making him nervous but I wasn't finished.

Now I was on a roll. I said, "Let me clear things up for you just so you understand what happened today. That guy you were about to stab—I saved his life. But guess what, asshole? I saved your life too!"

He looked a little puzzled and didn't know what I was getting at. So I kept going. "You were about to kill a guy . . . right in front of a cop! Do you know what that means? That means twenty-five to life. No bullshit plea deals. No parole. That means twenty-five to fucking life. You'd be an old man before you got out of prison."

I explained that right now all he was looking at was a bullshit attempted robbery and a misdemeanor weapons charge. And that he would most likely be out of jail in a few days.

He kept trying to look away, but I wouldn't let him. I continued, "So guess what? Looks like I saved your life too!"

He wasn't stupid. It took a second, but I saw the lightbulb go on over his head. He knew I was right. He knew he had every intention of killing that guy in the park and didn't care who was watching. You're not giving your defense attorney too much to work with when you commit murder right in front of a cop.

I let go of his shirt and calmly finished up. "Now. Do you need to go to the hospital?"

Prisoners can piss you off but they can also make you laugh. And what he did next made me laugh.

He rolled his head around to the right, then around to the left, like a boxer trying to loosen up. He pulled his knee up to his chest and rubbed it a few times. Then he did a few deep knee bends and followed that by running in place for a few seconds. After shaking it loose and stretching like he was getting ready to play a basketball game, he turned to me and said, "Nah, I'm fine."

I was trying not to laugh but it was funny. That instructor in the police academy was one hundred percent right. I really did have a front-row seat to the "greatest show on earth." And sometimes it's a comedy!

I asked him again, "Are you sure?" He just smiled. He thought it was a little bit funny too.

I was sure that if I got into a foot chase with him, I'd have a hell of a time catching him. After we ironed things out he was a model prisoner. I gave him a soda, a bag of chips, and a cigarette. Then he laid down on the bench and went to sleep so I could finish my paperwork.

After it was over, all I could do was laugh. The lieutenant thought I was a loose cannon and the crowd thought I was an overzealous, brutal cop. I did what I had to do and that was that. No more, no less. And in the end only me and the two drug dealers knew what actually happened that day. Or even cared.

2

Never Do That Again

Rookies do dumb things. That's just the way it is, and I was certainly no different. The thing about police work is, physically it's a young man's job but mentally it takes maturity and experience. Having balls doesn't necessarily mean you have brains, and in police work you need both. I had plenty of the first but I was still working on the second.

Desperate men will do desperate things to stay out of jail, so you need to be prepared to go toe-to-toe with some bad guy. You have to be prepared to do whatever it takes to get the job done because cops don't run away when things get tough. We don't give up just because a situation becomes difficult or because some guy who thinks he's tough doesn't want to go to jail. It just doesn't work that way. But it takes experience and street smarts to know what's important and what's not. What's worth getting killed over and what's not. You need to know when it's appropriate to go all out and do whatever it takes to get the bad guy. And you need to know when it's time to say, "Fuck it, it ain't worth it, I'll get him next time."

I was young, strong, fast, and eager, and it didn't take long before I realized I loved "the job." I loved catching bad guys. It pissed me off and I took it personally when they sometimes got away.

In the beginning, when you walk down the street you try to look like a hard-ass so nobody messes with you, but your spit-shined shoes and stiff leather gear make you stick out like a broken thumb. You're not fooling anybody. Everybody you walk past knows you're a rookie. Kids call you a "new jack" because of your shiny new jacket. And the dumb young look on your face doesn't help either.

The day I got sworn into the police department there were seventeen hundred of us sitting in a big auditorium at the Fashion Institute of Technology waiting to take the oath. That may seem like a lot of people, but this was an average-size NYPD class. We had more people entering the academy than most police departments in this country have police officers.

Cops can be real ball breakers and have a sick sense of humor sometimes. That doesn't mean we're not funny, it just means we have a fucked-up way of looking at things. The crowded auditorium was really quiet as we sat there filling out a stack of paperwork. I was printing my name, address, and Social Security number for the twentieth time when one of the instructors got up onstage and approached the podium. He had this shit-eating grin on his face as he grabbed the microphone and started to talk. It was obvious he had something funny to say—or at least he thought it was funny.

He said, "You guys like trivia?" Every baby-faced recruit in the room dropped their pen and looked up waiting to hear what pearl of wisdom the instructor was going to bestow on us.

He continued, "There are seventeen hundred of you in the room. Statistics show that one in every hundred police officers will die in the line of duty over the course of a twenty-year career . . . take a look around . . . that means seventeen of you are not going to make it."

He stopped smiling, making his long dramatic pause seem even more ominous. He continued, "Seventeen of you are going to die a violent death in the line of duty."

He paused again, letting that little tidbit of information sink into our young impressionable minds. Then he cracked up laughing again as he walked off the stage. It seemed like a well-rehearsed line. A line he had obviously used many times on previous academy classes before us.

We all looked around wondering who the seventeen were going to be. The big auditorium suddenly got smaller while the other instructors laughed their asses off also.

Not that cops getting killed is funny, but fucking with rookies is. At the time he was quoting some statistics from the seventies, so his numbers were a little high. But a few guys in that room would be shot and a few would die. I know because a couple would become friends of mine.

The amazing part is, I went back to finishing my paperwork without giving it a second thought. I think the reason the instructor said it was to thin out the herd. Get rid of the weak right at the beginning. If that little statistic scared you off then you shouldn't be in that room waiting to raise your hand. But the funny thing is, we all went back to finishing our paperwork. Nobody left the room! You would think there would be a mad dash for the door but there wasn't. Cops aren't like normal people.

As I went back to writing my name into little boxes I made a mental note of the statistic. I never wanted to forget it. Plus I figured it might be useful in picking up girls in bars.

When I first went out on patrol I was a little nervous—but definitely not scared. Cops don't get scared, or at least we never admit it. I knew this was going to be a life of adventure and couldn't wait for it to begin. And I didn't have to wait long.

I was assigned to NSU 12, one of the worst areas of Brooklyn. We covered the Six Seven and the Seven One precincts in Crown Heights and East Flatbush. The day I graduated from the academy, the ceremony was held in Madison Square Garden. I was standing out front in my shiny new dress uniform when one of my instructors asked me where I got assigned. When I told him, he just smiled and said, "You're gonna learn how to survive—real quick."

At the time I didn't know what he was talking about, so I just smiled back, with that young dumb look.

My first day out of the academy I'm walking a foot post in the Six Seven when I see this huge drunk guy in the middle of the street throwing punches at the passing cars. The guy must have been at least six foot seven inches tall, and he had on these dusty, dirty clothes and a tool belt around his waist. He was obviously a construction worker who had probably stopped off for more than just a few beers after work.

My first reaction was, that's dangerous, somebody should do something about that. Somebody should call the police before he causes an accident. It took a few seconds but then I realized, I was the police! I was that somebody that had to do something about it.

When I was a kid growing up, I lived in a fairly tough blue-collar neighborhood. Getting into a fight was no big deal. But when a cop gets into a fight it's very different. You don't have any friends standing around to break things up before anyone gets too hurt. When you're rolling around in the street with some guy you know from the neighborhood, chances are nobody is going to get killed.

In police work the total opposite is true. You don't know the individual you're going toe-to-toe with. You don't know how crazy or desperate he is. You don't know if he's armed. You don't know if he is wanted for a homicide somewhere and is willing to do anything to stay out of jail. You just don't know!

I fished around under my coat, grabbed my radio, and asked Central to send me over one car for backup. I was a rookie but I wasn't stupid. I fully expected to be rolling around in the middle of the street with this guy in another minute, and I wanted to call for assistance before I was out of breath.

I marched up to him with my nightstick gripped tightly in hand. This was my first taste of police work and I was determined to do my job. I looked up at him, and with the best authoritative voice I could muster, I pointed to the sidewalk and said, "Get the fuck over there."

I'm only about five nine so the guy towered over me. We stood there in the middle of the street, cars passing on both sides of us, staring each other down for what seemed like a long time. He was staring—way down—at me with his drunken bloodshot eyes, and I was staring—way up—at him with a look of "don't fuck with me" in mine.

I could feel my knuckles turning white as I gripped the night-stick in my hand. If he wanted to fight, I was ready to lay that stick right over the top of his head and end this thing quick. I hoped. He had no problem throwing punches at passing cars, so I figured he would have no problem throwing one at me either.

People passing by stopped and stared, waiting for the show to begin. Everybody loves a good fight in Brooklyn, especially when they think the cop is going to get his ass kicked.

But to my surprise he put his hands down and started stumbling toward the sidewalk just like I told him to do. He suddenly slouched over, hung his head down, and gave up. It was like he was a Macy's Thanksgiving Day Parade balloon and somebody just let the air out of him. I was utterly astonished. I was a twenty-three-year-old kid who had never told anyone what to do in my entire life except my little sisters, and even they didn't always listen to me. But now I'm standing in the middle of bad-ass Brooklyn enforcing the law. It was kind of a rush.

When we put him in the back of the car for the ride to the station house, he was so tall he had to duck his head down. That seemed easy enough. I wrote him a summons for disorderly conduct and I had my first arrest. It wasn't the Lindbergh kidnapping, but it was a start. And since this was Brooklyn, I didn't have to wait long for another collar to come my way.

Two hours later I'm walking my foot post again when I see a guy running down the same block. I'm only a few hours into my first day on patrol and I still had no idea what I was doing, but something wasn't right. I didn't see a bus coming and it wasn't raining either. I figured this guy must have done something, so I started running after him. He was fast, but I was faster. I was young and dumb, but I was in good shape.

I chased him for two blocks, and when I tackled him into a parked car he had a gold chain and crucifix in one hand and a knife in the other. He had just robbed some kid and his girlfriend around the corner, and I had my second arrest. Police work was fun and seemed easy. A little dangerous, but easy.

A week later I'm walking a foot post again when a teenage girl walks up to me and says she was raped by two guys in an apartment not far away. I went over to the apartment, dragging the victim with me, and found one of the perps. BAM! Just like that I had another felony collar. I was starting to get the hang of things. After just one week I had a rape, a robbery, and a disorderly conduct.

Not long after that a woman approached me all hacked up. Her hands, arms, and back had been slashed by a razor. She and her baby's daddy had an argument over some money and diapers he owed her and it got a little heated. He pulled out a razor and did a real nasty job on her.

When I went up to the apartment to lock him up and get her baby back, she felt the need to warn me about his bad temper. I smiled and assured her I would be fine. I told her that I would explain to this asshole that this was inappropriate behavior toward his baby's mama. She could read between the lines. She understood that I wasn't going to take any bullshit from this guy like she had to. As the blood pooled on the ground around her feet, she smiled back at me, eager to see this prick in handcuffs.

Unfortunately by the time she had found me out in the street and by the time I made it to the apartment, the guy had fled. That pissed me off because I really wanted to lock the guy up. I found the baby in the apartment unharmed and returned the kid back to the mother, but there was not much else I could do except fill out a complaint report referring the case to the detective squad. Somebody else would get to lock this guy up.

I quickly learned I was falling in love with the job. I loved the metallic clicking noise handcuffs make when you're slapping them on some bad guy's wrists. I wasn't smart enough to be a doctor so I probably wouldn't find a cure for cancer, but in some small way I knew I was doing something worthwhile in this world. For a guy starting out in life with just a high school diploma and a driver's license, I was making a difference and it was gratifying.

I still didn't really know what I was doing, but just like my instructor on graduation day told me, I was learning how to survive. I laugh when I hear cops say they hardly ever pulled their gun out in their entire career. In Krooklyn (gangster for Brooklyn) my gun was in my hand a couple of times a day.

Back in the eighties, New York City was like the Wild West, all you had to do was go out on patrol and something was going to fall into your lap whether you wanted a collar or not. The Big Apple was a great place to be a cop, and if you didn't mind rolling around out in the street and getting your hands dirty you could learn fast.

My new life of adventure was everything I had hoped it would be. Especially when my cynical, sarcastic, and hard-to-please training sergeant would sometimes grumble, "Good job, kid." He even put me in for a medal for my robbery collar. It wasn't that big of a deal, it was the lowest medal there is, an EPD (Excellent Police Duty). But when I got that I was strutting around like a rooster. I couldn't pass a mirror without stopping and looking at it. I was hooked, I wanted more.

Ever since I was a little kid with a toy cowboy hat on my head and a plastic cap pistol in my pocket, I had known that this was the life for me. I was a couple of months into the job and I looked like a cop and felt like a cop, but really, I was far from being one yet.

The trouble with rookies is, once you learn a little and start to get the hang of things, you get cocky. And that's when you get into trouble. You start to take chances and sometimes do stupid things.

About a year later I was working in Manhattan and feeling pretty good about myself. I had made more than a few collars since those first ones and was starting to think I knew what I was doing. I had a handle on all the required paperwork to process an arrest and could maneuver my way through the dingy labyrinth called Central Booking and the criminal court system, but I still had more balls than brains and was about to learn a big lesson.

I was out on patrol with my partner taking a slow ride up Sixth Avenue. It was in the middle of the day and the streets were packed with people and cars. Manhattan is not as bad as Krooklyn, but you still have to be careful because danger comes in many forms and I wasn't expecting this one.

As we cruised up Sixth Avenue approaching Eighth Street, I see a guy running out of a grocery store with the manager chasing after him. The manager was waving his arms and yelling for someone to call the police.

Okay, here we go! The adrenaline kicks in and the fun is about to start. I don't know what he did, but he's flying down the block like he just committed a serious crime.

Sixth Avenue is four lanes of congested traffic going in one direction—north. And just our luck, the perp runs past us going south. There's no way to turn the car around and go after him, so we're a little screwed. It's a lot easier to chase a guy with the car than on foot. Just stay with him long enough till he runs out of gas, then jump out, grab him, and slap the cuffs on him. He's out of breath and you're nice and fresh, just in case he wants to fight or try something else stupid.

I turn around in my seat and see him starting to disappear into the maze of cars and pedestrians behind us, and in a few more seconds we're going to lose him. My partner was a big Italian guy who wore size-twelve combat boots. He was good to have around in a fight, but he wasn't much of a sprinter. So I tell him, I'll take the guy on foot and you whip it around the block and try to cut us off.

Splitting up with your partner is always a dumb idea. It may look good on TV, but in real life it can get you killed. We work in teams for a reason, it's a hell of a lot safer than going it alone.

I bail out of the car and start running after the guy. In the distance I can see he starts to slow down slightly. He obviously thinks he has gotten away. As he turns and looks over his shoulder to see if anybody is following him, there I am, a rookie, a new jack, and catching up to him in a hurry. My jacket was unzipped and waved in the breeze behind me as I sprinted after him. I'm now close enough to see that "Oh shit" expression on his face as he sees me coming and proceeds to kick it into high gear.

He must have had his getaway planned because without hesitation he runs down into the subway station at Waverly Place with me right on his heels. Perps can really motor when they have to. I'm running hard because I want to catch him, but he's running hard because he wants to stay out of jail.

He jumps the turnstile like a deer over a fence and then runs down the steps and onto the platform, weaving through the crowd like OJ through an airport. This just gets me more excited. I keep thinking, this guy must have done something real bad or he wouldn't be running this hard to get away. I figured he must have robbed the store. Only cops, and especially rookies, think this way. But I'm actually hoping he has a gun on him or at least a knife. That would be a nice collar to bring into the station house.

He continues running down another set of steps and onto the lower platform with me right behind him breathing down his neck. Both of us are weaving through the crowd and pushing people out of our way as we go. I'm hoping to see a transit cop on the platform and maybe get a little help because I'm sure I lost my partner out in the street somewhere. And to make matters worse our radios don't work in the subway so I can't even call for backup.

When he reaches the end of the platform I'm thinking, "I got you now, asshole." But he doesn't stop, he just keeps on going along this little catwalk, then jumps onto the tracks and runs into the tunnel. He doesn't even hesitate one second. He just keeps on running like he knows exactly where he's going and then disappears into the darkness.

Two seconds later I reach the end of the platform and stop. I stand there for a moment staring into the dark tunnel, a little hesitant to follow. I knew going any farther was a bad idea. A very bad idea.

As I tried to decide what to do next, I looked down at the catwalk and there was a scuffed-up, worn-out black loafer sitting there. He ran right out of his shoe!

When we were in the the academy they gave us a "Track Safety" class. All day long the instructor was telling us to look out for this and look out for that. He said watch the third rail, it has six hundred volts flowing through it. He showed us how to read the traffic lights in the tunnel and tell when a train was coming. He said, don't step on a switch along the rail because if it closes it can crush your foot. The yellow stripes on the wall mean there is no clearance between the wall and the train, and you will be squished if the train comes. He said in a worst-case scenario, if the train is going to run you over, you could duck into a cutout in the wall or lay down in the trough between the rails. Neither one seemed like fun. The cutouts were shallow and hard to fit into, and the trough was filled with garbage, rats, and stagnant water.

Like good rookies we all took notes and tried to remember everything. The instructor, a salty old transit cop with a sadistic sense of humor, finished up the class by acknowledging he threw a lot of information at us. He said it would be difficult to recall it all in a stressful situation, so he summed it up by giving us one golden rule that would be easy to remember: "STAY OUT OF THE FUCKING TUNNEL. IT'S DANGEROUS DOWN THERE."

We all shook our heads in agreement. That seemed like a good idea, and it would be easy to remember.

I stood at the end of the platform and watched my perp for a second as he ran into the darkness and started to disappear. I could hear the instructor's voice in the back of my head telling me to stay out of the tunnel, but I could also see all the people on the platform looking and laughing at me as my perp got away. They weren't really laughing though, it was just my pride getting the best of me. I didn't like this guy getting away and my great robbery collar was disappearing down the tunnel while I stood there feeling like a dope.

I thought about it for a few seconds and then decided, fuck it, I'm not giving up that easy. So I jumped down onto the tracks and trotted into the abyss. I ran down about forty or fifty yards then stopped, looking and listening. He was only a few seconds or so ahead of me, but I soon realized he was gone.

There are lots of places a person can hide if you know where you are going. There are rooms and storage areas and escape routes that lead back up to the street. There were homeless people living down in the tunnels who knew their way around just as well as the transit workers. He must have been one of them because he obviously knew where he was going.

If you have never been down a subway tunnel it's kind of peaceful. When there is no train coming it's very quiet and serene. I could see why homeless people would want to stay here. It's not exactly the Waldorf Hotel, but it's better than some cardboard box out on the cold street. Or sleeping on a cot in a dorm at the men's shelter with a hundred other drug addicts, alcoholics, and violent mental patients.

Most of them would explain that they chose the tunnel over the shelter because the shelter was just too dangerous. It made sense to me. I'd been in the men's shelter plenty of times looking for perps or breaking up fights. It's hard to sleep when you're worried that the maniac next to you with nothing to lose and little to live for will cut your throat just to steal your half-empty pack of cigarettes.

The tunnel was warm and peaceful, but every few minutes the ground and walls would start to shake like an earthquake. The shaking would be followed by a hurricane-like wind, as the one-hundred-ton train blasted its way from one station to the next. I guess that was easier to sleep through than all the farting, burping, and arguing you hear at the shelter.

I shined my flashlight around but it was useless. I couldn't figure out where this guy might be hiding. The walls, ceiling, and floor were all painted black and covered with steel dust and dirt. About fifty feet farther down the black hole the tracks curved to the right, so I couldn't see past that. There are several trains that stop at this station: the A, C, D, E, and F trains.

There were tracks going in different directions here as well as up on the platform above me. I was no train expert, but it was obvious I was standing in a very busy area where several tracks merged. Not a good place to be while I tried to figure out where my mystery perp disappeared to.

I stood there for a moment catching my breath while listening to the clicking of the switches and watching the traffic lights change

from red to yellow to green. As I was appreciating the tranquility
of the subterranean lifestyle I felt the slightest breeze cross my face.
At first I didn't realize what it was or which direction it was coming from, but within seconds the slight wafting breeze turned into
a gale-force wind. I wasn't sure if it was me or the shaking ground
below me, but instantly my body was trembling because I knew
what was about to happen next.

I looked behind me and there it was—two glaring headlights
and a big letter "F" heading right for me. Bright blue sparks flew off
the six-hundred-volt third rail, lighting up the tunnel in an eerie
disco-like glow. In about five seconds I was going to get FUCKED
big-time by the northbound F train.

At that moment I felt scared, but more than anything I felt
incredibly stupid. This was a stupid, stupid way to die. From now
on I would be known as the idiot who ran down the tunnel and got
run over. In every Track Safety class for all eternity I would be the
example of what not to do.

In my overenthusiasm to catch the perp and make a nice collar,
I never planned on the likely event the train would come. Now, I
only had a few seconds to think of something before I became a
hood ornament.

I could just barely see the face of the engineer driving the train
in his darkened cab, but he looked as shocked as I was. When he
came around that curve he never expected to see someone standing
there.

I had a quick choice to make. Lay down in that dirty filthy
trough or try to squeeze into a small space behind me that separated the track I was on from the next one over. I chose the space—
but to reach it I had to jump over the third rail.

I jumped as quickly and carefully as I could. It wasn't that high
of a jump, but the thought of six hundred volts between my legs
made it seem like I was leaping over the Grand Canyon. That death
would not be any more pleasant than getting hit by a train.

I thought about running onto the other track behind me, but
with the wind, the noise, and the darkness there was no telling if a

train was coming on that one also. I was literally stuck between a rock and a hard place.

As I leaped over the third rail I could feel a strange tingling in my ball bag. I'm sure it wasn't any actual electricity flowing through my testicles but it did feel that way. More likely it was the thought of six hundred volts cooking my goodie bag that made it tingle.

Behind the third rail and between the two tracks were steel girders going up to the ceiling that were set into a cement divider. If I could somehow jump onto the divider and manage to hold on to the girder, I figured the train would probably miss me. It wouldn't miss me by much, a few inches or maybe a foot at the most, but I was running out of options. So the divider it would be.

I leaped up onto the divider and wedged myself between two steel girders just in time. Instantly the train was passing less than a foot in front of me. The floor and walls were shaking and the wind was hurtling past me at hurricane force. The screeching noise of the steel wheels against the steel rails was deafening and terrifying. I was scared to death and trying not to piss in my pants.

I was holding on as tight as I could, but the wind was sucking me forward and closer to the train. I couldn't hear myself, but I was screaming something like "Oh shit! Oh fuck!" Everything around me was dark except the inside of the train as it sped by. I could see the passengers' faces whooshing past me inside the brightly lit cars as they passively stared out the windows. They had the thousand-yard stares of bored, tired commuters heading home after work, oblivious to me screaming and holding on for dear life just a foot away from them.

I'm sure a couple of them must have seen my screaming face for a split second as I whizzed by right outside their window. They probably just shook it off, thinking they imagined it.

I looked down and saw my unzipped jacket flapping furiously in the breeze. It was within inches of the speeding train, and all I could think of was, if my jacket catches on to something it's going to pull me forward and squish me between the steel girder and the train. This was bad. This was real bad. I would rather be shot or stabbed. I couldn't think of a worse way to die.

I held on with everything I had. Every muscle in my body was tense and taut, holding me firmly in place. Then just as suddenly as it started, it was over. The noise, the wind, the shaking walls and floor all stopped. The train was gone, speeding down the tunnel into the station. Everything was quiet again, and the peacefulness of the subterranean lifestyle returned. The serenity was comforting and gave me a chance to gather my thoughts.

I made it! I survived! I'm alive!!

I jumped off the divider onto the tracks and headed for the cat-walk and out of that tunnel. The bright lights on the platform seemed warm and reassuring. My clean uniform was black from steel dust and my shiny shoes were scuffed, but somehow I made it out of that fucking black hole in one piece. And I swore to myself I would never do that again.

A few people were watching me high stepping it from the cat-walk back onto the platform. I was trying to act cool, or about as cool as I could be under the circumstances. I wanted it to look like . . . everything went just as I had planned it.

I wasn't happy about the perp getting away, but I was anxious to get the hell out of there and back up into the fresh air and sunshine. I started walking down the platform toward the stairs, brushing steel dust off my jacket, and debating whether I was going to tell my partner exactly what happened, when I see him running down the steps. I could see he was a little pissed at me for running off on my own the way I did, but he was also relieved he found me. It's never a good idea to split up the way I did, but my partner was a good cop and I knew he would find me sooner or later.

He asked me where the perp was. I was still a little shook up and out of breath, so I just pointed over my shoulder with my thumb toward the tunnel. My partner was a hard charger like me, but sometimes he could be a little more sensible. He took one look down that black hole and said, "Fuck it, let's go get coffee."

We started up the stairs with me chalking this up to a learning experience, when I remembered the shoe. My perp lost his shoe on the catwalk and I figured he probably wouldn't like hopping around that tunnel on one foot, so he might just come back for it.

I wasn't ready to give up just yet. I convinced my partner to give it a few minutes and see if the guy would come back out. When it comes to stakeouts I have the patience of a fisherman. I can wait all day and all night for some guy that I'm after. I love the thrill of the hunt. I find it exciting. I would probably be a great stalker.

We took a position behind the stairs where I could peek through the railing and keep an eye on the shoe. We hung out for a while as nonchalant as possible, but people were watching us and wondering what we were up to.

I was a little surprised because it didn't take as long as I thought it would. Within a few minutes Mr. Tunnel Rat walked out, right underneath the big NO TRESPASSING sign. He picked up his shoe, put it on, and sauntered down the platform like he didn't have a care in the world. It was like he was walking out of his bedroom and going to work. Except for the slightly ratty-looking clothes he was wearing, he looked like he belonged down there. He obviously spent a lot of time in his subterranean home and strutted around like he owned the place. The only thing he didn't do was whistle while he walked.

I was still eyeballing him from behind the stairs as he walked toward us, oblivious to our presence. And before he knew it we jumped him. I had no intention of chasing this asshole again, so I skipped the "Police, don't move" part, and he went down to the ground hard and fast. Before he could even think of resisting, he had handcuffs on. He was quite surprised to see me. He obviously thought I had given up. I took that as a compliment.

We grabbed him by both elbows and yanked him up to his feet so I could toss him. I asked him if he had anything sharp on him or anything else that might hurt me. Sheepishly he shook his head no. He was homeless, jobless, and now under arrest. Life wasn't going so good for him.

I checked his waistband first, then started going through his pockets, careful not to get stuck by anything sharp—especially a hypodermic needle. Not to sound cruel, but most of these guys are in this situation for the same reason, they're junkies.

Tossing him took a few minutes because he had on two coats, a hooded sweatshirt, and three pairs of pants. Most of the stuff he had on him was crap, and he stunk like he hadn't seen a shower in weeks. I kept searching, and cradled inside his coat pocket, carefully wrapped up in a wad of tissue paper, was a crack pipe and a cigarette lighter. No big surprise, he was a crackhead. I was happy I finally caught this guy, but my great collar didn't seem so great anymore.

I was peeling clothes off him like he was a giant onion, going through every pocket I could find. Finally I found what I was looking for. There was something heavy buried deep inside one of his many pants pockets, but it wasn't the gun I was hoping to find. It was five packs of Duracell AA batteries. My robbery collar was quickly turning into a petit larceny.

I looked at him and growled, "All this over some fucking batteries." I wanted to strangle him. We both could have gotten killed over twenty dollars' worth of batteries that he was probably going to sell for two. He hung his head and seemed slightly contrite but mostly unapologetic. He was just doing what crackheads do—they steal.

We walked him up to the street and back to the store. There were several more police cars on the scene because the store owner had called 911 to report a "robbery in progress." I explained to the sergeant that I saw the perp running from the store and chased him down into the subway and apprehended him.

I left out the part about the tunnel and the train and how I almost got killed over a bullshit collar. In the past he had always liked my eagerness and thought I showed some promise. No sense ruining that.

The victim positively identified the perp and his property and gave us a good statement as to what happened. It ended up being pretty simple, a ground-ball petit larceny and trespassing collar.

On the ride back to the station house I swore to myself I would never do that again. I learned a big lesson that afternoon about being eager and never giving up. I realized that in police work having balls is a great thing, but having brains and common sense is what keeps you alive.

3.

Growing Pains

A wise old cop once told me that police work takes a young, strong body but an experienced, mature mind. It was still early in my career and like most cops my age I had plenty of the first but was still working on the second.

My fingers were fumbling as I tried to pin my shield and the one medal I had on my uniform shirt. Next I grabbed my gun belt, strapped it on, and shoved my gun in my holster. My pounding headache and nauseous stomach made getting dressed a little difficult. I slammed my locker shut and ran up the stairs, taking them two at a time because I was late for roll call. As I sprinted up the steps my head was pounding like there was a woodpecker inside trying to get out and my stomach was doing flips. I had a little bit of a hangover. That's why I was late.

It was Sunday morning, and I was scheduled to work a day tour, but that didn't keep me from going out the night before. I was single, twenty-five years old, and like a dog in heat I was out on the prowl. It was summertime, so a couple of buddies and I had headed down to Seaside Heights to try to pick up some drunk Jersey girls hanging out in the clubs.

Having to work the next day meant little to me. I could party all night, catch a few winks on the sofa in the precinct lounge, then work all day. I could handle anything life, or the streets, could throw at me, because I was young, strong, and didn't know any better.

I finally made it to roll call a few minutes late, and slipped into the back row. For a second I thought I made it without the sergeant noticing, but a cocked eyebrow in my direction let me know I was bagged. I was normally a good worker and rarely gave the boss any trouble, so it wasn't that big of a deal and he didn't break my balls. Sunday day tours were the quietest, most laid-back tour of the week. Everybody was in a relaxed mood, expecting an easy day.

My partner took one look at me, laughed, and grabbed the car keys. I was glad because I had just raced up the Garden State Parkway and was in no mood to do any more driving.

Usually on Sundays we took the car to the car wash, but this time my stomach was up in my throat and my head was ready to explode, so I told my partner, "Fuck it. First I need some aspirins, then let's go get some breakfast."

We hit a diner, got egg sandwiches and coffee, and then headed over to Washington Square Park to chill out. While my partner was watching the girls jog by in their tight shorts and giving me his usual play-by-play commentary, I was massaging my temples, popping aspirins, and trying to put something in my stomach.

It was early in the day, but it was already eighty degrees outside and getting hotter by the minute. It was August, and the weatherman on the radio was describing it as hazy, hot, and humid. I was half tempted to take my vest off and throw it into the trunk, but instead I turned the air conditioner up full blast and pointed the vents right into my face. I reminded myself that staying up late last night was a stupid thing to do and taking my vest off would be another dumb decision.

After a little while my stomach started to feel better, and the woodpecker finally escaped. I swore to myself I wouldn't do this ever again, but in the back of my mind I knew I was full of shit. I would be out again next Saturday night doing the exact same stupidity.

As we sat there having breakfast and watching the girls jog by, the dispatcher called our unit to give us a job. Neither one of us was in the mood to start working just yet, but we were rookies and you do what you're told. Like most rookies we were both adrenaline junkies so we hoped that it was a "man with a gun" or maybe a "robbery in progress" and not some bullshit job.

But instead of the "gun run" or the robbery, we got the worst possible job in all of police work, a report of a "foul odor." The dispatcher gave us the address of a building over on Tenth Street and told us to see the super. We both looked at each other with that "Oh shit" look on our faces. This could mean only one thing, a DOA. I couldn't believe it, a rotten, smelly, stinking DOA in the middle of summer—and I was still hungover.

Chasing a guy with a gun or grabbing some perp that just did a stickup is a walk in the park compared to handling a ripe, stinking DOA. Just the thought of it had my stomach flipping again. I wrapped up my egg sandwich and put the lid back on my coffee, afraid anything I ate might be coming back up again in a little while.

Cops deal with death on a regular basis, it's a big part of the job, and it's something you learn to get used to. But it takes a little time before you can look at a dead body and have the only thing on your mind be paperwork and notifications.

Before becoming a cop, like most normal people my only experience with death was seeing some dead relative in a funeral home. They were always dressed up nice, with plenty of makeup to give their cheeks and lips that rosy color. The room was always filled with flowers, giving the air a pleasant, sweet smell.

Police work is a little different. We get to see them right where they fall, usually lying in a pool of blood. There are no flowers to mask the smell, and there's no pink or rosy cheeks, just a gray ashen face with half-opened eyes staring back at you. And it's not unusual to be stepping over somebody's brains or entrails lying on the sidewalk. Real death isn't pretty, but the more you see the more you get used to it.

My first homicide was a guy shot because he was fooling around with somebody else's girlfriend. The victim hears the doorbell ring and when he answers it, *pow*, one through the chest. Small hole and very little blood. The round went right through his heart and came out his back. He sort of looked like he came home drunk and passed out on the floor.

The thing I remember most about it was his wife wailing and sobbing and rolling all over the floor in the other room. This went on for hours, the whole time we were there, and it wasn't easy to listen to. I guess she hadn't figured out why he got shot yet.

Since that time I had a few more dead bodies, but I was nowhere near being used to dealing with them.

We found the address and parked the car in front of a fire hydrant out front. The building was a typical pre–World War II Manhattan five-story walk-up with a couple of steps leading up to the entrance. The first thing I noticed was the front door propped open with a few Chinese menus and some undelivered junk mail. This was not a good sign. And as soon as my foot hit the top step I realized why. The smell hit me like a punch in the face. Once you smell it you'll never forget it for the rest of your life.

If you ever had a mouse drop dead behind the stove or refrigerator and you can't find it, you know the smell I'm talking about. A mouse weighs a couple of ounces. Imagine one hundred and fifty or two hundred pounds of decaying flesh.

I put my hand over my nose and mouth. The lingering aroma of bacon and eggs on my fingers was a relief. I think.

When we walked in, a male Hispanic stepped forward eager to meet us. Obviously he was the super. He had the generic drab green matching shirt and pants supers like to wear, with the name "Jose" stitched over the front pocket. I gave him my generic cop hello: "Somebody call the police?"

Jose gave us the story. He had a young female, mid-twenties, living in a second-floor apartment that he hadn't seen or heard from in a few days. Apparently the girl's parents hadn't heard from her either and called Jose to ask if he could check up on her. So Jose being the helpful—slash—busybody super, he went and knocked on her door. After knocking a few times and getting no answer, he put his ear to the door in order to listen more carefully, but the only thing coming through the crack was silence and the smell of putrid, decaying flesh.

Jose had been at the super game for a long time and knew exactly what the smell was. This wasn't his first "foul odor" job. But before calling the parents back and telling them there was a problem, he wanted to be sure, so he climbed down the fire escape and through the window. After checking things out and satisfying his own curiosity, he left the apartment through the front door, and when he did, he let the odor out that had been building up for the last few days. Now everybody in the building understood why cops hate responding to a ripe DOA.

Jose gave us the girl's pedigree info and said the parents were upstairs waiting for us. Right away I was relieved—this was turning out to be an easy one. The victim was properly identified and the parents were on the scene, so there was no need for a missing persons report. Some quick paperwork, have the sergeant and detectives respond, and we would be done in no time. I hoped the boss would have some rookie with even less time on the job than I had sit on the body until the medical examiner's wagon showed up, and we could save the rest of the day. Maybe even make a collar later.

I grabbed the apartment keys off Jose and headed for the stairs, but before I could get too far he blurted out, "Hey man, we got a problem."

He explained to me that the mother had wanted to go into the apartment to see her daughter, and when he told her no she got mad and almost ripped his head off. She was adamant about seeing her daughter and nobody was going to tell her no.

Now that the police were on the scene it wasn't Jose's problem anymore, it was mine, and angry moms can be a real pain in the ass when it comes to their kids. Especially dead ones.

The smell in the lobby was sickening, so without even going upstairs I already knew I was never going to let Mom step foot in that apartment. I didn't know what was waiting for me up there, but I sure as hell knew it wasn't going to be pretty. And there was no way I was going to let a mother see her child like that.

I walked up a couple of steps, then stopped. I had to take care of some unfinished business with Jose. I turned and said, "You know you shouldn't have gone into the apartment. You should have waited for the police."

I didn't have to explain any further. Jose knew exactly what I was talking about. It wasn't unusual for the super to go into a DOA's residence and clean it out of jewelry and cash before the police could safeguard it for the family.

I put on my dead-serious cop face and told him, "If there is anything missing, I'm coming to look for you first." Jose gave me his best puppy-dog eyes and said, "Oh no, Officer, I would never."

I walked up the stairs to the second floor, and with every step the smell got worse. You can't see it, but it's thick and heavy and hangs in the air like a fog. It clings to everything it touches, the inside of your nostrils and throat, even your clothes.

When we got to the apartment, there were two middle-aged people waiting for me, Mom and Dad. I started to introduce myself, but before I could get a word out Mom charged me and very firmly stated, "Officer, I want to see my daughter!"

The daughter was in her mid-twenties, the same age as me, so when I looked at Mom and Dad they could have easily been my parents. I was in uniform, with my shiny new silver shield, and my one medal for good police work, but at that moment I felt like a little boy being scolded and I instinctively backed up half a step.

As Mom was reading me the riot act Dad was standing a few feet behind her just watching. He had the kind of face that had "nice guy" written all over it. I looked over to him for a little help, but right away I could tell that wasn't going to happen. I don't know if Mom normally wore the pants in the family, but today she was definitely in charge.

Before we went up Jose had given me a little family history. Our deceased had suffered from diabetes all her life, and about a year ago she convinced her parents to let her move out and get her own apartment. Apparently this was not an easy decision for her parents because she was an only child and very sick. I could tell already the parents were holding a lot of guilt. Maybe if they had held their ground and said no to moving out, we would not be here gagging on the smell of decaying flesh.

I don't know how it was possible, but apparently Mom was in denial. I think she was hoping there was some other explanation for the smell seeping from under the door, and she was not going to believe her daughter was dead until she saw the body.

I let Mom vent for a minute or so and just politely nodded as she warned me that she was going to see her daughter and there was nothing I could do to stop her. As Mom harangued me I glanced over to Dad a few times again looking for help, but I got nothing. I could tell *he* was looking to *me* for help.

As Mom paused to catch her breath I put my hands up and said, "Okay, okay, I understand. Just let me go in first and check things out."

She must have thought she was making some progress with me, so she calmed down and reluctantly agreed to let me go in first. At this point all I was doing was stalling, hoping my sergeant would show up soon. He was a great guy with a lot of time on the job. He always knew what to do and what to say, and I was sure he would know how to handle Mom.

I don't know why, maybe my uniform made me look older and wiser then I actually was, but for the time being Mom was listening to me and Dad seemed to be trusting me.

As I stood there in that hallway letting Mom vent, and looking into Dad's helpless eyes, the feeling of being a little boy being scolded by his mother was suddenly replaced by a huge sense of responsibility. I felt terrible for these people. I knew there was no hope. I knew there was no possible explanation for the smell coming out of that room other than a dead body. My partner was a great cop. I trusted him with my life on a daily basis, but he had all the compassion of Attila the Hun, so I knew this was up to me to deal with.

I put the key in the lock and opened the door just enough for my partner and me to slip in, then slammed it shut. I didn't want Mom trying to peek inside.

I figured we could hang out in the apartment and stall until the boss arrived and let him deal with the mother. The situation was getting tense, and I was looking forward to getting out of that hallway for a few minutes and letting things settle down a little. When we got inside I couldn't believe it. The hallway was bad, but the apartment was unbearable. Right away I put my hand over my nose and mouth and tried to suck in the last lingering aroma of bacon and eggs.

The apartment was a small studio, and as soon as you walked in, the bed was in front of you. And on the mattress, stained with body fluids, and covered with flies and maggots, was the body of Karen.

Jose had described her as young and pretty, but not anymore. Now you couldn't tell if it was a man or a woman, young or old. Her body was black and bloated, and flies and maggots were feasting on the eyes and swollen tongue. The only way I could tell it was a female was by the red painted finger- and toenails, and the pink and white cutoff girlie pajamas. The type a woman would wear when going to bed on a hot summer night. And by the looks of things I could tell she went to "sleep" at least a few nights ago.

I couldn't help but notice the air conditioner in the window next to the bed was turned off. If she had only put it on before going to bed this mess wouldn't be half as bad.

I stood there for a moment with my hand over my nose and mouth, swatting away flies and breathing the most shallow breaths possible. Old-time cops will tell you to go down to the corner store and buy the fattest stinkiest cigar you can find and light it up. Another trick is burning coffee grinds in a pot on the stove. We even have DOA crystals that you sprinkle on the floor. They smell sweet, kind of like bubble gum, but nothing was going to help here. This was the worst I had ever seen.

I looked around, and the tiny apartment seemed to be undisturbed. It was clean and neat, and the sun was shining in the windows. It looked like a girl who was proud of her first apartment lived here. I could see the half-open window that Jose had climbed into, but everything else, the dresser drawers, the closet, all seemed to be undisturbed. Maybe Jose wasn't a bad guy after all.

When I looked around I saw on top of the dresser a picture of a pretty girl with long brown hair leaning up against a tree in some park on a nice day. This was obviously our victim. She seemed happy, pretty, and full of life. Somebody I would have liked to meet.

I grabbed the radio off my belt and had the dispatcher notify the sergeant and the detective squad that we had a "confirmed DOA" at our location and needed them to respond. I wanted to get them over here as soon as possible, so we could get some help with Mom, and get out of the apartment. But the next thing I heard was the sergeant's gruff voice advising us that he would be responding "with a delay." He told the dispatcher to put him out at the station house "administrative" for a few. I knew exactly what that meant: it was eight o'clock on a Sunday morning, and he wasn't done having his coffee and reading the paper. The boss was a good guy, and I'm sure if he knew what I was dealing with he would have rushed over. But there was no way of explaining it to him over the radio, so we were on our own until he finished his "administrative duties."

We had come into the apartment to stall for a while, but I couldn't take it anymore, and by the look on my partner's face under his hand I could tell he couldn't either. I really didn't want to deal with Mom again, but I had to get some air.

When Jose had told her she couldn't come in she almost ripped his head off, but I was hoping my uniform carried a little more weight than his.

We opened the door and went back into the hallway to face Mom. I slammed the door shut and shoved the key deep in my back pocket. After witnessing what was in that apartment there was no way in hell I was going to let her in there. Even if I had to wrestle her to the floor and handcuff her, she was not going in. I figured I was going to get a civilian complaint over this but so what,

I didn't care. The last image of her only daughter was not going to be what was lying in that room.

Mom was staring straight at me, ready to charge. She wanted an answer and she wanted it now. Dad was standing behind her and he wanted help. Jose was staring at me wanting to know what was going to happen next. My partner was standing in the background watching everyone and covering my back while my mind raced, searching for just the right words.

This had the potential to get ugly real fast. My mind was racing as I tried to think of the right thing to say, but nothing was coming. I was a kid dealing with someone twice my age.

It was quite an awkward moment that seemed to last a very, very long time. I had never told a parent their child was dead. Cops do it on a regular basis, but I had never done it before. I was only about a year out of the academy and had no experience with this type of situation. At this point in my career I had very little experience with anything police-related besides making arrests and filling out the most basic paperwork.

In the academy they teach you the law and police science. You learn how to shoot a gun, drive fast, and handcuff a perp, but nothing could possibly prepare you for this. At the time I was only twenty-four, so I had very little life experience to fall back on.

Ever since the first time I stepped out on the street in uniform I had always felt a sense of pride and duty. I was proud to be a cop. I was always proud to walk down the street wearing my uniform, and I tried to do the job as best I could. But at this moment I was screwed. I was at a loss and didn't know what to say or do. It was a very delicate situation that needed to be handled just right, and I was completely unprepared to deal with this. But I felt bad for these people, and I was determined to get this right. I put one hand on Mom's shoulder, and with the other I motioned to the steps leading upstairs and said, "Please."

She understood, I wanted her to take a seat. At first she hesitated, because telling someone to have a seat could mean only one thing—bad news was coming. She slowly shuffled over and sat down on the steps. She clutched her purse, holding it tight into her chest and got prepared to hear what she most certainly knew already.

Dad, the super, and my partner stood off to the side waiting to see what was going to happen next. And to see if my head was the next one she was going to try and rip off. My heart was pounding and my mind was racing as I struggled for the right words.

I got down on one knee and knelt right in front of her. We were eyeball to eyeball and only a few inches apart. I reached out and took her hand in both of mine. To anyone watching it might have looked like I was proposing marriage, but I wasn't. I was about to tell her that her only child was dead, only a few feet away, and that she would not be allowed to see her one last time.

At that moment I was winging it. And again I was stalling. Every second seemed like an hour while my mind was going a hundred miles an hour trying to figure out what to say and hoping my sergeant or the detectives would show up just in time.

I kept trying to figure out just the right words, but nothing was coming. My mind was blank, and I knew that if I said the wrong thing this whole scene was going to explode into an ugly mess, and Mom and Dad deserved better than that. They needed me to rise to the occasion.

As I knelt there on one knee, holding a woman's hand that I didn't even know, a Zen-like calm came over me. I can't really explain it, but I stopped trying so hard to find the right words and just let it happen. I stopped thinking, and started feeling.

Mom wasn't saying anything or even holding my hand back. I could tell she was just letting it happen also. Call it divine help or wisdom or whatever you want, but my lips started moving without any thoughts from my brain.

I said to her, "Karen is gone. . . . She's been gone for a few days now and I know you want to see her and say good-bye but I don't think that's a good idea."

I was speaking in a slow but very deliberate way. I needed to sound compassionate but authoritative. I needed her to trust this baby-faced police officer kneeling in front of her who was half her age.

I continued, "You see, when a person dies the body goes through certain changes. Now it's not a bad thing, it's natural. And I guess that's the way God intended it to be, but it's not a pleasant thing to look at and I don't want you to see her like that. I want your last memories of her to be happy ones, like that picture of her in the park I saw on the dresser. Now I know you don't know me, we kind of just met, but I need you to trust me on this. I think it's the best thing to do right now."

I had Mom's limp hand held firmly in both of mine. I wanted her to squeeze back, but nothing. I wanted some sort of acknowledgment that I was making sense to her, or that she was even listening. She just sat completely silent, clutching her purse to her chest and staring toward the floor at the same sensible shoes my middle-aged mom likes to wear.

I gave her a moment to think about what I had just said while I waited for an answer. The moment seemed to last a very long time. Without looking up I could feel Dad, the super, and my partner staring at us. We were all nervous and wanted to know what the answer was.

Finally after what seemed like an eternity I leaned in and said, "I need you to trust me on this . . . please."

I watched as Mom pulled her purse to her chest even tighter, hugging the only thing she could. Any fight she had left in her seemed to be long gone, and any hopes she had for one last kiss or a face-to-face good-bye were gone as well, as the reality of the situation set in.

There was not much more for me to tell her. This baby-faced kid in uniform, kneeling down in front of her, holding her hand and begging her to listen to reason, was right.

What I had seen in that room would be difficult for anyone to look at. It would be unbearable for a parent, and I wasn't going to let that happen. If she continued to insist, I was prepared to paint a more graphic picture. I was even prepared to physically stand in that doorway and block her from going inside. I'm glad it didn't come to that.

I finished by saying again, "Will you please trust me?"

It wasn't easy for her to do, but finally, I felt her hand squeeze back, as she very softly said, "Okay."

I quietly breathed a sigh of relief as everyone around us did the same. I couldn't believe I had done it. I fully expected her to scream at me, or to try and push past me, but none of that happened. She was just a very sweet woman who needed a little help getting through what was probably the greatest tragedy of her life.

It was time to wrap this up, so I told her, "Maybe it's a good idea to go home now. I'm sure you have some arrangements to make, and I promise you my partner and I will stay here and take care of Karen."

She seemed to appreciate the idea that my partner and I would stay there and take care of her daughter, and that she would not be left alone in that room. I motioned with my hand for Dad to come over. He grabbed one arm and I grabbed the other, and we helped her up off the step. He put his arm around his wife's shoulder, and as he helped her down the hall he turned toward me and mouthed, "Thank you."

In the past year or so I had more than a few gratifying moments in my short career, graduating from the academy and making a couple of pretty good collars, but none of them made me feel more like a cop than Dad's "thank you."

I watched Mom continue to hug her purse as her sensible shoes shuffled down the hall. And as Dad eased her past the apartment, she paused and placed her hand on the door. It was as close to a good-bye, and touching her child, as she would be allowed, and my heart broke for her. She stood there for a moment with her finger-tips on the door, almost caressing it, and whispered, "I love you."

A few hours later when I finally walked out of that building I realized somewhere in the middle of all this my hangover had disappeared. I also realized something had changed inside of me.

I wasn't that dopey twenty-four-year-old drinking beer and doing shots, trying to pick up girls in a Jersey Shore bar anymore. I had grown up, more than just a little.

I was a young, inexperienced cop with a difficult job to do, but somehow I got the job done. Cops call it "the job," but police work is more than that. It's more than just going toe-to-toe with some bad guy and hauling him off to jail. Anybody with a young strong body can do that. It's being there in people's lives during times of crisis, and knowing what to say and what to do.

I wish I could say that the words coming out of my mouth were calculated and well thought out. They weren't. I don't know where they came from, but I'm grateful they did come when I needed them. Sometimes in life, and very often in police work, you are faced with a situation that forces you to grow up and to be a better, wiser person. It forces you to rise to the occasion.

When I walked into the building on that Sunday morning I had the strong body all young cops have, but when I walked out a few hours later, I was a small step closer to being the older, more mature cop I wanted to be.

4.

Dentist

I parked the car on Ninth Street and Fifth Avenue facing west, figuring this was as good a place to sit as any. There was a bank one block behind us, and two more just around the corner on Eighth Street, and all three had been hit in the last couple of weeks. The one right behind us had been hit twice.

Most people passing by had absolutely no idea we were cops. We were working anti-crime (plainclothes) and our job was to blend in—and we were good at it. My partner George's idea of plainclothes was a Hawaiian shirt and a big fat cigar dangling under his handlebar mustache. I was a little less fashionable—a cutoff sweatshirt worked for me. Our car was a baby-blue Buick LeSabre with crushed velour seats and a couple of dents the police department was too cheap to fix.

I took the lid off my coffee cup, hit the lever under my seat to lower it a few inches, and nestled in for what might be a long night.

My partner and I were looking for a guy they dubbed the "Silver Gun Bandit." He had been doing gunpoint ATM robberies all over Manhattan South. The guy was a maniac, a one-man crime wave—he had done over twenty of them in about eight weeks. Finally enough was enough, he was driving up the robbery stats and the big bosses were pissed. They wanted the guy caught and they wanted him now!

The heat was on, so we had to catch this guy, and we had to do it soon. For the past couple of days there had to be at least fifty of us out looking for this guy, and everybody involved wanted to be the one to drag him in, in handcuffs.

The big plan they had come up with was for the Robbery Squad and a bunch of the anti-crime teams to do surveillance. We were told to pick a bank we thought looked good and sit on it. We hoped the perp would hit one of them while we were watching, and if everything went right, he'd be in for one hell of a surprise when he tried coming out.

The perp we were looking for was a fairly nondescript guy, white male, average height, average build, and neatly dressed. His MO was simple: he would follow his victims into bank lobbies, pull a silver handgun on them, and force them to take cash out of the ATM machine.

Normally robberies in Manhattan are no big deal, but when you do over twenty you start pissing off the police department. Also when you do them in a short period of time, all of them in the same area, hit a couple of banks twice and use the same distinctive weapon and MO, you start attracting some attention to yourself.

A smart robber, and there aren't too many of them, tries to keep a low profile. If he had done a couple in the Bronx, a few in Brook-lyn, jumped around from Manhattan to Queens, nobody would have put two and two together for a long time, but he didn't. He liked robbing people in downtown Manhattan.

Probably he was afraid to do stickups in the Bronx. You pull a gun on somebody up there and they might just point one right back at you.

Also, in the beginning he started out slow, doing them maybe once a week, but after a while he was knocking them off every other day. This dumbass was either stupid, or had balls on him like an elephant. But either way, he was just begging to be caught.

He was what we call a "pattern robber." And once we figure out the pattern it becomes a lot easier to track and catch him. We usu-ally get several of these a year, and this dope became Manhattan Robbery Squad pattern number twenty-three. That means starting January first of that year, twenty-two other brain surgeons just like this guy attracted undue attention to themselves.

Out of the other twenty-two individuals, twenty had been caught, due to good police work. The other two just stopped, seeming to fall off the face of the earth. That usually means they are either dead or in jail on some unrelated matter. If they just start up again, that means they were in jail for a while. If we never see or hear from them again, that usually means they're dead. I doubt if any of them actually went to church, lit a candle, and saw the error of their ways.

Tonight my partner George and I took this spot because our guy seemed to like the area. I liked it because it was a busy corner, so it was easier for us to blend into the crowd. Plus we could keep ourselves amused watching the world go by, especially the girls.

When you see stakeouts on TV they probably seem exciting, but they're not. They're usually ninety-nine percent boredom, but the fun part is when the one percent excitement happens. There's nothing better than coming face-to-face with some real bad guy that you've been hunting for a while.

I alternated between the faces in the crowd and the wanted poster we had rubber-banded to the visor above my head. The poster was a sketch done by a police artist based on information provided by some of the victims. As sketches go this one wasn't too bad; it had a lot of detail.

Most times sketches are useless. The victim gets a few seconds to look at somebody who is sticking a gun or a knife in their face and threatening to kill them if they don't do what he says. Of course the perp looks like the boogeyman, and the sketches reflect that. Usually the victim can give you a good description of the weapon but not the person holding it. That's because they can't help but be focused on the gun pointed between their eyes.

But this dope robbed so many people, and believe it or not he was polite about it—except for the one victim he shot in the leg, ending the man's professional dancing career—that some of the victims got a good look at him.

As I sat there sipping my coffee, watching the world go by and looking for some armed robber, I started thinking, I love this job! I mean, what could be better than this? I call this work, but to me it really isn't. I'm hanging out with my partner, who is also one of my best friends. I'm in Manhattan, watching girls and catching bad guys. I love this shit!

George and I have been "partnered up" for about two years now. Four years ago, the first day I walked into the precinct, I saw him standing in the muster room. He had a big smile on his face and an even bigger handlebar mustache. I didn't know him at the time but I caught good vibes off him. I thought he seemed like a cool guy and I wouldn't mind working with him someday.

Sure enough, two years later here we are working anti-crime together. And like a lot of partners we quickly became best friends. We hang out together after work and on our days off. We even go on vacation together. The reason is, you don't partner up with a guy unless you like each other. You spend eight hours a day together cooped up in a car. It's like being roommates in a very, very small apartment.

But an even bigger reason is because you trust each other. And I don't mean you trust him just to pay the rent on time or not to hit on your girlfriend. I mean you trust him with your life. You don't do the kind of work we do unless you trust the guy sitting next to you to be there when the whole world turns to shit. So I consider myself a very lucky individual. I'm doing the job I love with one of my best friends.

Every precinct has an anti-crime team. It usually consists of a sergeant and about five cops. Usually they are the best cops in the precinct. The commanding officer handpicks the most active cops, puts them in plainclothes with unmarked cars, and lets them go out and tear up the streets.

It takes a couple of years of proving yourself before you get picked, so just being in anti-crime is kind of prestigious. We were sort of the cowboys in the precinct. We only went after the most serious stuff and we always brought in the best collars.

For me there was no better feeling in the world than dragging some bad guy into the station house in handcuffs, slapping a gun on the desk, and telling the lieutenant, "I got one for robbery."

While sipping my coffee, scanning the crowd, and listening to the police radio all at the same time, I asked George, "If we don't get anything good tonight, do you think you're going to be thirsty later?" He knew exactly what I meant. I wanted to know if he was up for a beer after work. His handlebar mustache wrinkled for a second while he thought about it and he said, "You might be able to twist my arm a little." We both knew it wasn't going to take too much arm-twisting.

Just then, as we were sitting there bullshitting, drinking coffee, and girl watching, this dude walks right past the front of our car. He looks right at us and you can tell he's bugging out. This guy is freaking! He's got panic written all over his face.

I look at him, then I look at the sketch. My eyes are going a mile a minute, darting back and forth between the sketch and this guy's face. George is doing the exact same thing. It didn't take long until we both reached the same conclusion. He looks exactly like the sketch!

One thing is for sure, this guy made us and he's freaking the fuck out. But it can't be this easy. Everybody in Manhattan South is looking for him and he walks right past the front of *our* car! I couldn't believe we could get this lucky, but what the hell, why not? I'll take it. A lot of times good police work comes down to luck. Being in the right place at the right time.

Now George and I are both professionals. On the inside we're racing, we're doing a hundred miles an hour, but on the outside we remain cool. I said, "What do you think?" George shot right back, "Looks good to me, bro, let's jump him."

I'm thinking, sketches aren't perfect but this guy is way too close. We've got to grab him and get a better look, but the problem is he made us. We lost the element of surprise.

The best way to grab a guy like this is to "shock the shit" out of him. We run up on him, jump him, and BAM! The next thing he knows is he's face first against the wall with a gun screwed into his ear. He never gets a chance to try something stupid. But he made us and now he's got the advantage. If he's our guy he could just

whip out the gun and light us up—ending *all* dancing careers—
before we ever get out of the car.

So we decide to let him take a few more steps. We want to put a
little distance between him and us, so we sit tight for a few seconds
just playing it cool. But as we're watching him, he's watching us.
You could see him peeking out of the corner of his eye trying to see
what we were doing.

He was walking south on Fifth Avenue toward Eighth Street
and was now past the corner of the building line we were sitting
parallel to. It was time to make a move, so I grab the sketch,
shove it in my pocket, and jump out of the car. We hustled up
to the corner and start to peek around, but when I got there he
was gone. He was nowhere in sight. I was pissed. I turned toward
George, who was right on my heels, and said, "He fucking took
off on us!"

We jogged down the block looking all over for this guy, but
nothing. Now we were the ones who were bugging out. We had
him right in our mitts, and now in ten seconds we'd lost him.

My mind was racing, "Shit, shit, shit, I can't believe this. Everybody in the world is looking for this guy, and we had him, and lost
him." Because George and I are both calm, cool professionals who
may have just fucked up big-time, we're raging on the inside, but
on the outside we're keeping it together.

"All right, let's think about this. We were only a couple of seconds behind him. He couldn't have gone too far," I said.

I started looking around, trying to figure out where he could
have ducked into. I looked back along Fifth Avenue where we just
ran from. There was one building, but it was a nice one with a doorman in the lobby, and there was no way the doorman would have
let him in unless he lived there. And if he lived there he probably
wasn't our boy.

He didn't run all the way south on Fifth Avenue toward Washington Square Park because we could have seen him. He didn't run
west on Eighth Street because we would have seen him cross Fifth
Avenue.

The only place he could have run to was east on Eighth Street. So we tear ass down to there, but still nothing. The guy was gone. He was nowhere in sight. We looked around trying to size things up.

It was a long run from Fifth Avenue to University Place. George and I both looked at each other and realized the same thing, he must have ducked into one of the stores. We both relaxed a little because if we were right we were going to get him.

We started walking up Eight Street because there was no need to run anymore, he was close, I could feel it. I reached into my back pocket and turned down the radio, no need to let him hear us coming. Then I reached under my shirt and unsnapped my holster. Out of the corner of my eye I saw George was doing the same. We were side by side, step for step, and walking with a purpose. I kind of felt like Gary Cooper in *High Noon* walking down a dusty street. We were ready for a gunfight.

The first place we passed that he could have ducked into was a bank. I looked through the window but nothing. At the same time George kept scanning the street just in case the guy popped out somewhere else.

We continued walking. Next was a pharmacy. The window was covered with posters and merchandise and I couldn't see inside, so I opened the door and slowly eased my way in. George covered the doorway. He was watching my back, but he was still keeping an eye on the street.

I took a quick look around and everything was quiet. There were a couple of people shopping and everything seemed normal, except for me. I must have appeared pretty suspicious, eyeballing everybody while holding something big and black under my shirt. I glanced over to the clerk, who was watching every move I made, and I could tell he was bugging out a little himself right now. He probably thought he was getting robbed, so I pulled out the shield that was hanging on a chain around my neck and said, "Police. Did anyone come running in here?" The clerk shook his head no. He seemed very relieved that I was a cop.

We continued walking up the block, taking everything in and

becoming more and more aware of our surroundings. We were looking at everybody and everything. Just sucking it all in.

Next was an indoor parking garage, which I knew was going to be a pain in the ass. It had two levels that went down into the basement and probably had over a hundred cars parked in there. It would take both of us to do this right, which would leave the street not covered.

As we approached the garage I was thinking about calling for another anti-crime team to back us up. I was a little hesitant because I didn't want to have to explain how we had the guy and then lost him. Things like that can be embarrassing.

Just as I was reaching for the radio in the back pocket of my jeans, I saw him. Holy shit—there he was! He's peeking from around a corner inside the garage. I see him but the problem is, he also sees us.

George and I have done this hundreds of times. There's no need to talk about who does what or how we're going to approach this guy. It's like it's choreographed.

Okay, here we go! It's showtime. I pulled out my shield, whipped out my gun, and charged him. I started yelling at the top of my lungs, "POLICE, DON'T MOVE, DON'T MOVE MOTHERFUCKER OR I'LL BLOW YOUR FUCKING HEAD OFF!" George was right next to me yelling similar profanity-laced instructions at him.

And that's how real cops do it out in the street. Don't believe that bullshit you see on TV where the cop talks in a normal tone of voice and tells the bad guy to put his hands behind his head and walk backward to the sound of his voice. That might work out in L.A. or someplace like that, but it don't work here. New York bad guys would just laugh at us and run away.

Anytime you pull a gun on a person, it's stressful for all parties concerned. Especially when you think the other guy has a gun also. There's never a "Go ahead, make my day" scenario in real life.

And don't think that we just start yelling like that for no reason. The reason we start yelling like maniacs is to shock the shit out of him. We want that survival instinct of his to kick in. We want him to think that he's about to die. We want him to think that if he makes one wrong move that we don't like we're going to kill him. And even if he is a real hard-core bad guy, in the end, he really doesn't want to die, so he does what we tell him.

What we do is, we give the guy zero chance to think. He gets no time to try something stupid, or even think about trying something. He gets no time to react. It's intimidating and disorienting all at the same time. If it goes well, it's all over in about five seconds, and the next thing the perp knows he's facedown on the ground in handcuffs.

It may seem like we're being a little rough on the guy, but it's safer for him and us. We want to end this thing, fast. Without anybody getting hurt—him or us.

So I'm pointing my gun right between his eyes and yelling at the top of my lungs for him to come out and keep his hands up. I'm cursing and yelling at him to show me his hands or I'll blow his fucking head off.

And it worked just like it always does. The guy was stunned. He didn't know whether to shit or buy a motorboat.

But as he comes out, trying to do what we're telling him, he's holding his arms across his head and face, and he's crying like a baby. He's covering his head and and yelling back at us, "Please don't kill me, PLEEEEEASE, PLEEEEEASE, PLEEEEEASE, I'm sorry. PLEEEEEASE don't kill me."

Just then he falls to the ground and curls up into a ball, like in the fetal position. You could tell he was trying to cover up his vital organs because he thought he was about to be shot. And all the while he keeps crying, "PLEEEEEASE DON'T KILL ME."

I have done this hundreds of times before, but I never had this reaction. My method always worked well in the past, but never this good. Now I was the one who was stunned. George and I both lowered our guns a few inches to get a better look at the guy. Then we kind of glanced at each other and shrugged in disbelief. I could tell at that moment we were both thinking the same thing: "What the fuck is going on here?"

At this point we both knew this probably wasn't our guy. I doubted the armed robber we were looking for was a crybaby. By this time in my career I had locked up a lot of bad guys, and none of them had cried like this when we grabbed them.

I stood there for a moment looking at this guy lying on the ground begging us not to kill him. I put my gun back in my holster and stepped closer. George keeps his gun out. He's covering me because right now we don't know what's going on.

I inch up closer and tell him, "Relax, man, we're the police, take it easy." But he doesn't hear a word I'm saying. He's still curled up into a ball with his head and face covered up. This time he's rapid-fire whimpering and sobbing, "Please don't kill me, please don't kill me. I'm sorry. I'm sorry. I'll never do it again. I'll never do it again, I'm sorry, PLEEEEEASE, PLEEEEEASE DON'T KILL ME . . . I'M ONLY A DENTIST."

Apparently this guy did something to somebody, and right now he's sure as shit sorry he did it. I don't know what it is yet, but I'm thinking it's got to be something really bad because he thinks he's about to be killed over it.

Now George and I are the ones bugging out. I don't know whether to laugh or what. I walk closer to the guy and bend down next to him. He's shaking and crying, and I'm thinking I've got to snap him out of it before he has a heart attack on us.

I'm holding my shield out in front of me so he can see it. It's been out all the time, but this guy never saw it. And I know we yelled "Police" because we always do, but apparently he never heard me say it.

I get down right next to him, and I'm practically shoving my shield into his face and yelling, "LOOK AT ME!—LOOK AT ME!"

After a few seconds I finally get through to him and he looks up. He's got boogers coming out of his nose, tears streaming down his face, and his lower lip is quivering. I point my shield right between his eyes and in a nice, calm, soothing voice I tell him, "We're the police. Relax, nobody's going to hurt you. It's okay, just relax."

Now that I have a better look at him, the guy is dressed kind of nice. He has on expensive dress slacks, a button-down shirt, and some nice shoes. But now he's lying on the dirty floor so I help him up.

I give him a hand up, but he's still a little wobbly and I have to hold on to him so he doesn't fall back down. At this point I have to get a little firm with him, so I say, "Knock it off, man! You gotta relax! Nobody's gonna hurt you." But this guy is really shook up. He shaking like a leaf and I'm starting to feel bad for what I just did to him.

Just then I realize there are two parking attendants standing behind us watching the whole thing. One of them motions to a chair sitting a short distance away outside their office. I help the guy over and sit him down. On the desk inside the office are a few napkins, so I grab a couple and hand them to him. I tell him, "Here, blow your nose."

As he blows his nose and gets himself together, I take the wanted poster out of my back pocket. George and I both look at it and god damn if he didn't look just like the sketch. As George and I are looking back and forth between the sketch and our boy's face, the parking attendant, Tony, is peeking over my shoulder. He starts yelling, "That's him, man! You got him! That's the dude." Tony's sidekick, another parking attendant, is bobbing his head up and down fast and furious, confirming Tony's suspicions, and says, "Fucking A, bro, that's him, you got him."

Now I don't feel so bad about almost giving this guy a heart attack. Tony and his sidekick agree, this guy looks *exactly* like the sketch.

But George and I both knew this wasn't our robber. Armed robbers don't usually fall on the ground sobbing like five-year-olds. By now our guy had regained his composure a little, so I took the sketch and held it in front of his face so he could take a long hard look at it. Then I said, "Who's this?!"

For a second he seemed slightly amused at seeing his face on an NYPD wanted poster. With a little bit of a smile on his face he looked up at me and said, "I guess that looks a lot like me."

I shot back, "No shit it looks like you!"

Then with puppy-dog eyes and a very sincere tone in his voice he countered, "But I assure you, it's not me."

At this point things lightened up a little. I knew he wasn't our guy, and he knew he wasn't about to be killed, so we all started to relax. But something wasn't right about this guy, and I wanted to know what it was before we parted ways.

I put my serious face on again and it was back to business. I said, "I know NOW it's not you, but something's going on here and you better tell me what the fuck it is."

I looked over my shoulder and saw the two parking attendants standing a short distance away, arms folded . . . waiting. They wanted to know what the fuck was going on here too. We all wanted to know what was going on. There had to be a story here somewhere.

To make a long story short, Doctor Crybaby here really *is* a dentist. And a very successful one because he lives a few blocks away on Fifth Avenue. He goes on to tell us that a few months back some Mafia guy from Brooklyn brought his girlfriend in for a little dental work. Well, I guess the little Italian princess took a liking to the doc's soft sensitive side, and he started working on more than just her teeth. He filled more than just her cavity—if you know what I mean.

She probably latched on to the doc because I'm sure he's the opposite of her Mafia tough-guy killer boyfriend. I'm sure the doc is cuddlier and probably sleeps over when he's done. He probably even makes breakfast for the two of them before he leaves. As opposed to Vinnie Bag o' Donuts, who probably shows up at her apartment, the one he pays for, bangs the shit out of her, then leaves. But not before having her make him a sandwich.

But Vinnie is no dummy, and it didn't take long for him to figure out something was up, and when he does he sends a message to the doc that he better knock it off before something very *very* bad happens to him.

I could just picture this chick, she must have been smoking hot, with the tight jeans and high heels, popping the bubble gum. I wanted to ask him if he had any pictures of her. I really wanted to see what this chick looked like. I wanted to see what was worth getting killed over. But I couldn't ask for a picture. That wouldn't be very professional.

Anyway the doc just can't resist her charms and he keeps on seeing her. But the whole time he's sneaking around, he's looking over his shoulder waiting for something very *very* bad to happen to him. And when he sees me and George sitting in the car right down the block from his building, he thinks that we are two of Vinnie's guys coming to *whack* him.

Believe it or not, I'm a little bit of a people person and after hearing his story I believe him. He had business cards in his wallet that said he was a dentist. He had all the right answers. Everything was making sense.

But now I felt kind of bad about scaring him the way we did. We were a hundred percent right doing what we did, but I felt like I had to make it up to him somehow. So I figured I'd give him my best Father Flanagan advice.

I put my hand on his shoulder and in my most sincere, caring voice I told him, "Listen, Doc, I don't care what this broad looks like, it's not worth dying over a piece of pussy. I don't care how good-looking this chick is—you can get plenty of girls. You're a dentist!!!"

He was still staring at the floor trying to stop the shaking, and without looking up he just nodded his head in agreement. He knew I was right. This little episode seems like it really taught him a life lesson. It was a real learning experience for him.

I continued, my voice a little firmer this time, "Now, I want you to go home and call this girl. You got to tell her you can't see her anymore. This is no good for her. It's no good for Vinnie and it's *definitely* no good for you. You seem like a nice guy, and I don't want to hear you caught two in the back of the head and ended up in the weeds out in Staten Island."

I only knew this guy for about five minutes, but for some strange reason I was starting to like him and I didn't want to see anything happen to him. He seemed like a nice guy who got himself into some deep shit over some big-breasted tight-assed Italian broad. And who hasn't done that once or twice in their life?

I was probably never going to see him again, so this was my last chance to drive the point home. So I got real serious and said, "Look at me!"

He looked up at me, still kind of dazed and shaken up. He looked like a guy with a lot of thinking to do and a lot on his mind. I continued, "Now *promise* me you're never going to see her again."

He looked at me, nodded in agreement, and said, "Okay, I promise."

He paused for a moment, thinking about what just happened. He was shaking his head and said, "I can't go through this shit again."

It was time to part company, so we shook hands, no hard feelings. I felt bad about scaring him the way we did, but if he went home and did what I told him maybe we saved his life. Or at least his kneecaps.

As he wobbled off down the block, George and I started to head back to our car. We had real criminals to catch. When we turned to leave, Tony and his sidekick asked if they could have the poster so they could keep an eye out for our armed robber. Police work must have seemed like fun to them. I laughed and told them thanks but no thanks.

As we walked back to the car, George and I couldn't take it anymore. Finally we both burst out laughing. I said what we both were thinking, "You can't make this shit up."

I could not believe this guy's bad luck. He looked just like the armed robber we were looking for, and we looked just like the two hit men he imagined Vinnie was gonna send to whack him. What were the odds?

5.

Hot Dogs

It was my day off, and I was back in the precinct again. Actually, I was sitting on a bench in Washington Square Park, which was in the confines of my command, the Sixth Precinct, Greenwich Village. I was enjoying a nice sunny afternoon, reading the paper, drinking coffee, and watching the world go by while I waited for my girlfriend to finish up with her dentist's appointment right across the street. (No, it wasn't the same guy.)

She had called me up yesterday and asked if I could take her, and of course I said yes. We had only been going out for a few months, but I could already tell things were getting a little serious—she had me hooked from day one. She was smart, very pretty, and to me there was something exotic about her. She was from Spain, and had just moved back to New York after living in the Canary Islands for a while, so she had a nice tan to go along with those full, pouting lips that purred when she said her *R*s. Most of the girls I had been going out with so far in my life had been from the exotic Island of Staten, where I lived, or maybe some far-off place like Brooklyn or New Jersey. So the Spain thing was making me a little nuts.

Her plan for the day was a quick dentist visit, then off to my apartment, cook dinner for me, and maybe a movie. My plan was to order out and try to get lucky—then maybe a movie. I was trying to keep her out of my kitchen as much as possible because her last adventure there didn't go so good. Having a boyfriend with his own apartment had her domestic juices flowing, and she wanted to learn how to cook. The last meal she made for me was "Cinnamon Stuffed Shells." That's right, she put cinnamon in stuffed shells. She wanted to try her hand at Italian and found this recipe on the back of some box that she thought looked easy enough. My mother is Italian, and a great cook, so she wanted to make a home-cooked meal just like Mom would make.

The recipe called for some kind of brown powder, what it was I do not know, and the only thing she could find in my sparsely equipped bachelor's kitchen was cinnamon—so she figured that was close enough. I was always working and hardly ever home, so the only condiments I kept around were ketchup, mustard, salt, and pepper. Where she found the cinnamon is a mystery to me. It was probably left over from the previous tenant.

To add to my culinary experience she dimmed the lights and served it in the romantic glow of candlelight. I was glad the lights were low because it helped hide the look on my face when I took that first indescribable bite. And because things between us were getting serious, she made about ten pounds of the stuff. She was worried about me not eating right and wanted me to have enough vitamins, minerals, and general Italian goodness to last a week.

Several times during that week I stood over the garbage can looking down, tray of shells in hand, but I couldn't get myself to do it. She had tried so hard and the thought of dumping it made me feel bad. At first, when she tried it, even she admitted, "It tastes kind of funny." But I protested, "Oh no, this stuff is great." So during the course of an entire week I ate the whole frigging thing! After a few Rolaids and a lot of small bites, I finished every last bit of it, and came to the same conclusion as she did—things between us were getting serious. When my mother asked about her cooking skills, I replied, "She's really pretty."

Like most cops I met my girl while I was working: she lived right around the block from the station house, which made things convenient for me. But it also meant I was spending seven days a week in the neighborhood where I worked. Normally most cops don't like hanging around where you work because if you're active, meaning you make a lot of arrests, guys get out of jail and don't necessarily have fond memories of you. You don't want to have to deal with them when you're off duty, especially when you're with someone you care about, like a girlfriend. It's not that you're afraid of these guys, it's just you have better things to do with your free time than getting in an off-duty confrontation.

One evening after work I was sitting in a gin mill having a beer, when all of a sudden the bartender comes over, slides another beer down in front of me—one that I didn't order. That's when he points to a guy sitting across from me and says, "That's from your friend." When I looked over, it wasn't any friend of mine but rather a guy I had locked up for a robbery about a year earlier.

Whenever I arrest somebody I give them my usual speech: "You act like a gentleman, and I'll treat you like a gentleman. You act like an asshole, and that's the way I'm going to treat you, and I guarantee you're not going to like it." When I saw this guy's face I remembered him right away. He had acted like a gentleman and that's the way I treated him. Besides, his was a ground-ball case, and he knew it. I just happened to be driving by the street corner while he was banging some dude's head on the sidewalk—what we call giving him a concrete facial—and taking his money. So there was no bitching and moaning like some guys do. "This is all a big misunderstanding" or "You got the wrong guy."

Looking back I can honestly say I was really careful about who I locked up. Everybody I put cuffs on, I felt, deserved to go to jail. If I didn't have a good case on you, I'd rather let you go than lock you up. If you're a real bad guy, you'll be out doing some stupidness again tomorrow and, I always figured, I'll get you next time. But jails are filled with innocent guys, or at least that's what they like to tell you, and they prefer to blame their fucked-up lives on you instead of themselves.

So I sat on the park bench drinking my coffee and reading the paper and waited for my girlfriend. It was a nice, sunny day so there were a lot of normal people hanging out, but there were also the regular drug-dealing shitheads, some of whom knew me. I was only half looking at the paper because I had to keep one eye on everything that was going on around me. I didn't want somebody sneaking up behind me and cutting my throat while I was reading the sports page.

If you're a people watcher like me the park is a great place to hang out and pass a little time. It helps if you have a newspaper and sunglasses so you don't look like you're staring too much, and today the park was jumping with plenty to watch. Not too far away was the fountain, the centerpiece of the park, which street performers of all kinds use as a stage and then pass the hat around trying to make a few bucks. There were break-dancers, magicians, jugglers, kids doing tricks on bikes and skateboards, you name it, it was here. Today there was a guy with a tinfoil crown on his head, a gold cape, and silver hot pants who ran back and forth, flipping pots and pans in the air in a clumsy attempt at juggling. He sucked, he kept dropping the frying pan on his head, but people were clapping and laughing anyway. I think it was the gold cape that had them amused.

Scattered around on the grass were the NYU students doing their homework and contemplating their future. Then there were the freewheeling hippies, sneaking a joint, playing the bongo drums, and contemplating the universe. And in the middle of all this, mingling in the crowd, were the drug dealers, looking for buyers and watching what the cops were up to. Some I knew and some I didn't, but you can always tell who they are if you look closely enough. They're always walking, constantly moving, but they never seem to go anywhere, and they watch everything and everybody—just like cops do.

The thing about being a cop is after a while you become one inside and out. The way you walk down a street, the way you talk, even when ordering a coffee, it all says cop. It's the way your eyes scan a crowd, sizing everybody up, constantly looking for bad guys or anything that might be a threat. And the loose-fitting, fashion-deprived shirts and jackets we wear aren't bought because we like the way they look, we need them to cover up the steel bulge we're always trying to hide.

Everything about you says cop, but more than anything it's that cold, confident aura that surrounds you and follows you everywhere you go. I could be standing in the middle of a crowded Grand Central Terminal, and I could pick out another cop on the other side of the big room just by their look—and bad guys can do the same. The same way I can ride down a busy street and pick out the shitheads, they can do the same with us. It's self-preservation, and it becomes a way of life for both of us.

I was halfway through reading my paper and drinking my coffee when all of a sudden a real salty-looking dude comes walking by, slows down, and gives me a long hard look. I didn't recognize him, but I can tell he smells cop. I smell drug dealer. I can see him out of the corner of my eye, and I can feel his annoying presence just a few feet away, but I don't look up. I keep looking at my paper and refuse to give him the benefit of a reaction because that's what he wants. Right now he's not sure who I am or what I'm doing, but I've shot his bad-guy antenna up, so he's staring at me, pushing it, trying to feel me out.

Cops do the same thing to see if you get nervous and make that involuntary movement toward the gun in your waistband, or maybe even start running. Bad guys do it to see if you get scared and look away. If you do they smell victim, but if you give them a hard stare back, they smell cop.

My head is down, and I'm looking at the paper, but I'm also watching Salty's feet, making sure he doesn't get any closer. Right now we're both playing poker and Salty is starting to annoy me. What I would like to do is grab him, turn him upside down, and dump him into a nearby garbage can headfirst. But then he would win the staring contest. So I keep reading my paper, playing poker, and after a little while he saunters away.

I look at my watch, hoping my girlfriend will be done with her appointment before anything else happens, but no such luck. A few minutes later two more hard-core-looking assholes emerge from the crowd and come walking by, eyeballing me hard. These guys are a little older and better dressed than the other dealers in the park, so I figure they must be the managers. Salty must have told them I was here, and they came over to check me out. They slow down right in front of me and give me their best well-rehearsed, jailhouse tough-guy look. Narcotics is always sneaking around trying to catch these guys, it's a cat and mouse game. They obviously want me to know that they made me. It makes the mouse feel like he won something.

Finally enough is enough, everybody knows who everybody else is, so I close up my newspaper, look them right in the face, and give them my best well-rehearsed "go fuck yourself" look. I made sure nothing got lost in the translation, and they got the message loud and clear, so after a few seconds they started walking. But they kept looking over their shoulders, walking that slow, shuffling bad-guy walk—feeling like they won something. And I keep giving them my slow, shuffling "fuck you" look.

I glanced around to see if anybody else noticed our little nonverbal sparring match, but nobody seemed to notice or care. Even the guy sitting right next to me wearing the "I'm with Schizo" T-shirt, with the arrow pointing up to himself, didn't notice. They seemed to be floating around in their own little universe.

I hardly ever go anywhere without a gun, because in a cop's life you're never really off duty, so under my jacket, tucked into a little shoulder holster, is a five-shot .38 revolver. I press my arm up against my side and give it a slight squeeze just to make sure it's there. I know it's there, because it's always there, but it's comforting to feel the steel bulge hanging under my arm just in case I need it. I have friends, also, five of them.

I go back to reading my paper and drinking my coffee, feeling relatively inconspicuous to most of the park goers, when all of a sudden a black dude walking by stops right in front of me. He takes one look at me and I can tell, without even looking up, that he's flipping out, his eyes are popping out of his head. From a few feet away he just stands there and stares at me with this really astonished look on his face, like he can't believe what he's seeing. His head is moving left and right, and forward and backward, like he's trying to focus his eyes and get a better look. He looked like he spotted Bigfoot out in the woods when he least expected it.

Now I'm starting to get a little pissed off, all I want is to be left alone so I can read my paper like a normal person, but a cop's life is anything but normal.

Finally I look up, wondering what the hell does this guy want? We weren't friends, buddies, or cousins and we didn't go to school together, but from the look on his face he obviously recognizes me from somewhere. After a few seconds of staring and getting his eyes focused, he puts his two hands out in front of himself like a traffic cop trying to stop a speeding car and says really loud, "Stay right there, don't move." That's when he takes off running across the park as fast as he can.

I looked around to see if anybody saw what just happened, but again, nobody seemed to notice or care. The hippies were still sitting on the grass banging their bongos, contemplating the universe, and the NYU students were still doing their homework. And when I looked over at schizo sitting next to me, he—or they—didn't seem to notice either.

The guy obviously recognized me and didn't want me to go anywhere, but why? I didn't recognize him, but that doesn't mean anything. Every day I go to work and deal with countless people, and most of them don't leave a lasting impression. I kept thinking maybe I locked him up, or maybe I just threw him out of the park for doing something stupid. That happens all the time. But why did he want me to stay here, was he going to get a gun and come back and shoot me, or get a couple of his drug-dealing buddies and try to tune me up? I didn't think so, that would be a ballsy move, especially in a crowded park, but why was he so adamant about me staying here?

Was he with the guys I had the staring match with earlier? I didn't know, but all I could think about was that this couldn't be good. I thought about getting up and leaving, but I didn't want the drug dealers to win. But the last thing I wanted to do was get into a confrontation with some shitheads while I was off duty. It's an unhealthy situation that the police department really frowns on, but I didn't want them to think they scared me out of the park. My girlfriend was going to be finished with the dentist soon, and my plans for the day did not include getting shot or shooting somebody else. So I sat there for a moment and debated what I should do.

I must have been debating this a little longer than I realized, because all of a sudden the guy came back. I could see him on the other side of the fountain running toward me as fast as he could, but this time he wasn't alone. This time he had some girl with him. I was a little relieved it was a girl and not some crazed-out crackheads, but I was still wound up and ready for a fight, if that's what he wanted.

He was dragging the girl by the hand, and she was running as fast as she could trying to keep up with him. As they got closer, he was pointing at me, and I could hear him say, "That's him! That's the guy! That's the guy I told you about!"

I kept looking at his face, but as hard as I tried I couldn't place him. I wanted to remember him because then I might have a better idea where this was going. I didn't know him, but this nut job seemed positive that he knew me, so I guess I must be the guy. As I watched him get closer I got ready for a fight, or at least some kind of confrontation, but what was throwing me off was that he was smiling from ear to ear. He didn't seem like a guy who wanted to fight, he seemed like a guy who was very happy about something. Now I was really confused, so out of habit I squeezed my arm against my side again, just to feel that the steel bulge was still where I needed it.

They ran right up to me and skidded to a stop, both of them panting and out of breath. When I looked at the girl, she seemed nice. She was dressed conservatively in a plain blouse, a pleated skirt to the knee, and sensible flat shoes. She didn't seem like the type who would be interested in helping somebody slit a cop's throat. And just like him, she was smiling also. She had this big dopey grin on her face and seemed just as glad to see me as he was.

There was a slight awkward moment when I didn't smile back. While they huffed and puffed trying to catch their breath, they seemed surprised that I wasn't as happy to see them as they were to see me, and that's when he said, "Don't you remember me?"

I looked up at him with my best "don't fuck with me" look and shot right back, "Sorry bro, I don't know you." And I underlined it with a tone of voice that said, "Tell your story walking." He seemed a little disappointed that I didn't remember him. Apparently whatever happened between us was a lot more memorable for him than it was for me. Undeterred, he continued, a little more enthusiastically this time, and said, "Come on, you remember me, you arrested me a couple of years ago. I was selling crack down the block on Sixth Avenue."

Telling me that I arrested him didn't help my memory either. By this time in my career I had locked up a lot of guys, and after a while they all start to look alike, smell alike, and become one big ugly blur. Many of them you forget, but some leave a lasting impression, usually because they did something incredibly stupid, funny, or heinous, but this guy didn't seem to fall into any of those categories.

I could feel my muscles start to tense up, and I told him again that I didn't remember him and that he must have me confused with someone else. But this guy wouldn't give up, and that's when he leaned a little closer and said, "Don't you remember—THE HOT DOGS!" It took a second, but as soon as he mentioned the hot dogs it all came back to me.

*   *   *

A while back my partner and I were out on patrol, working a four-to-twelve tour in uniform, and I was looking to "collar up"— meaning make an arrest. Years ago, in the bad old days of New York City, crime was everywhere, so making a collar was as easy as shooting fish in a barrel. Any day of the week I could leave the station house and within an hour come back with a felony collar, and if you couldn't find a quality arrest like a robbery, assault, or maybe a guy with a gun, you could always grab a drug dealer, since they were everywhere. Everybody in or around Greenwich Village knew that if you wanted crack, weed, or maybe a little cocaine, just head over to Washington Square Park and it wouldn't take very long to find a dealer.

We always had a few cops assigned to the park, so the dealers would sometimes steer the buyers down to Sixth Avenue and "hit them off" down there. So I told my partner, let's check out Sixth and see what we can find.

We took a slow ride up the avenue starting at West Houston Street and checked out every storefront, doorway, side street, and subway entrance—looking for the guy who is always walking, but has no particular place to go. Another reason the dealers steer the buyers down to Sixth Avenue is because it's always crowded. Any time of the day or night there are people and cars all over the place, and it's easy to mingle in the crowd and do your business. And just like the crowds and the cars help the dealers, they also help us. It's not easy to sneak up on drug dealers when you're in uniform and driving a nice shiny police car with a big red light on top. Dealers, just like cops, have eyeballs in the back of their heads, always watching everything and everybody.

We cruised up the avenue nice and easy, my partner driving and me in the passenger seat, and to anybody watching it looks like we're just two cops out cruising around. But nothing could be further from the truth. My partner is checking one side of the block and I'm checking the other, and we're eyeballing everybody and everything, until we find what we're looking for. With all the thousands of people coming and going in different directions, it might seem impossible to find that one drug-dealing shithead slipping something very small into somebody's hand—which only takes about five seconds. And to makes things more difficult, sometimes the dealers will have the buyer hand the money to one person, then have him walk down the block and get the drugs from someone else. Instead of a five-second "hand-to-hand," I have to watch for two exchanges in the middle of a busy Manhattan street. But my partner and I are good at this.

After passing at least a half a dozen guys that I knew were dirty but not doing anything illegal at the moment, I found what I was looking for—a skinny, scraggly crackhead talking to a very well-dressed Wall Street–type businessman. They were on the west side of Sixth Avenue just before Fourth Street, and if you weren't looking carefully enough you'd drive right past them. The crackhead's baggy pants were ready to fall off his skinny ass, and the business guy looked like he was wearing a nicely tailored Brooks Brothers suit, and they were involved in this intense conversation. To the rest of the world passing by this was no big deal, these guys sort of blended in, like they were two old buddies happy to see each other—but not to me. When I saw these guys my spider sense started tingling because I know at any other time or place Mr. Brooks Brothers wouldn't piss on Mr. Baggy Pants even if he was on fire. But right now they're best buddies, and that's because Baggy Pants has what Brooks Brothers needs—crack. You wouldn't know it by looking at the suit and briefcase, and I'm sure his boss in that tall glass building he works in doesn't know it either, but Brooks Brothers is a crackhead too, he's just better dressed.

When I first spotted them I could see Brooks Brothers had his hand balled up into a tight fist out in front of him—that was the money—and Baggy was counting out something small in his hand—that was the crack. Brooks Brothers was oblivious to the rest of the world, as he kept staring down at Baggy's hand like a dog waiting for a treat. He wanted his shit and he wanted it now. Baggy was a little more careful. His head was on a swivel, looking for the cops while he counted out tiny vials from a plastic bag. They might as well have had a big neon sign over their heads with arrows pointing down at them saying DRUG DEALER and DRUG BUYER.

I wanted to grab them, but I had a bit of a problem. I didn't spot them until we drove past them, and if I jumped out now and they saw me coming across the street, they were probably going to start running—in two different directions. On TV when two perps run in opposite directions, one partner chases one and the other partner chases the other, and they usually get them both, but it doesn't work that way in real life. In real life that's a good way to get yourself killed. In real life we both chase after the guy we want most—hoping that's the fat, slow guy—and then we try to catch number two, and if we're really lucky, we get both. Besides, my partner was a big Italian guy who was not exactly light on his feet, especially with the size-twelve combat boots he liked to wear. He was great to have around in a fight, but chasing skinny crackheads fleeing for their freedom was not his forte. So I told him to whip it around the block and I would get them when we come back around.

There was not much to talk about. In the past year since we became partners we had made plenty of collars together, and he knew exactly what I was thinking. We would whip it around and I would get out about a half a block behind my two crackhead buddies, then I would blend in with the crowd and sneak up behind them. My partner would drive past them, cut them off with the car, and we would have them boxed in between us. Most of the time they would spot the car first and start running away, usually in the opposite direction, and right into my waiting arms.

We made the right on Fourth Street, then another right on Mac-Dougal Street and stopped dead. The traffic light was red, cars were backed up, and we were stuck. I was pissed because I knew the heartwarming friendship between my two friends was not going to last very long. We couldn't hit the siren because I didn't want to let every drug dealer in a two-block area know we're up to something, so my partner very quietly jumped the curb and drove down the sidewalk. We left a few angry pedestrians in our path, but we made it around the traffic and we were back on Sixth Avenue in no time.

When we got back around I spotted Baggy Pants, who was all smiles as he counted his money, but Brooks Brothers was gone. I knew this friendship wasn't going to last very long. But it was no big deal, I figured I'd grab Baggy, cuff him up, throw him into the back of the car, and then go looking for Mr. Wall Street because he couldn't have gotten very far.

I jumped out of the car, hurried over to the sidewalk, and used the sea of unsuspecting pedestrians to get lost in. Across the street a couple of other salty-looking dudes saw me sneaking through the crowd and started high stepping it off the block. They didn't know who I was after, but they obviously figured it was a smart idea to go hide for a while and dump anything they might have on them.

I looked over my shoulder to check on my partner. He was laying back, waiting for me to get closer to Baggy Pants so he could race up and cut him off. This is the exciting part, as I'm bobbing and weaving through the crowd trying to get closer, I can see Baggy has his head down still counting his money, and he has no idea that he's about to be collared.

When I saw Baggy counting out the bills I knew he was a one-man operation. He wasn't part of a team: steerer, moneyman, hand-to-hand guy, and maybe a stash guy or girl. No, he was an independent operator, so I knew I was only getting two collars out of this, Baggy and his buyer.

I kept creeping closer, twenty feet, ten feet, I'm almost there, a few more steps and I'm going to grab him by the jacket, yoke him around the neck, and get him down to the ground before he can try to run. But just like cops have a spider sense, bad guys have it also, and his must have started tingling because just as I was about to grab him, he turns around. You should have seen the look on his face, his eyes were popping out of his head like a cartoon and he had that "Oh shit!" expression.

I grabbed the back of his jacket and that's when he tried the classic perp evasive maneuver. If the front of the jacket is open, just point your arms backward, lean forward, and start running—right out of your coat. The next thing the cop knows he has a handful of empty jacket and you're off and running, I know because it's happened to me before. But it didn't go so well for this guy because both his hands were balled up into fists—one had the money and the other had the stash, and he wasn't about to drop either. I'm sure his brain was telling his fists to open, but the fists weren't listening, and they got caught inside the sleeves.

When his hands got caught I grabbed him around the neck, jumped on his back, and rode him to the ground, hard. When we hit the sidewalk there were loud groans—from me because I banged my knee and elbow, and from him because two hundred pounds of cop just landed on him when he wasn't expecting it. He threw a couple of punches, kicks, and elbows trying to get away but it wasn't working, I was all over him like a bum on a baloney sandwich, and the next thing he knew he had one hand behind his back and I was slapping a handcuff on it. I tried to get the other hand but he wasn't giving it up, and that's when I saw why—in the other hand was a clear plastic bag with twenty-eight vials of crack in it.

In a situation like this, desperate men do desperate (or stupid) things, and that's when he popped the bag into his mouth and tried to swallow it. The bag was big, and I don't know if he really thought he could swallow it, but he was giving it a good try. He had it in his mouth and his jaws were chomping up and down like he was chewing a giant wad of gum. He looked like a pelican trying to swallow a fish that was a little too big for him to handle.

I finally reached around and pulled his other hand behind his back and got it cuffed—now he's mine and he knows it. I rolled him over and told him to spit the bag out, but he wasn't giving it up that easy. His bottom jaw was bouncing up and down as he stretched his neck out, doing his best to get that bag down his skinny, scrawny throat where he thought I couldn't get it.

This is another common maneuver with drug dealers. They think they're slick, they think no evidence equals no collar, but it only works if I don't see you doing it. Sometimes they get it down and sometimes they don't, but it doesn't work with a bag this big and it never works with a cop sitting on your back. As hard as he tried he couldn't swallow it, and now it was getting stuck in his throat. I couldn't care less if he choked on it and died, one less drug dealer in the world, but if he did swallow the bag I'd have to sit in the hospital with him for the next twelve hours waiting for it to come out the other end.

Just then my partner comes screeching to a halt and runs over. I told him to watch my back and that I would take care of the perp. I wasn't as worried about the perp as I was about getting hit in the head with a flying beer bottle thrown by some cop-hating shithead in the crowd.

Again I told him to spit it out, but it was no good, he wasn't giving it up, so I decided if he wanted to play hardball so could I. I wasn't going to stick my fingers in his mouth, that's disgusting plus it's a good way to get a thumb chewed off. So instead I grabbed him by the throat and pinched his windpipe, cutting off his air supply. Now he was the one with the problem. If he wanted to breathe, he would have to spit it out—and that's when I leaned over and whispered ever so gently into his ear, "Spit it out, motherfucker, or I'll strangle you."

As soon as I grabbed this guy, a small crowd of concerned citizens had gathered, wanting to see the show. Everybody in New York loves a good fight. The crowd had no idea what was going on, but they seemed to be more on Baggy's side than mine. It wasn't a problem until they started moving in a little too close and yelling for me to leave him alone. My partner is big and intimidating, so he took care of the crowd and I could hear his deep voice behind me barking at the crowd to "start fucking walking."

Finally Baggy Pants realized that he couldn't swallow that big bag, plus he also realized that if he wanted to breathe again he was going to have to spit it out, so with a cough and a burp, it flew out and landed on the sidewalk. I patted him on the head and said, "Good boy." It was disgusting: the bag was covered with phlegm, spit, and whatever other slimy crap he had down his throat. I had the bag, but I needed to make sure I didn't miss anything, so I flipped him over and told him to open his mouth. He knew the routine. I shined my flashlight in his mouth and down his throat while he rolled his tongue around to show me I had gotten it all. We were now both out of breath, and glad this was over.

I grabbed Baggy by his belt and jacket and lifted him to his feet and started putting him into the back of the car. That's when some do-gooder got up into my face, blocking my path, and started yelling that Baggy Pants wasn't doing nothing, and that he wanted my name and shield number so he could make a complaint. I'd had enough. My knee and elbow ached from rolling on the ground, and I had crackhead saliva all over my sleeve from Baggy coughing up the stash. So I informed Mr. Liberal that if he didn't shut the fuck up and get out of my way, he'd be joining Baggy in the back of the car for a ride to the station house. The lib was concerned, but not enough to go to jail, so he took my advice and started walking.

It always amazes me how people right away want to think the worst about the police. Without knowing all the facts they just assume we're the bad guys. Police work is a difficult and dangerous job, and it rarely goes as clean and neat as it does on TV—which is where most people get their information about cops and police work. I just want to do my job with as little hassle as possible and go home in one piece—and without germ-filled crackhead saliva all over me.

I threw Baggy into the back of the car, then went to get the stash, which was still lying on the ground. My partner was standing over it so nobody would scoop it up and take off with it. I knew there were other junkies standing in the crowd drooling over it, and they didn't care how disgusting it was, they would have smoked it anyway. When I went back, my partner was standing there with a rubber glove in his hand. The glove was for me, and he had that smile on his face that said, "Your collar, you pick it up."

I scooped it up, threw it into a brown paper envelope, then we jumped back into the car and took off. I wanted to get out of there because I wanted to get away from the annoying crowd, but also because I wanted to go look for Brooks Brothers—I hadn't forgotten about him. We checked the surrounding blocks, and I even ran down into three different subway stations looking for him, but no luck. The guy from Wall Street was in the wind. Once a junkie gets his shit, he gets happy feet—he takes off like a squirrel with a nut and wastes no time looking for a nice quiet place to go get high. I just hoped he wasn't the guy managing my 401(k) tomorrow morning.

I grabbed the radio off my belt and notified the dispatcher that we were going into the house with "one under" (into the precinct with one arrest). I was a little pissed that I didn't get my second collar, but that's the way it works sometimes. I hoped he'd get grabbed by Narcotics someday—I was sure this wouldn't be his last vial of crack. That's the thing about crack, you chase it like a gerbil on one of those little wheels, and the wheel never stops until somebody else makes it stop.

The ride into the station house was quiet. Sometimes perps will try to talk their way out of things. "Officer, this is all a big mistake, you got the wrong guy." Or sometimes the cocky ones will mouth off and tell you, "This is bullshit, my lawyer will beat this." But not this guy, he was quiet. I had him good and he knew it, there was no way he could say the stash wasn't his—I found it down his throat. And there was no way he could argue that it was for personal use, because twenty-eight vials is way too much for one person, so he just sat there staring off into space contemplating his future like the NYU students and the hippies in the park. I figured he must have more than a few collars on his rap sheet and he knew he was going to do a little time for this one.

We got back to the precinct, and I brought my prisoner before the desk. In every station house the desk is the focus of attention, everything and everybody that enters or leaves stops and notifies the desk officer. It's the center ring of a three-ring circus.

Today's desk officer was a grumpy old lieutenant who wore tiny Benjamin Franklin glasses and had very little use for rookies. While I stood there waiting to be acknowledged, I emptied my prisoner's pockets and wrote down his pedigree information so it could be entered into the command log. After an appropriate amount of time had passed and the lieutenant let me know where I stood in the police department hierarchy, which was on the very bottom, he looked up, grumbled, and acknowledged my presence. I informed him that I had one under for criminal sale of a controlled substance and showed him the now moist brown paper envelope with the plastic bag containing the stash.

I left my gun with the lieutenant because no guns are allowed in the cell area, and walked my prisoner back to the holding cells. The cell attendant was old and crusty just like the desk officer, but not as smart. He couldn't pass the sergeant's or lieutenant's test and was a cop just like me, so I just told him I had a collar and walked right past him.

I found an empty cell, marched my prisoner in, and uncuffed him. He stood on one side of the iron bars looking out, while I stood on the other side looking in, both of us staring at each other, waiting. We both knew what was going to happen next, and neither one of us was happy about it. I told him to hand over his jacket, shirt, pants, shoes, everything he had on. I had to check every pocket, cuff, and hem. I was looking for guns, knives, needles, razor blades, ballpoint pens, matches, paper clips, cigarette lighters—anything sharp or pointy or that could conceivably be used as a weapon, plus anything that could be used to facilitate escape. I also took his shoelaces, belt, and even the string from his hood so he wouldn't try to hang himself, or choke me.

Slowly and methodically I checked every possible hiding spot in his clothing. When I was done he stood there barefoot, in his bikini Speedo shorts, waiting for what was coming next. He had been collared many times before, and he knew the routine. I had made many collars before, and I knew the routine. That's when he turned around, dropped his shorts, and bent over, and from about six feet away I shined my flashlight up the last place a perp could hide something. When I was a kid watching *Columbo* or *Adam-12,* I don't remember ever seeing them shine a flashlight up some prisoner's ass. Real police work isn't half as glamorous as people think it is.

I gave him back his clothes and slammed the cell door shut as he got dressed. The door must weigh a few hundred pounds, and when you slam it shut there's a loud boom as the floor and walls shake. I do it on purpose, as it lets the prisoner know he's not out on the street anymore—he's in my world now.

I went out to the arrest-processing area with a stack of paperwork that had to be filled out and found an empty desk and typewriter. On the wall was a poster of a distraught-looking cop, deep in thought, and underneath him was the phone number for the suicide hotline. This was a good place to put it.

After about two hours of typing I was starting to get hungry, so I went out to the vending machines and got a bag of chips and a soda. I had given my perp the "if you act like a gentleman, I'll treat you like one" speech, and ever since the swallowing episode out in the street, my guy was acting like a gentleman, so I got him a soda and a bag of chips as well.

When I went back to the cells he was lying on the wooden bench staring up at the ceiling. You could tell he was contemplating his dismal future. I could also tell he was skinny as a fence post. It looked like he hadn't eaten in days. When you become a crackhead you forget about everything: eating, sleeping, bathing, and even sex takes a backseat to getting high. I pushed the soda and bag of chips through the bars and said, "Hungry?"

It was like I rang the dinner bell. He leaped up, holding on to his pants while trying not to step out of his shoes, because I had taken his belt and laces, and then snatched the chips and soda. He squeezed the bag in his hand, crushing the chips into dust, then opened it, and poured them down his throat. Then he popped open the soda, drank the whole thing, and burped me a "Thanks." It was obvious the guy hadn't eaten in a while, so I handed him my chips and soda and went back to doing paperwork.

And don't believe all the crap you hear about cops beating prisoners. Some guys want to be hard-ons, so you have to put them in their place, and explain the rules to them, but most of my perps have been through the system before and just want to make it as painless and comfortable as possible. So I feed them, give them a cigarette, and talk nice to them. I usually tell them, "Don't worry, you'll be out in a few days." Most of the time they know I'm full of crap, but it gives them something to hope for and it makes life more pleasant for everybody.

And not to sound like a softy, but my perp wasn't such a bad guy. A lot of individuals I deal with are evil, rotten-to-the-core motherfuckers that walk the earth bringing misery wherever they go. This guy wasn't one of them, he just did some stupid things in life and got caught. And as I watched my skinny friend lying on the hard wooden bench trying to get comfortable, I was a little pissed because Brooks Brothers wasn't in the cell also, trying to hold up his pants.

I finished up my paperwork, and it was time to head down to Manhattan Central Booking. I grabbed my partner and perp and headed out to the car, but not before stopping by the desk to get my gun back and have my paperwork signed by the lieutenant. I still had to wait to be acknowledged this time, but not as long as when I first came in. Desk officers always want to get the prisoners out as soon as possible—one less thing to be responsible for.

We jumped into the car and headed downtown. My partner was driving and I was sitting in the back with the perp. The whole ride down my stomach was growling. Processing a collar takes time and I hadn't had a chance to eat, but lucky me, I spotted a hot-dog wagon parked outside the courthouse. I told my partner to pull over, I needed some nutrition. You can't do police work without your vitamins and minerals.

When we pulled up next to the wagon, I rolled down the window and told the old guy to give me two with everything and a Diet Coke. Like an old pro who has done this a million times, he slapped them together and handed them to me through the open window. When I opened up the aluminum foil wrapping, the smell of onions, sauerkraut, and mustard was filling up the car—it was a beautiful thing. But as I hoisted one of those heavy dirty-water dogs up to my lips, I could see out of the corner of my eye that my perp was staring at me, and he was practically drooling. Obviously the chips and soda didn't do the trick.

I could have been a hard-on and told him that dinnertime was over for him, tough shit, that the chips and soda were all he was going to get, but I didn't. The fact is, I did not like him, but I didn't dislike him either. He was a criminal and I was a cop. He does what he does and I do what I do, and I learned a long time ago that you don't take these things personally—it's only business.

Besides he was a good prisoner and didn't give me any trouble, and it doesn't hurt to be nice once in a while, so I said to him, "You still hungry?" He didn't say anything, but his head bounced up and down, doing all the talking for him: "Fuck yeah I'm hungry!" So I said, "How do you like 'em?" He was still staring at the hot dog in my hand, he hadn't taken his eyes off it, and that's when he very politely said, "Those would be fine."

As soon as I decided to feed him I realized that I had a problem: he was rear cuffed, and my kindness only goes so far. There was no way in the world I was going to hand-feed a crackhead a hot dog. I thought about my predicament for a second and realized there was only one thing to do: I had to uncuff him.

When I reached for my keys I could see my partner's eyes glaring at me in the rearview mirror. He didn't have to say a word, his eyes said it all: this is a stupid thing to do, you never uncuff a prisoner. And he was absolutely, one hundred percent right, but I had no choice. But before I did it, I leaned in and explained to my prisoner that if he tried anything crazy, I was going to fuck him up, big-time. Hunger pains would be the least of his problems. He knew exactly what I meant, there was no need to overstress the point, and that's when he shook his head back and forth and said, "No, no, no, I promise, I'm just hungry."

So I uncuffed him, and just like he never took his eyes off my hot dogs, I never took my eyes off him. I watched his two hands, one with a pair of cuffs dangling from the wrist, as he hoisted that heavy, aromatic, dirty-water delicacy to his lips. If his hands moved a half an inch toward the door handle, I was going to be all over him. You never, ever let your guard down when dealing with a prisoner, especially when you're being nice. Never let them mistake kindness for weakness, that's how you get hurt.

It was incredible, I never saw anything like it. I thought I was at a Coney Island hot-dog-eating contest because in seconds the two dogs were gone. I looked at him as he wiped mustard and onions off his chin and asked, "Still hungry?" Again his head bounced up and down: Yes! I probably could have fed this guy a tray of cinnamon stuffed shells and he would have eaten the whole frigging thing, but I couldn't do that. There's a law against cruel and unusual punishment. I got him two more, and while he was stuffing his face I ordered a couple for myself. The old guy was as happy as could be because money and hot dogs were flying back and forth through the open window. Finally, after six dogs and two sodas my prisoner was full.

My partner didn't find any of this amusing, but I did. If it weren't for the dangling cuffs that were smacking him in the chin as he ate, we probably would have looked like two guys sitting at Yankee Stadium enjoying a ball game and a couple of dogs. All we needed were two beers. In the middle of all this I had asked my partner if he wanted any, but he told me he doesn't eat that shit. Too bad, he missed out. And when my perp was finally done, without me having to say a word, he leaned over and put his hands behind his back so I could put the cuffs back on, just like a gentleman. That little gesture impressed the shit out of me.

On the ride over to Central Booking he stared out the window watching the world go by and actually seemed content in life. His belly was full and he'd had a nice nap back at the precinct while I did paperwork. But when we reached Central Booking things changed. This was the foyer to the criminal justice system, and when the steel door shuts behind you, that's when reality sets in. You're surrounded by concrete floors and walls and iron bars, and the place stinks like horrible body odor. The claustrophobic ambience lets you know your days of fresh air and sunshine are over—there's no green grass under your feet around here. And dirty-water hot dogs are the things you dream about.

I walked him over to the bullpen, which is a large holding cell about twenty feet by twenty feet, packed with prisoners waiting to go to arraignment. I led him by the arm to the steel door as he shuffled along trying to hold on to whatever dignity he had left. It wasn't easy because he was struggling to hold up his beltless pants, and trying not to kick off his laceless shoes. But he would soon have company, because the bullpen crowd of lost souls and evil motherfuckers (sometimes it's hard to tell them apart just by looking at them) were all having the same problem.

I grabbed a pair of handcuffs from the central booking sergeant and switched cuffs so I could get mine back. As I was unlocking and locking the steel bracelets my prisoner asked what I thought was going to happen to him. Actually he knew what was going to happen, he had been locked up numerous times before, and even in New York City, eventually some judge will give you some serious time inside. But I gave him my regular feel-good speech I gave to all my perps—a happy prisoner is a cooperative prisoner—and I didn't want him trying anything stupid before I left, like hanging himself.

I told him to relax, what I had him on was no big deal, that he would see the judge in the morning and probably be out in a day or two, but he knew better. He knew the criminal justice system as well as I did, and with twenty-eight vials of crack it would be difficult for his lawyer to argue that it was for personal use. He knew he was going for sale this time.

He nodded politely as he listened to my feel-good bullshit, and that's when he said something I didn't see coming. I was completely surprised when he blurted out, "Thanks for the dogs, man."

I was kind of taken aback by his gratitude. Prisoners rarely thank you for anything, they all have that entitled, "you have to take care of me" attitude. I told him don't worry about it, that it was no big deal, but he got real sincere on me and said, "I know you didn't have to do it—but you did it anyway. Thanks."

That's when I warned him, "You better not go sick on me." Who knows what those dirty-water dogs would do to an empty stomach, and I didn't want to get stuck sitting in Bellevue emergency room for a couple of hours because he had a tummy ache. We both laughed, he thought it was funny too.

And as we were talking, and I was switching handcuffs, it suddenly dawned on me that we were both talking really low, like we were whispering, and I knew why. He was whispering because he didn't want the other prisoners in the bullpen to think that he was being chummy with the cops, and I was whispering because I didn't want the other cops to think I was a liberal.

I put him in the cell and watched as he shuffled and melted into the crowd. In seconds he seemed to disappear, swallowed up by the sea of beltless, laceless lost souls and evil motherfuckers. Inside the bullpen, instead of thirty individual sad and sometimes heinous stories, there seemed to be a collective misery that hung in the air like the body odor that never seemed to go away.

I slammed the door shut with a booming thud that shook the floor and walls, and that was that. He was now incarcerated, and on his way to becoming an inmate of the New York City Corrections Department.

In reality we were two ships that pass in the night, never to meet again. When you lock somebody up, most of them take a plea. Ninety-nine cases out of a hundred never go to trial and you rarely ever see them again unless you arrest them on something else, or bump into them out in the street. The last thing I told him was have a nice life and good luck with the case. I figured, like most of my collars, he would go his way and I would go mine, never to meet again unless it was in the courtroom.

*   *   *

And now here we are, a few years later on a sunny afternoon in Washington Square Park, and not only does this guy remember me, but he picked me out of a crowd of about a few thousand people. I didn't recognize him at first because he put on a few pounds, plus he was cleaned up and healthy looking. He didn't look anything like the shell of a man I tackled to the ground and choked a few years ago.

As he and I talked, the girl just stared at me and smiled like we were old friends. Apparently this guy must have told her the hot-dog story about twenty times, and she must have felt like she knew me. And because he and the girl were both smiling so much, and seemed genuinely happy to see me, I eased up a little and forgot about the steel bulge hanging under my jacket. He obviously wasn't pissed off about being arrested and didn't want to put a bullet in me, so in return I lightened up a bit and said, "How you doing? I haven't seen you around in a while. You staying out of trouble?"

That's when the girl jumped into the conversation. Up until this point she just stood there, smiling and letting him do all the talking, but when I asked if he was staying out of trouble, she leaped in and said, "Yes sir, Officer! I'm making sure of that!"

She was a petite girl with kind of a high-pitched voice, but I could tell by the way she said it, she could be as tough as a cranky old desk lieutenant when she had to be. He finally introduced her: this was his girlfriend and soon-to-be wife.

He went on to tell me that he took a plea on my case and did a few months on Rikers Island and had a difficult time dealing with it. That may not sound like a long time, but it is. Even hard-core bad guys have a difficult time dealing with Rikers for more than five minutes, and this guy wasn't hard-core. He was just a guy with a problem who did stupid things in life and got caught. He was one of the many people in this world who teased that big dog named Crack and got bit in the ass.

He told me about how he met his girlfriend when he got out of jail and with her help he straightened himself out. Jail was no fun and he was determined never to go back.

It was amazing. The next thing I knew we were laughing and talking like we were old pals. She asked me if I was married or had kids. I said no, but that I had a new girlfriend and things were getting serious. I had to tell them that she was from Spain, so they both oohed and aahed. It sounded very exotic to them also. I was kind of surprised how open I was about my personal life with someone I arrested, but the moment was pleasant and seemed to sweep the three of us away. Cops and robbers time was behind us and now we were just three human beings having a nice moment.

We talked for a few more minutes, then just as quickly as it started, he stuck out his hand and said, "We've taken up enough of your time, it was really nice to see you again." I stood up, stuck my hand out, and we shook like we really meant it. And not to sound like a liberal, because I'm not, but it was a really good feeling. I actually felt warm all over because in my line of work happy endings are far and few between.

When they turned to leave, my new buddy stopped for a second, then he pointed to a hot-dog wagon and asked, "Can I get you one?" We both laughed while I politely declined. I didn't want to mix some dirty-water dogs with whatever my girlfriend had on the menu for tonight, the mix might be more then a human stomach could handle. And off they went, just a nice couple holding hands, enjoying a sunny afternoon in the park. And I would never see them again.

I sat back down on the bench, taking in the sun-filled scenery, and that's when I spotted the three dealers from earlier standing about fifty feet away. They had been watching us the whole time. Out of habit I pressed my arm against my side, checking to make sure my other friend, the steel bulge, was where it was supposed to be. It's nice to have friends. I glanced at my watch and realized time had flown by and it was time to go meet my girl. That's when I stood up, and real slow and deliberately walked past the three shitheads and gave them my final "go fuck yourself" look. Then I sauntered out of the park. Now I was good and ready to leave.

When I picked my girlfriend up she asked me how the park was. I couldn't tell her about the three drug dealers I had the staring match with. She knew that I was a cop and thought it was really cool, but she didn't really understand what a cop's life is all about just yet. It can get edgy even when you're off duty, and I didn't want to scare her off. Good thing, because in a few years she would become my wife. I thought about telling the story about my new friend and the hot dogs, but stopped. I didn't know how to explain to her that my job is this: I chase a guy down out in the street. I choke the living shit out of him. I shine a flashlight up his ass. Then I buy him dinner. So I just told her, "I met an old friend in the park."

6

Home

It took a while, and I was starting to get a little frustrated, but it finally happened. I found a place to call home.

A year earlier I was promoted to sergeant and was sent to Midtown North for my first six months. Most people think working in Midtown is a primo spot, but it isn't. It sucked, and I hated it. It was insanely busy, which is what I like, but it was all nonsense. I spent most of the night stuck in traffic and supervising more cops than I could count, or possibly keep track of. And every stupid little thing is a big deal when it happens in Midtown. I couldn't wait to get out of there.

Then they sent me to the Fifth Precinct, Chinatown. Hated it. It was dead, nothing happened. There was a million people coming and going in all directions, but no real crime. I had to get out of there also.

Finally I couldn't take it anymore. I was miserable, so I put in for a transfer to the Ninth Precinct. The Fifth and the Ninth were on the same radio frequency, and all night long I would hear gun runs, shots fired, and robberies in progress over in the Ninth, while in the Fifth, nothing was going on. I was bored out of my mind.

When I asked the lieutenant if there might be a problem getting me over there, he just laughed. For as long as anybody could remember, the Ninth had been a shit hole, and if you got sent there, it was either bad luck, or you were being punished. Especially when it came to supervisors—nobody with half a brain in their head wanted to be a boss there. The cops there were a salty bunch, and if you didn't have your act together and know what you were doing, they would eat you alive. But they were a tight bunch, and every-body watched each other's backs.

Right away they put me on midnights, 12:00 a.m. to 8:00 a.m. Most people hate midnight tours, it's the busiest for real crime and has the least number of cops working, but I liked it. It suited me. Most of the normal world was home in bed, so it was just us and them: the bad guys and the creatures of the night, all of us roaming the streets, looking for trouble.

My first night there I got stuck on the desk. I really wanted to be out on patrol, but the way it works is, we "whack it up." Tomorrow night the other sergeant would be inside, and I could go out in the street. Besides, I was just happy to be here and out of the Fifth, and Midtown was quickly fading into a distant memory.

It didn't take long for the fun to begin—I was only about an hour into my first tour. I was admiring the cracks in the walls and the peeling paint on the ceiling, when all of a sudden, I hear a commotion outside. Then without warning—BOOM!—the front door flies open and a guy comes running in, screaming, "Help me, help me!"

His head is split wide open, and there's blood flying all over the place. And running right behind him is another guy chasing him with a three-foot piece of steel pipe, screaming, "Motherfuck-errrrrrr!"

Right away me and some young cop I hadn't really met yet leap over the desk and tackle the guy with the pipe. Two seconds ago I was sipping my coffee, reading the paper, and admiring the dingy decor, now I'm rolling all over the dirty floor with some nut job.

I had this maniac's one arm, trying to wrestle the pipe out of his hand, while the young cop is trying to slap cuffs on the other, and the guy wouldn't stop fighting. It was amazing, he could give a rat's ass he was in a police station. He was pissed, and really wanted to kill the other guy. And all the while we were fighting, the victim is hovering over us screaming at the top of his lungs, "Fuck him up! Fuck him up good!" And every time he screamed there was spit and blood flying all over the place.

What made it worse was that both of these guys stunk really bad. They were two homeless drunks that liked to hang out on the park bench across the street, and they reeked of booze, body odor, and some other delightful aromas I didn't want to really think about.

At the same time my PAA (police administrative aide), a civilian woman in her fifties whose job is to take reports from victims on minor stuff, tried to help. She pulls a nightstick out of her desk drawer—the stick she's not authorized to have—and comes running over yelling, "Hit him with this, Sarge!"

Just then two cops come charging through the front door and jump in. They saw the commotion from down the block and figured I might need some help. Finally, after a lot of kicking, punching, and screaming, I get the pipe out of the guy's hand, and we get him cuffed. Then we wrestle him over to the holding cell and throw him inside, headfirst.

I sit the victim down and try to get a story out of him, but it isn't easy. He was bombed, his blood alcohol level would have humbled a college frat party. Plus there was blood rolling down his face, into his mouth, ears, and watery eyes. And every slurred syllable out of his mouth was accompanied by blood, spit, and booze breath. Real police work is not as glamorous as you might think.

Turns out these two best friends were fighting over who took the biggest sip from the forty-ounce beer they both chipped in for. And believe it or not, after hearing the story, it all made perfect sense. Out on the street what's fair is fair. Guys get killed over less.

I grabbed a radio and notified the dispatcher that we had "one under," inside the station house. I'm sure that got a laugh from everybody that was listening. Around here you didn't even have to leave the station house to make a collar! I also requested an ambulance for the victim, while the cops started banging out an arrest report for the perp. Just another night in the Ninth Precinct—loser goes to the hospital, and the winner goes to jail.

I grabbed some alcohol wipes and scrubbed my hands raw, then I went back to the locker room to change into a clean uniform shirt. The shirt I had on was now a biohazard. I thought about throwing it in the garbage, but if I did that every time something like this happened, I'd go broke buying new shirts.

When I got back to the desk, it was amazing, it was like nothing had happened. The young cop on the telephone switchboard went back to doing his crossword puzzle, and my PAA went back to filing her nails. It seemed like nobody felt this was anything unusual. In most precincts it would be something out of the ordinary—but not here.

As I took my place behind the desk again, I couldn't help but stare up at this big piece of peeling paint on the ceiling. It was huge. I was wondering how long it had been like that, and how long it would be before it fell on somebody's unsuspecting head. I wondered when the last time was that anybody had painted or even really cleaned this place. The building was a hundred years old and looked every minute of it.

What I liked about being a New York City cop was the history, and the tradition. We're the oldest police department in the country, and I felt like I belonged to something special. On the wall behind me were several plaques with the names and faces of police officers killed in the line of duty. This place had a lot of history.

A short time later, I was trying to decide whether I was going to order out for eggs or a cheeseburger, when, believe it or not, it happened again. BOOM! Suddenly the front door flies open. I jumped out of my chair, ducked, and put my hand on my gun, thinking "What the fuck now?" And that's when a guy comes marching into the station house—playing the bagpipes. It three o'clock in the morning, and this guy kicks open the front door of a police station and comes marching in playing the bagpipes like he's something out of *Braveheart*.

He doesn't acknowledge me, or any of the cops standing around. He just starts marching back and forth in front of the desk playing this ear-splitting music. And the funny part is, when I looked around, nobody really acknowledged him either. I glanced over to the cop on the switchboard, and he was still doing his crossword puzzle. I looked over at my PAA, and she barely stopped filing her fingernails. Just like the fight, only an hour before, nobody seemed to think that this was unusual.

Turns out he was just another one of the neighborhood nut jobs. Almost every precinct in the city had their regular psychos that liked to hang around the station house, and the cops usually let them, as long as they didn't become too much of a pain in the ass. Usually they're harmless, and they kind of become the precinct mascot. I would soon find out that the Ninth had more crazies than most.

After doing a couple of laps in front of the desk and playing that earsplitting music, he marched back through the front door and out into the night where he came from. As I listened to the music fade away in the distance, the young cop on the switchboard smiled and said, "Welcome to the Ninth." Then he told me he was ordering coffee and asked me if I wanted one. All I could think was, I don't need coffee to stay awake in this place.

Not long after that I was back on patrol, but this time I was assigned to Tompkins Square Park. About a year and a half earlier, the city had kicked out all the squatters that lived there. Over the years the park had become sort of a shantytown. It was filled with junkies, crackheads, homeless, runaways, anarchists, and any other kind of miscreant you could think of, all looking for like-minded companionship. Twenty-four hours a day there were subhuman-looking creatures huddled around barrel fires smoking crack, shooting dope, and drinking forty-ounce bottles of beer. It was something out of this world. You might as well have been on Mars surrounded by aliens.

The grass refused to grow anymore, and if the trees could have picked up and moved, they would have. They were tired of being peed on.

Some well-intentioned do-gooders had given the homeless tents and sleeping bags to help make them more comfortable, so the park had become crowded with cardboard shacks, campfires, and brightly colored domes. Some of the bigger tents were for community use. They had one tent just for "shooting up." Junkies like a little privacy when they're cooking their shit and sticking a needle in their arm. Then there was the sex tent. If a crackhead couple needed some alone time to make a crack baby, there was a quiet, romantic place for that.

If the police had to go in there, you would never go alone—you were just asking for trouble. We were always outnumbered, so we would always go in there in groups of two, three, or preferably more. It seemed like almost everybody hated us, especially the anarchists.

Surprisingly, though, not everybody wanted to throw a brick off some roof and hit us in the head. There was one guy who every time he saw me came over to say hello. He was a pleasant, soft-spoken fellow who looked like Jesus, with long sandy-colored hair and a scruffy beard. For short periods of time I actually found him amusing. Sometimes he would make me laugh, and he could carry on a normal conversation, unlike many of the other park inhabitants. He would talk my ear off until I got tired of him and told him to take a hike. Sometimes I would see him walking around the neighborhood with a live chicken. One day I asked what the bird was for, and he gave me this creepy smile and said, "Dinner."

A year or so later, his girlfriend, a ballet dancer, would end up missing. Through some good police work, the detectives quickly figured out that he killed her, then chopped her up, boiled her in a big pot, and made soup out of her. As if that wasn't freaky enough, he said that he fed the soup to his homeless friends. He probably told them it was chicken. I heard they found her skull in a five-gallon bucket up at the Port Authority bus terminal in Midtown.

Even for a place like the Ninth Precinct, this was definitely unusual, so the story, and his picture, made the front page of the paper. You can guess what happened next: somebody asked him to autograph it, and they hung it up on the wall in the Detective Squad. He signed it, "To the boys in the Ninth, I'd love to have you for dinner."

The park, and everybody in it, was a three-ring fucking circus.

After the city kicked everybody out and started the infamous Tompkins Square Park Riot, they surrounded it with a ten-foot-high fence and vowed never to let them back in. After the riot, the city had no intention of giving back one square inch of this valuable Manhattan real estate. So every day, twenty-four hours a day, whether we had the manpower or not, at least two cops and sometimes a sergeant were assigned there in order to keep the former tenants from moving back in. Tonight, I was the "Park Sergeant."

Some of the people that got kicked out stayed around. They hung out across the street, just staring at us, and that ten-foot fence that was put up by the Man. You could see that crazed look on their faces as they tried to figure out how to get back in, or at least how to hang a banner on the fence proclaiming SQUATTERS' RIGHTS.

It was like a Mexican standoff. I felt like I was at the Alamo.

A few hours later I felt like I was in a slow-motion Daytona 500—and I was starting to get dizzy. I had a car with two cops locked inside the park covering the interior, and my job was to drive in circles, covering the perimeter, and we were not supposed to leave under any circumstances. If one of these morons managed to get back in and damage some park property, or at least hang a banner saying something like FUCK THE MAYOR, I would get my nuts cut off. So I was stuck riding in circles.

On one of my laps around the block a homeless woman leaped from between two parked cars and landed in the middle of the street, right in front of me. I had to jam on the brakes to keep from hitting her. When my tires stopped screeching, my front bumper was only inches from her. And in the bright glow of my headlights, she turned, smiled, then pulled down her pants and pissed right in front of a marked NYPD police car.

She had this kooky grin on her face, as she squatted dangerously close to my front bumper. Half her teeth were missing, and those she had left were black and crooked, but the smile made me believe she was really enjoying herself. I don't know if she did this to other passing motorists, or just to police cars, but she was nearly pissing on my front bumper, and having a great time doing it.

I was a little startled because I almost ran her over, but the pissing thing was a little surprising too. When she was done, she pulled up her pants and took off running up Avenue A, laughing like crazy.

For the briefest moment I thought about chasing her—but why? What the fuck for? I didn't want to catch her. I didn't even want to touch her. I was running out of clean uniform shirts. And if I did catch her, then what? Tie up a sector car for a couple of hours while they sat on her at the Bellevue psych ward? We only had three sectors working that night, and crime never stops in the Ninth. It would be a total waste of manpower.

I looked over and saw a few of the park zombies laughing their asses off. They seemed to enjoy it as much as she did. What to do? But after thinking about it for a second, I started laughing with them. Finally something we could all agree on. Then I went back to riding in circles.

A little while later, a "gun run" at East Third Street and Avenue B came over the air. The dispatcher stated there was a male white and a female Hispanic inside a blue auto, and the male was armed with a gun.

I heard Nine Adam pick up the job, but nobody was answering to back them up. We only had three sector cars, the other two were probably busy handling their own jobs, and the Park Car was locked inside the ten-foot-high fence. The dispatcher called out again, "Any available Nine unit to back Adam on a report of a man with a gun?" No answer. I decided the hell with it, I'm going.

The southeast corner of the park is at Seventh Street and Avenue B, so I could practically see Third Street. I figured I could shoot right down there, back up the sector car, and get back before any of the park zombies knew I was gone.

I only drove about a block, when a blue car with a male white and a female Hispanic flew past me going the other way. I figured, this has got to be them, so I pulled a U-turn and started to follow. The car was moving a little fast, and by the time I made the turn they were about two blocks ahead of me, so I hit the gas and tried to catch up. I snatched the radio off my belt and told the dispatcher, "I'm following a possible from the gun run at Three and B."

They made the left on Seventh Street, and I was having a little bit of a tough time catching up because he was hitting green lights all the way. I couldn't use my red lights and siren, because if he saw me coming, the chase would be on. The best way to do this is to get in behind him and try to grab him when he's stuck in traffic. We always try to avoid a car chase whenever possible, but it was four in the morning and there wasn't much traffic, so I was a little screwed.

He made the right on First Avenue and stopped at the red light on St. Mark's Place. This was it, I couldn't wait for another car to back me up because when the light turned green, he would be off and running again, and I'd be following him to the Bronx before he hit another red light.

So when the traffic light turned green, I flipped on my flashing red lights and bleeped the siren, and much to my surprise he pulled right over. That was easy enough, I thought. I pulled in behind him and waited a moment. I figured I could stall for a few seconds and give one of the sectors a chance to swing by, but when I grabbed the radio to tell the dispatcher that I had the vehicle stopped, the driver's door on the blue car had swung open. The next thing I knew, a big white guy with a goofy grin on his face stepped out and started walking toward me.

It was dark out, but it was easy to see, and I had no doubt about it. In the glow of my high beams and flashing red lights, I could see the butt of a gun sticking out of his waistband. When he got out of the car his shirt lifted a little, and there it was right in front of me—and getting closer.

This is it—this is a cop's life. Every minute, of every day, this is what you wait for. This is what you think about, and this is what you prepare for: The Man with the Gun.

I looked at the gun, then at that dopey grin on his face, and I thought, this guy is going to try and shoot me—and he's pretty fucking happy about it.

All that thinking took about one second. Then I dropped the radio, grabbed my gun, yanked the door handle, and shoved it open with my shoulder—all in one move.

I jumped out of the car, pointed my gun right in his face, and yelled, "PUT 'EM UP! PUT 'EM UP, MOTHERFUCKER, OR I'LL BLOW YOUR FUCKING HEAD OFF!" Now his dopey grin was replaced by an "Oh shit" look.

Again, much to my surprise, he threw his hands right up and did exactly what I told him to. When I threw him onto the trunk of his car, he was trying to say something, but I couldn't really hear him. I was wound up, and all I could hear was my heart pounding in my ears. I had him spread-eagled on the car with my gun screwed into the back of his head while I reached into his waistband and grabbed his gun.

While dealing with him, I had to keep one eye on the female in the car. I didn't want her getting out and jumping on my back, or trying something else crazy because she wanted to help her man. Out in the street, a woman can be just as nasty and vicious as any guy can be, and a lot of times they're worse.

Then I heard him say it again, but this time he yelled it, "I'm on the job." That caught my attention. He was trying to tell me he was a cop.

"I'm on the job" is the universal NYPD jargon for "I'm a cop." If he had said, "I'm a police officer," I would have known he was full of shit. But in a situation like this, this was the correct—and the only—response.

I looked at the gun I just pulled off him, and saw it was a Smith & Wesson .38-caliber five-shot revolver—the standard NYPD off-duty gun. That's when he mumbled, "My ID is in my back pocket."

I shoved his gun into my pocket, then reached for his wallet, and when I opened it, there was an NYPD shield and ID card. That's when he turned and said, "Can I take my hands off the car now?"

I unscrewed my gun from the back of his head, and we all started to relax. Turned out he really was a cop and worked in the Ninth, and the woman in the car was his girlfriend. He went on to tell me that the shitheads over on Third Street didn't like the fact that a neighborhood girl was dating a white cop, so sometimes they would call 911, just to break his balls.

Under normal circumstances, I would have been pissed at him for getting out of the car the way he did, but he thought he was getting pulled over by one of his buddies. He apologized profusely and said he didn't even know there was a new sergeant working midnights. After he explained everything, it all made perfect sense, so there was no need to make any more out of this than it was.

I took a peek into the car and very casually said, "How you doing?" The girl was petrified. She just sat there staring straight ahead, afraid to move an inch. She mumbled back a very soft, petite "Hellooooo."

Just then Nine Adam pulls up, and now they have that "Oh shit" look on their faces. The new sergeant has one of their buddies pulled over, and this can't be good. I explained to them what happened, and we all had a good laugh over it—cop humor. I told them to give back the gun run as a 10-90Y (Unnecessary), and I would do the same for the car stop.

We shook hands, introduced ourselves, and he said, "Welcome to the Ninth." A year later he would be working in my squad, and we would become good friends. And a few years after that at their wedding, we would all laugh about how the wedding almost didn't happen because the new sergeant almost shot the groom.

We all went on our way and I raced back to the park, and just as I feared, on my first lap around I caught one of the anarchists climbing the fence. He almost shit himself when he heard my tires screech to a halt behind him. He must have figured I was gone for the night. The jerk-off figured wrong.

I yanked him down and threw him onto the hood of the car, and when I did he was clutching something inside his jacket. I reached in and pulled out a large white bedsheet, and when I opened it up, spray-painted in big red letters was FREE REPUBLIC and SQUATTERS RIGHTS.

I really just wanted to kick this guy in the ass and send him on his way. Locking this guy up was a waste of manpower also, but this was a big collar to the police department, so I slapped cuffs on him and notified the dispatcher that I had "one under."

I gave the collar to one of the cops and went back to riding in circles—and getting dizzy again. The Mexican standoff continued.

* * *

It was after five in the morning, and things were starting to settle down. The radio was getting quiet, and the creatures of the night, watching me from across the street, had faded away. Where they went, I do not know. They probably found some abandoned building or an empty lot to squat in.

I hadn't eaten in a while, and I was starting to get tired. I needed coffee and a bagel. I knew it was a bad idea to leave the park, but my stomach was growling and I needed a caffeine fix. I was new to the command and didn't have a regular coffee spot I trusted, so I decided to go to a joint I liked over in the next precinct. Leaving the park was a little risky, but I hate bad coffee, and my stomach was telling me, "Fuck it, let's go."

I was driving as quick as I could, and I figured I could get there and be back in ten, maybe fifteen minutes, tops. When I got there I ordered my regular—a large coffee and a bagel with cream cheese. The counter guy knows me and likes me, so he really lays on the cream cheese, but when I feel how heavy the bagel is, I start to think, maybe he really doesn't like me, maybe he's just trying to clog my arteries and kill me slowly.

I jumped back into the car and started racing back to where I belonged, when all of a sudden, I saw two guys "high stepping" it down Houston Street. They were't running, but they were walking fast and had "guilty" written all over their faces. I looked back in the direction they just came from, but I didn't see anything. I knew these guys were fleeing from something—I could feel it. By this time in my career I had been involved in a lot of collars, put handcuffs on a lot of perps, and I knew what I was looking for. And these guys looked good.

My old partners and I had a long-running joke, if I saw somebody that I thought looked good, my Spidey sense would start tingling. But my Spidey sense was located in my ball bag, and right now, my nut sack was buzzing like a cell phone on vibrate.

And it's not racial profiling—it's called good police work.

Houston Street is wide, six lanes across, and I was on the opposite side from them, and these guys were so zoned out in their own little world, they didn't even notice me watching them. What I should be doing now is calling for another car to back me up and then grabbing them—what people refer to as a "stop and frisk." Obviously I didn't know for sure these guys did anything—just a gut feeling. Or in my case, a tingling in my ball bag. Try explaining that to a judge.

But my problem is I'm a little off base. I'm on the other side of the precinct, when I should be in the park. All I need is for the Duty Captain to hear me on the radio, ten blocks from where I'm supposed to be, getting involved in who knows what. He'd cut my nuts off, and where would I be then without my Spidey sense? So I decide to make a quick U-turn and take a look down the block to see if anything is going on before I let the whole world know what I'm up to. Besides, the streets are quiet, and I know I can find these guys in a hurry if I have to.

I made the U-turn, and it only took about thirty seconds for me to figure this caper out. Standing on the corner was what used to be a well-dressed businessman in an expensive suit. His jacket and shirt were ripped, and his tie was yanked up around his neck from when he was being choked. He was dirty all over from being thrown on the ground, and blood was shooting out of his wrist. As soon as he sees me, he runs over and starts crying about how two guys just stabbed him and stole his watch. He started to tell me what they looked like and which way they went, but I didn't need to hear it, it was my two high steppers—no doubt about it. I told him to stay where he's at, and that I'll be right back. The guy was drunk and looked like a typical Wall Street overachiever who partied too much tonight and stayed out a little too late. Somebody like him is an easy meal for a couple of hungry bad guys at five in the morning.

I turn around and race down the block, and I'm back on these guys in no time. I'm driving fast, but not too fast. There are no screeching tires or flashing red lights and siren. There's no need to spook these guys just yet. If I do, I'll only end up in a foot chase.

As I pull up behind them, I grab my radio to call for another car, but suddenly I have another problem: they just looked over their shoulders, and they now see me coming. And if they see me sneaking up behind them and talking on the radio, they're going to start running in two different directions, which means I can only catch one.

I love making robbery collars. I've made lots of them over the years. It's always been my favorite collar to make, and I'm good at it, but also I'm greedy. I don't want only one—I want two. I want both these fucks.

We were now about two blocks away from the scene, and I could tell they had calmed down a bit. The high stepping had slowed to a brisk walk, and the guilty look had eased into a "job well done" happy face. They obviously started to relax because they thought they got away with it—and if that's what they think, great, there's no sense making them think any different. I figure I can play it real cool, grab them, then call for another car, and I can get both of them.

Besides, they only have a knife—I have a gun. Sounds like a fair fight to me, if there is one.

I pull up next to them, roll down the window real calm, and say, "What's up, guys? How you doing tonight?" Suddenly their happy look is replaced by panic and quivering lips. Their eyes are popping out of their heads. They don't know whether to shit or go blind.

Then I say, "Where you going?" I can tell by the dopey looks on their faces that they are thinking fast, trying to come up with just the right answer. That's when they both point in different directions and say, "That way." They obviously haven't had a chance to get their story together.

I get out of the car, all smiles, and follow it up with some calm reassuring words, like "I got to ask you a question. Do you mind? It will only take a second."

I could tell they were all confused right now, they didn't know what to do. Every other time they got stopped—and I'm sure this wasn't their first or their tenth—the cops jumped out real fast, threw them up against the wall, and probably weren't very nice about it. But not all stop and frisks are done that way, this time we were doing things a little different. This time I had my "Officer Friendly" face on, and they were giving me their best "We're not doing nothing" look. This time, we were all playing poker.

I get out, grab the first guy, and throw him onto the hood of the car. It goes smooth, no problem, so I start thinking, "Good, I'm halfway there, the nice-guy routine must be working." But when I go for the second guy, he tries to back away from me, so I reach out, grab him by the shirt, and throw him onto the hood. But as soon as he goes down, he bounces right back up again, and when he does, he's reaching into his waistband trying to grab something. Suddenly my ball bag is on fire.

I know he's got something, so right away it's a race, I go for whatever he's going for, and when I reach into his waistband, there it is—a gun! I try to get it first, but it's too late, he's already got it in his hand, and he's pulling it out.

Now I'm in some deep shit. I'm up against two guys, one armed with a gun, and the other probably has the knife. And they just did a stickup, and obviously have no intention of going to jail. To make matters worse, I'm alone.

In about a half a second, a simple stop and frisk turns into a life-and-death struggle. Most people go to the gym because they want buns of steel, or rock-hard abs. A cop goes to the gym because one day, when he least expects it, he might be fighting for his life.

The bell has rung, and the fight is now on, so I have no way of grabbing my radio and calling for help. I'll have to deal with these guys myself. To make matters worse, the guy with the gun is tall, real tall—six four at least. I'm barely five nine when I'm lying, and

I can't see over his shoulders. I have him from behind in a bear hug with my arms wrapped around his waist. My face is buried in his back, and his shoulders are over my head, so I can't even see what I'm doing or what his partner is doing. I can't see the gun—I can only feel it. I'm definitely in some hot water.

We're both struggling for the gun, but he got to it first, and now he has a pretty good grip on it. All I could get was a little bit of the barrel, and a small part of the grip. He's pulling one way, and I'm pulling the other, but he's got more gun to hold on to.

My first thought now was, if I can't get the gun away from him, maybe I could get my finger inside the trigger guard and try to squeeze off a shot. All I needed was one shot and I figured I could give him a tingling in his ball bag that he would never forget, but it wasn't working. He had these big hands and really long fingers, and he had them wrapped around the gun pretty good.

I remember thinking how dry and scaly his hands were. Funny the stupid things you think about at a time like this.

I always liked going to the gym, lifting weights, and hitting the heavy bag, but anybody who's been in a real street fight will tell you, they don't last very long, thirty seconds, maybe a minute, tops. Then somebody wins and somebody loses. Somebody goes to the hospital and somebody goes to jail. But in this case I figured somebody was going to the cemetery.

I don't know how long we were fighting, but it seemed like a long time. He was trying to get off the car, and I was slamming him back down—trying to keep him from turning around on me. He was pulling one way on the gun, and I was pulling the other way, and I knew I had to end this thing quick, before I ran out of steam.

For a second I thought about letting go of the gun, then jumping back and going for mine. Try and turn this thing into a quick-draw contest, and whoever got the first shot off would be the winner, but that wasn't going to work either. The NYPD had been using the same old-fashioned leather holster for the past fifty years. It was made more for retention than for quick draw. Even if your holster was well broken in, it would still take you a couple of seconds to get your gun out. His gun was already in his hand. I was going to lose this quick-draw competition, no doubt about it.

We were right in the middle of the street and cars were whizzing by, driving around us. I was hoping a sector car might pass by and see me, but no such luck. There's never a cop around when you need one.

Just when I thought things couldn't get any worse, the second shithead jumps off the car and maneuvers around behind me. I can tell he wants to jump on my back, or maybe try to stab me. If one guy has the gun, then most likely the other one has the knife.

Not calling for another car to back me up was turning out to be a huge fucking mistake, and it was getting worse by the second.

I'm not a very tall guy, but I'm strong, and the only thing I could think of was to lift the first guy up off his feet and swing him around, and use him as a shield. I needed to keep number two off me, so when he moved left, I swung the big guy left, when he tried to go right, I swung right. It was working, sort of, but my problem was, my face was buried in the big guy's sweaty, smelly back. My eyes were right between his shoulder blades and I couldn't see. Number two was jumping back and forth trying to get behind me, and I'm struggling to see exactly where he's at.

While all this swinging was going on, me and the big guy were both yelling, not at each other, but at number two. I was yelling for him to "Back the fuck up." And the tall guy was yelling, "Do it! Come on, do it!"

It was dark out, and I could barely see around number one's shoulders, but when I did, I could see on the other guy's face a look of indecision. As number two jumped back and forth, trying to get behind me, I could tell in his movements he was hesitating a little. He knew exactly where this was going. They were going to kill a cop, and he wasn't a hundred percent sure he wanted to be a part of it. This whole encounter happened just as fast for them as it did for me, and it was spinning out of control for all of us.

This was the moment of truth for the three of us, there was no undoing what had just begun, and I was starting to run out of energy. I had to think of something fast or I was going to be the one going to the cemetery.

Our four hands and the gun were balled up into a giant fist right in the middle of the big guy's stomach, he was trying to rip the gun out of my hand, and I was trying to rip it out of his. I was running out of energy and options, and the only thing I could think of was to start squeezing. Not his hand, but his stomach. So I started yanking harder and harder, as hard as I could. I was giving him some kind of crazy Heimlich maneuver—trying to knock the wind out of him. I didn't know what else to do, it was the only thing I could think of. I couldn't let go of the gun and I couldn't let go of him, and number two was quickly working up the courage to jump in and stab me in the back.

So I yanked and squeezed so hard I thought I was going to break his ribs. I pulled that big four-handed fist deep into his stomach, and when it couldn't go any farther I pulled and squeezed some more.

I would later find out that these guys were high on crack, but I was wound up on adrenaline and fighting for my life. And to see my family again. So I was yanking, squeezing, and swinging for all I was worth.

And after a few hard yanks it started working! As I pulled that giant four-handed fist up through his stomach and into his diaphragm, he was making this kind of yelping and gurgling noise. I could tell he was in a lot of pain, and I was knocking the wind out of him. And the first rule of fighting is, if you can't breathe, you can't fight.

I squeezed and squeezed, and when he gasped for air and tried to catch his breath, I squeezed even harder. Then all of a sudden I could feel it, it was starting to happen—he was loosening his grip on the gun. So I yanked and pulled some more, and as soon as the gun loosened enough, I ripped it out of his hand.

It was a good feeling getting the gun, I was starting to win, but this fight was far from over, so as soon as I got the gun, I hauled off and smashed him right in the side of the skull with it. BAM! I nailed him right in the temple as hard as I could. Now he was out of breath, and seeing stars. That seemed to take a lot of the fight out of him. Then I pointed the gun at number two and yelled for him to back the fuck up and to put his hands on the car.

At this point I could have shot the both of them. I could have executed them right on the spot, and they would have given me a medal for it. Thinking back, I probably should have, the world would be a slightly better place without them. But contrary to what a lot of storefront reverends and cop-bashing politicians would like you to believe, cops aren't trigger-happy. Nobody wants to get into a shooting. Nobody wants to take a life if you don't have to. Not even these two assholes.

I pointed the gun right between number two's eyeballs and told him to get back on the car and if he didn't, I was going to shoot him right in the fucking face. I was a little spent from fighting with the first guy and had no intention of doing it all over again.

I finally get the both of them spread-eagled over the hood of the car. Number one is moaning a little because he's still stunned from that whack to the temple I gave him, and number two doesn't want to get shot in the face. I'm pointing the gun at one guy, then at the other, telling them to keep their hands on the car, and that's when I realize—I'm using their pistol to hold them down at gunpoint. I look at the little gun in my hand and it's a piece of shit. It's a silver .38-caliber revolver, a real Saturday night special—and I'm not even sure if it works. So I slap it into my left hand and pull out my gun. Now I'm in the middle of Houston Street with a gun in each hand, like in some movie, pointing them at their heads.

And all the while, cars, taxicabs, and early-morning delivery trucks are passing by. People could not care less. Back in the bad old days of New York City, a little gunplay in the middle of a busy street was apparently no big deal. So everybody just drove around us and kept on going.

Finally I shoved their gun in my back pocket, grabbed my radio, and told the dispatcher, "Central, Houston and Elizabeth, 10-85 me one unit forthwith—I got two under." That was all I had to say, everybody listening could tell I was out of breath, and the next thing I knew there were sirens in the distance racing in my direction. The cavalry is coming—it's a great feeling.

In the first car to respond were two cops I had known from my previous command, and when I told them the story we all had a good laugh. Cops have a sick sense of humor.

We did a show-up at the scene with the robbery victim, and he positively identified them as the individuals who stabbed him. I also showed him the watch I recovered, and he identified that as his property. This was turning out to be a nice, ground-ball collar—an easy one for any assistant district attorney who catches it. I was positive we weren't going to trial on this one.

I gave the collar to one of the sector cars and got ready to go back to the park—and riding in circles again. But before that, I had some unfinished business. I grabbed our victim and not so nicely asked him, "Why the fuck didn't you tell me they had a gun? You almost got me killed." He was very apologetic, and stammered on about how they stabbed him, and all he could think about was the knife.

I would later find out that a few hours earlier, they had robbed another guy at gunpoint on the Brooklyn Bridge. Turned out these pillars of society had been on a robbery and crack-smoking spree for the past three days! The detectives would end up doing some lineups and closing out a few cases on these two.

Two hours later, I was back at the station house, and the night was finally over. I had changed into civilian clothes and was hanging out behind the desk waiting to sign out. My first few days at the Ninth were interesting, to say the least, plus I had quite a few laughs. A normal person with a half a brain would have said, "Get me the hell out of here." But not me. I really liked the Ninth. I really liked the salty cops that worked here, and the station house that was crumbling around us. But more than anything I liked the neighborhood. It made you feel alive, and it made me feel like a cop. And as I stood there watching the day tour head out to go on patrol,

I looked around at the dingy floor, cracked walls, and peeling paint, and I couldn't help but think—I finally found a home!

*   *   *

A few days later I was behind the desk again getting ready for another night on patrol. I checked my mailbox, and inside I found the arresting officers had left me a copy of the paperwork from the two collars, in case I needed it for the grand jury. When I flipped through the packet I found the ballistic report from the lab: that piece-of-shit-looking gun was loaded and fully functional. It worked just fine!

Buried underneath the paperwork was a large manila envelope with a return address from the Manhattan South Borough Commander—the Chief. When I opened it, there was a nice-looking certificate inside for "Outstanding Police Work." I read the letter that came with it and couldn't help but laugh. It was for collaring the guy in the park for trying to climb the fence and hang the banner.

And in big bold letters—in the middle of the certificate—he spelled my name wrong.

7.

Midnights

When the sun goes down—that's cops and robbers time. That's when the real police work happens. The city may sleep but crime never does. And the later it gets, the busier it can get. During the day cops deal with all kinds of stuff, but at night is when the craziness starts. That's when the violence happens.

Especially after midnight, when the rest of the world is in their pajamas, safely locked behind closed doors, the creatures of the night come out to roam the streets. That's when it's just us and them: junkies, crackheads, prostitutes, drug dealers, rapists, robbers, and murderers.

During the day the world has some rules; people go to work, kids go to school, and stores open for business. But when it gets dark, and the normal people pull down their shades, and barricade themselves in for the night, the rules go out the window—and the bad guys get bolder. They're like vampires, and for some reason the lack of sunlight seems to energize them.

Even the regular, law-abiding people who were out for just a good time find themselves in trouble. After hours of boozing, partying, and barhopping, that's when stupidness happens. Motor vehicle accidents tend not to be just fender benders. More likely they're "rollovers" or "pin jobs," with the occupants trapped inside waiting for us to save them. Alcohol-fueled disputes often escalate quickly, with the winner going to jail, and the loser going to the hospital—or worse, the cemetery.

And when it comes to drunken nonsense, the girls are just as bad as the guys.

Years ago the Ninth Precinct on the Lower East Side of Manhattan wasn't the chi-chi hipster place it is now. There were no cafés with tables outside, and yuppies sipping their lattes. Back then it was the Wild West. Shootings, stabbings, and robberies happened constantly and bloodshed was a nightly occurrence.

The Ninth was less than a square mile, but it was filled with twenty-story public housing projects, tenement apartment buildings, and five-floor walk-ups. There were a lot of people crammed into a small area. Block after block was packed with residents, except for the countless burned-out buildings and empty lots. They were filled with homeless, squatters, junkies, and drug dealers.

And the neighborhood seemed to revolve around one thing: drugs. At any given time there were at least twenty or more spots dealing all hours of the day and night. Narcotics would come in and make collars almost daily, but it was useless. It was like swatting flies in a shit house. Crime was everywhere.

I had only been assigned to the Ninth for a couple of months, but I loved it already. It was the most interesting place I ever worked. If you wanted to do police work, this was the place to do it.

I got to work early, found a safe place to park my car, and walked into the precinct. I had that spring in my step that said I was happy to be here. It may sound crazy but I didn't want to be home curled up in bed, or out at a party somewhere. I wanted to be . . . *here*. And unlike most normal cops, I really enjoyed working midnights.

The station house and most things in it were almost a hundred years old, and they looked every minute of it. The building was a dump—everywhere you looked something was either cracked, broken, or peeling—but the place had character. It had an outpost-like charm to it. It was a sanctuary in a dangerous world where people could come for help—and a place that cops called home.

I was a rookie sergeant, young, in my early thirties, and still trying to get a handle on being the boss. I always felt that I was a pretty good cop, but being the man in charge, the one with the stripes on his arm, the guy everybody looks to when the world is turning to shit, is a lot more challenging.

But I was doing good, and catching on fast. Not because I was smarter than anyone else, but because it felt natural to me. It felt like home. Like this is where I'm supposed to be. I loved police work.

My eighth-grade English teacher, Sister Kathleen, would beat the crap out of me on a regular basis—usually for being a wiseass. She would preach to me about hell and tell me I was never going to make anything out of myself. I never got upset, because I never believed her. Deep down, I knew she was wrong. I knew I was going to grow up to be a cop someday. And five minutes after the beating stopped, I went back to being a wiseass again.

One of the things I liked best about working midnights was you hardly ever saw a boss above the rank of sergeant, and tonight there would only be two supervisors working. I had patrol and the other sergeant had the desk. So for the next eight hours everything that happened out in the street was my responsibility. And as usual I was shorthanded again.

I had three two-man sector cars, and a driver for myself. I also had a two-man Tompkins Square Park auto, but they were untouchable. Their job was to stay in the park and make sure the squatters that the city threw out didn't return and make camp.

It was the same in every precinct in the city. The late tour was always the busiest, and the least manned. We were the hardest working, least appreciated, and the most sleep deprived. Midnight cops are a different breed.

I checked the roll call, made some changes, and headed for the locker room. I opened my locker, ripped off the plastic dry cleaner wrapper from my uniform shirt, and got dressed. Sometimes it's easy to take for granted how dangerous police work can be, but when you strap on a vest, two guns, thirty rounds of spare ammunition, mace, and a nightstick it can be a little bit of a reminder. We don't carry all that cool shit for nothing.

I headed back downstairs twenty pounds heavier than I was before. The clock on the wall said it was time to get this show started, so in my best sergeant's voice I barked out to the cops mingling around the desk, "Fall in! Attention to roll call!"

Roll call went fast, there wasn't many of us, so there was no need to drag it out. I told them their assignments, then walked down the line of cops standing at attention and gave them a quick inspection. There weren't many sharp creases in their uniforms and not everybody's shoes were as shiny as they should be, but they were all really good cops. The tired looks on their faces told me some were probably in court all day processing arrests from the previous night. The rest were most likely working a second job during the day, just to make ends meet.

I gave them my usual pep talk about being careful out there. We were shorthanded, so we had to listen to the radio and watch each other's back. Midnight cops also tend to be a tight bunch.

The four-to-twelve guys were outside the front door waiting for me to finish so they could unload all their cool shit and go home. So again in my best sergeant's voice, I finished up by barking, "Take your posts! Fall out!"

The radio was jumping already, so there was no time for screwing around. We hit the streets taking two and three jobs at a time, trying to clear up the backlog.

First I took a ride over to Seventh Street. There was a "heavy bleeder" job. Turns out one of the neighborhood homeless guys had a little too much to drink, fell down, and busted his head open. There was a lot of blood but no assault. No arrest necessary, and no big deal. The only problem was the guy didn't want to go to the hospital. He didn't want to leave his shopping cart full of his "stuff" behind because he was afraid somebody would steal it. Finally we found a homeless buddy of his who promised to watch it until he got back.

He probably lost another half pint of blood while we figured out who was going to watch his shopping cart, but he didn't care.

He had some old keyboard with a dangling cord that was attached to nothing. But he thought it was a computer and must be worth something.

We handle the jobs as fast as we can because they just keep coming: dispute in the street, dispute in a bar, a family dispute, a "man with a gun," "shots fired." The radio never stops. Why can't we all just get along?

I look at my watch and it's one o'clock already. The night is flying by and I haven't had my coffee yet, so we head over to my favorite bagel joint and grab coffee and something to munch on. Then we find a quiet corner to park the car so we can eat without anybody staring at us. People always seem to want to ask you a question when you're wiping cream cheese off your chin.

I unwrap my bagel and just as I'm about to take a sip of coffee, Central interrupts and asks me if I'm available to handle a report of "shots fired." Tough luck for me, coffee is going to have to wait.

Shots fired over at Twelfth Street is usually no big deal. The neighbors like to call it in once in a while, so we could get it a few times a night. That block, and twenty others just like it, are what we call a "drug-prone location." The people living there get tired of seeing the dealers hanging out on the corner, so they call 911 saying one of them has a gun.

We usually roll up, throw everybody on the wall, and toss 'em. You'll never ever find a gun on any of these assholes. They're not that stupid. The guns are always hidden close by, usually in a mailbox, under a car, in some bushes, or even in a hole in a wall somewhere. But we kick everybody in the ass and send them on their way. It cleans up the corner even if it's only for a few minutes.

As I put the lid back on my coffee and wrap up the bagel, the dispatcher advises me additional calls are coming in, stating there is a "male shot" at the location. Without saying a word my driver hits the gas, and I can feel myself being pushed back into the seat as the engine roars to life. Additional calls usually means it's for real.

The turret lights on the roof illuminate everything around us in flashing red and white lights as we weave through the late-night traffic. When we're about a block away I unlock the snap on my holster, just in case all the fun isn't finished by the time we get there.

As we turn the corner some do-gooder in the street is waving to us with one hand while pointing to a small crowd gathered halfway down the block. Here we go—this one's definitely for real.

Driving down the block, my gun is now in my hand and my head's on a swivel. I'm checking out everybody and everything. Is the shooter still on the scene? Is anyone running away? Things happen fast and I'm trying to take it all in.

The crowd backs up a little when we screech to a stop and jump out. The street is dark, but the red and white turret lights swirling across the nearby cars and buildings light up the scene.

Everything was strangely quiet and under control. There was no yelling or screaming and nobody seemed too upset. Violence around here is a common occurrence, so nobody found this too unusual. In this neighborhood dying of natural causes includes getting shot.

In the center of the crowd, lying on the ground, was our victim. He was a short, thin male Hispanic and couldn't have been any more than seventeen years old. He wasn't moving or making any sounds. He was just lying there staring straight up, holding his stomach, with a scared look on his face.

I snatched the radio off my belt, keyed the mike, and told Central we had a "confirmed male shot." I also told her to advise EMS (Emergency Medical Service) "forthwith on the bus [ambulance]."

As I walked over to the kid, I was still scanning and taking it all in. I wanted to make sure the shooter was gone and all the excitement was over. I didn't want to get shot in the back by someone I didn't see or overlooked. We're here to save people and catch bad guys, but survival always comes first.

As I approached the crowd and the kid lying on the ground, I threw the question out to no one in particular, "Did anyone see what happened?"

My question was met with blank, uninterested faces and shrugging shoulders. I didn't really expect an answer out of these pillars of society, but you have to ask anyway.

Next, I knelt down next to the victim and told him, "Relax, kid, the ambulance is on the way. You're going to be all right."

Actually I didn't know if he was going to be all right, but I gave him my regular feel-good speech I give all my shooting victims. When someone gets shot, the bullet goes in one place, but then it can go anywhere and you can never tell how serious it is just by looking at it.

Once I had a guy with what looked like a minor gunshot wound to the arm, but actually the bullet went through his armpit and into his heart. He was dying as I was talking to him.

I recognized the kid and I'm sure he recognized me. I'd seen him hanging around with the dealers down the block. I'd thrown him and his buddies up on the wall more than a few times. When I asked him what happened, and who did this to him, he just turned his head to the side and closed his eyes. He was feigning unconsciousness.

At the age of seventeen this kid was hard-core already. He had no intention of answering me or cooperating with the police in any way. When I asked him for his name, he just kept his eyes closed, hoping I would go away. He wasn't giving up anything.

Out in the street there's no honor among thieves. They have no problem killing each other over the dumbest stuff, but don't ask them to be a rat. That seems to be the only thing these shitheads can agree on. Never talk to the police, and never be a rat.

Fuck it, if he wanted to play hardball, so could I. There was no reason to baby this little prick, so I explained to him that he was shot up pretty good and just might die. I didn't know if he was going to die or not, I just wanted to scare him into talking.

I asked him to help us and not let the guy who did this get away with it, but he didn't even flinch. He just kept looking the other way, ignoring me. He would rather let the guy who did this get away with it than die like a rat.

People in this neighborhood don't talk to the cops much, even in the face of death. The kid was a stoic little bastard, and I like to think I would be as tough as him if I was lying there with a bullet in my gut. I didn't know whether to be pissed or to admire him. Actually it was both.

As I was talking to him I lifted his shirt and saw the tiny bullet hole in his stomach oozing blood. To anyone watching, it must have looked like I was trying to help him—but I wasn't. I was checking to make sure he didn't have a gun on him. This kid was no choirboy and most likely got shot for a reason. I also patted down his pockets, looking for a wallet or anything with his name on it so we could ID him, but nothing.

Even on those rare occasions when the victims do talk to you, they usually give you a bullshit story. They try to tell you they were just walking down the street, heard a pop, felt a sharp pain, and realized they were shot. Ninety-nine percent of the time they're just full of shit and we know it.

EMS pulled up to the scene within a few minutes with one of my sector cars pulling in behind them. Now the entire block was aglow in swirling red and white lights.

Sector Charlie heard I had a confirmed male shot, dropped what they were doing, and came over to help. Midnight cops are always watching each other's back. We made some small talk and I filled them in on what I had so far—which wasn't much. We all agreed this dispute most likely started down the block on First Avenue, where the dealers all hang out. The kid probably ran with the shooter chasing him, maybe throwing shots along the way, until he caught him and finally put one in him.

I wanted them to rope off a crime scene, then walk down the block and do a "search for evidence": shell casings, drugs, money, broken windows, or cars with bullet holes in them. Anything that may shed a little light on what happened. Maybe if we got lucky we could find a witness who was peeking out a window, but I wasn't holding my breath on that one.

The detectives would be here soon, but some good police work by the first cops on the scene always makes their jobs a lot easier.

As I was talking to the cops, a Hispanic woman in her late thirties walking arm in arm with a teenage girl started to approach us. As they got closer I could tell they were both crying and visibly upset. Before they said a word I knew they had to be the victim's mother and sister. Apparently right after the shooting one of the victim's buddies ran to his house and told his mother what happened. It was a common scenario. Good, now maybe I can get this kid identified.

The tears really started to flow when the mother and sister saw the kid in the back of the ambulance with two EMTs sticking an IV in his arm and cutting off his clothes. I grabbed the woman and asked her if that was her son. In between sobs and gasping for breath she answered yes. Good, we're making progress.

I told her to relax and tried to get her to calm down by telling her that he would be all right. I tried to reassure her he was in very capable hands and the doctors at Bellevue Hospital were the best. Again I was just giving her my regular feel-good speech I give all victims' mothers. I needed her to settle down so I could get some information.

I pulled her off to the side so we could talk in private and I could have her full attention. I took out a pad and pen and started asking some questions, but as soon as I asked for her son's name the crying stopped. She put on her game face and said, "What name did he tell you?"

Un-fucking-believable! In this neighborhood even the victim's mother won't help you. She had no intention of answering me or helping the police in any way. She knew her son was a little prick and into some bad stuff, and she wasn't going to give me anything that might be useful to the investigation. And when I pressed her, all of a sudden she started speaking Spanish and made believe she didn't understand what I was saying. She was full of shit and we both knew it.

If she wanted to play hardball so could I, so I told her without identification the hospital may not treat him. This time she knew I was the one who was full of shit. The hospital treats everyone and she knew it. So then I tried telling her that if her son died, the morgue would not release his body until he was properly identified, and that could take days or even weeks. This she believed, and it seemed to bother her, so she started talking, and miraculously, her English got better.

As I was talking to Mom and the daughter I could see something distracted them. Suddenly their eyes popped open wide in terror and disbelief. They weren't looking at me anymore, but at something behind me, just over my shoulder. I turned just in time to see a woman with a zombie like thousand-yard stare on her face stumbling directly toward me. She was wearing a white nightgown that went from her neck to her ankles. She had no shoes, no coat, and was covered from head to toe in blood.

It was dark, but through the flashing red and white light from the nearby police cars and ambulance I could see she had stab wounds all over her body. Everywhere you looked blood was oozing out of a hole or an open gash. Somebody had hacked her up pretty good. I've seen a lot of people shot and stabbed over the years, but this was definitely a good one. We all had that "Holy shit" look on our faces.

I don't know why, but out of all the people standing there, she came straight for me. And as she got closer, she reached out with those bloody hands and tried to grab my arm. I didn't understand exactly what she was saying, but I knew she was pleading with me in broken English to help her.

I pointed to the curb and told her to sit down and relax, that we would take care of her, and she would be all right. Again I was lying. I was giving my standard feel-good speech I give all my stabbing victims. She was cut up pretty bad, and I really wasn't sure if she was going to make it.

She kept trying to grab me while I kept trying to back away from those bloody hands. It was obvious she wanted to latch on to me and pull me somewhere. I kept trying to ask her what happened, but she had no interest in answering my questions.

I looked at the open slash wounds all over her arms, neck, and scalp, and then I glanced over at my shooting victim in the back of the ambulance. The obvious question was: what did the stabbing have to do with the kid being shot?

I pointed to the kid in the ambulance and asked her what happened, but she just looked at me with that same vacant stare and didn't answer. She seemed to not know anything about the shooting, which confused the hell out of me.

I asked the kid's mother and sister if they knew the bloody woman. Both furiously shook their heads no.

I looked around to the now stunned crowd for help, but nobody seemed to know anything about this woman, or if the stabbing had anything to do with the shooting.

As I stood there for a moment trying to figure all this out, the woman reached out and tried to grab me again. And again I did my best to sidestep those bloody hands. Now she was pleading with me in English, but all she could say was "Help my sister. Help my sister."

She was in shock and her broken English wasn't that good, but I could tell she wanted me to follow her. I tried to ask where her sister was, but all she kept mumbling was "Help my sister. Help my sister."

She started to back away while frantically motioning with those bloody hands for me to follow. She obviously wanted to take me somewhere and show me something, and she wanted to do it—*now*.

I told the two cops in Sector Charlie to stay with the shooting. My driver and I would check out what was going on with this woman.

We followed her, barefoot and bloodied, as she led us down the street and around the corner. Along the way I was still peppering her with questions, trying to get some information, but in her zombie-like stupor all she kept mumbling was "Help my sister. Help my sister."

I didn't know where we were going, and I didn't know what she was leading me into, so at this point all I could do was follow. And as she walked she left little petite-sized bloody footprints on the sidewalk.

I don't like walking into a situation blind. I wanted to know where we were going, and what was waiting for me. I wanted to know if the person with the knife had a gun also. But she wasn't answering any questions. She just stared straight ahead, walking and mumbling.

She took us to an apartment building on Eleventh Street, an old five-story walk-up, and stood at the bottom of the front steps afraid to go any farther. She stood terrified and frozen, just pointing at the front door and crying, "There, in there."

I asked where? What apartment? But pointing at the front door was all I was getting out of her. Whatever happened to her happened inside of this building. And somewhere inside was her sister.

I grabbed my radio and notified the dispatcher that I had a "pickup" of a female stabbed and needed another ambulance. I gave Central the address of the building and said we were going in to search for a possible perp and another victim. I also wanted the dispatcher, and anyone else who was listening, to know exactly what building I was going into, just in case I needed help in a hurry.

I pushed open the front door and walked in. It was your average Lower East Side tenement, five floors with four apartments on each floor. I didn't know which apartment to go to, but I didn't have to be Sherlock Holmes to figure this clue out. On the worn-out, dirty tile floor were bloody footprints leading to a half-open door at the end of the first-floor hallway. We found the apartment a hell of a lot quicker than I thought we would. Lucky me.

I stood there for a moment taking it all in. Quietly looking and listening. There was no yelling, no screaming, no glass breaking, so there was no reason to rush anywhere. I was trying to listen for voices, children, a dog barking, anything that might give me a clue as to what was inside the apartment, and what I might be walking into. But nothing, only silence—and bloody footprints leading the way.

I pulled my gun and slowly walked down the hall toward the door, careful not to step into the blood. I now had another crime scene to protect. I also turned down my radio. No need to announce my presence too early, just in case the guy who did this was waiting for me on the other side of the door.

The entire building was eerily quiet, and nobody knew we were here yet. Tactically speaking, that's a good thing. I had the element of surprise on my side.

I approached the partially opened door as quietly as I could and waited for a second, still looking and listening—but I heard nothing, only silence. I don't get excited too easily, but this whole thing was a little spooky and my heart was pounding like a drum.

After listening for a few moments more it was time to go in. My driver was right behind me, gun in hand also. I turned around and whispered, "Ready?" I got back a whispered "Ready." The door was half open, so I gave it a soft kick, just enough to nudge it open the rest of the way. At this point in my career I had seen a lot, but when the door opened I was stunned. There was blood everywhere. It was all over the floor and the walls. It was across the refrigerator and in the sink. When I looked, up there was even splatter across the ceiling. I had been to many crime scenes, but this was definitely a good one.

The apartment was a typical Manhattan one bedroom—small. The front door opened into the kitchen, there was a tiny living room, a bathroom off to the right, and a bedroom to the left.

The kitchen table was pushed over, and the chairs were lying on their side. A fierce struggle clearly took place here. There were bloody hand and footprints smeared all over the dingy linoleum floor. It looked like someone had been scrambling on all fours trying to escape their attacker.

I quietly stepped through the door, my gun out in front of me, tightly gripped in a two-hand hold, looking and listening. Right now I was wishing I had about five more cops with me, but I didn't—and there was no time to wait. I had a sister to look for.

I was waiting for the guy from *The Texas Chain Saw Massacre* to jump out with a butcher knife in his hand, and if he did I was going to light him up. No questions asked. I was wound up like a top. I made sure my finger was off the trigger. I didn't want to let a round go because some cat ran across my foot.

It was easy to see there was no one in the kitchen, so I eased on over to the living room and poked my head in. It was tiny, with just a few pieces of ratty-looking furniture that had seen better days. There was no place for anyone to hide, so I stuck my head into the bathroom—nothing.

The last place to check was the bedroom. I was tiptoeing across the kitchen floor trying not to step in the coagulating pools of blood. Blood can be slippery, and I didn't want to fall on my ass. That would have been noisy—and nasty.

I walked up to the bedroom door as quietly as possible. We hadn't made a sound coming in, and the element of surprise was still on my side. If the perp was on the other side of the door, I was sure he didn't know we were here.

I stood along the side of the door frame with my ear to the crack, listening. Was the maniac who did this on the other side waiting for me? Who knew? But one thing was for sure, the apartment was small, and this was the last place he could be hiding. I waited and listened for a few seconds more but heard nothing. It was time to go in.

If I was sitting in a theater watching this scene in some horror movie I would be saying, "Don't go in there, you'll be sorry." I reached out to grab the doorknob and turned it as quietly as I could. To me the clicking of the lock sounded like thunder. I was thinking, "He's got to hear that! He's got to know I'm coming for him!"

I opened the door just a crack, then stepped back. It was showtime! I hauled off, landing my black boot squarely in the middle of the door, and kicked it open. My adrenaline must have really been pumping because the door just exploded open. I kicked it a hell of a lot harder than I needed or wanted to.

With a loud boom, the door flew open and crashed into the

dresser behind it, bouncing off. And just as violently as it flew open, it swung back and slammed closed in my face. Now I'm standing there, gun in hand, staring at a closed door, feeling like a dope.

Things don't always go as smoothly in real life as they do in the movies. When I think about it now, it seems funny, but it wasn't so funny back then.

The boom was so loud the people in the upstairs apartment must have heard it. I'm pissed because *now* I lost the element of surprise! He has to know I'm out here, so I have to move fast. I step back and kick it again. This time I stop the door with my foot to keep it from closing on me.

I stepped through the door, gun in one hand, flashlight in the other. I was looking left and right, and up and down, as fast as I could, ready to shoot if I saw a hand with a knife in it. I had already decided that if I saw a guy with a knife and he stepped two inches in my direction, I was going to light him up.

The room was dark, but the curtains were ripped down from the window. There was just enough ambient light from the apartments across the alley to let me see. There were two small beds in the tiny room—one against the far wall and one under the window to my right. The mattress on the bed against the wall was half on the floor, and there were bloody handprints smeared high across the wall. It looked like someone had run across the bed trying to climb the wall in order to escape from the knife-wielding psycho chasing them.

I shined my flashlight around the room, under the bed, and in the closet, but nothing. For sure, I was relieved there wasn't some maniac behind the door waiting for me, but I was also a little disappointed. I wanted to get this guy!

It looked like most of the excitement was over, so I holstered my gun and turned on the lights. I looked around at the bloody hand- and footprints on the walls and bed. This must have been some fierce struggle. I couldn't believe one of the neighbors didn't hear it and call 911. But New Yorkers, especially in this neighborhood, don't like to get involved—even if your neighbor is getting butchered.

I walked around the apartment looking for anything that might shed a little light on what happened: drugs, money, or the knife. Maybe this was a drug deal gone bad. Or maybe a home invasion-type robbery. Or a really violent family dispute.

I stood in the middle of the kitchen looking around. The apartment was quiet. There was no television or radio on. The only sound was the hissing of the air conditioner. I stood perfectly still staring at the hand and footprints and pools of blood on the linoleum floor. The whole scene was eerie and was getting spookier by the minute.

The air conditioner was on, but it was still stifling hot. I wanted to get the hell out of there and get some fresh air, when suddenly, I thought I heard something. I didn't know what it was, but it was something.

I stood there for a moment trying to figure out what I just heard—but nothing, only silence. It was all quiet except for the hissing A/C and my own breathing. I stood very still for what seemed like a long time, just listening, and just when I thought maybe I had imagined it, I heard it again. A very soft, very faint moan.

I looked around the room again, but there was no one here. And the sound didn't come from the living room or the bathroom. It must be coming from the bedroom!

All I could think of was "Oh shit, I missed something." A small person or a child hiding somewhere. I rushed back into the tiny bedroom and did a quick search. I flipped over the beds, nothing. I pulled the clothes out of the closet, but nothing.

I looked around a little confused. With all that adrenaline pumping through my body, were my ears playing tricks on me? I was sure I heard something, but what? Then suddenly I heard it again—a very faint moan.

The sound seemed to be coming from the window. It was open about a foot, and outside the window I could see a fire escape. Okay, it's showtime again. I pulled out my gun and stepped toward the window. I wasn't crazy about sticking my head outside because I still hadn't found the nut job with the knife. Was he out there waiting for some dope to stick his head out? No person with a half a brain would go sticking their head out that window, but I had to see who or what was making the noise.

I pulled open the window and shined my light outside. Still nothing. Very cautiously, I poked my head out just an inch or two, gun in one hand and flashlight in the other. As I stuck my head out into the night air the moaning was getting a little louder, and when I looked up, there she was. Another woman in the exact same nightgown, covered in blood. This must be the sister!

She was sitting on the steps up on the second floor curled up into a ball, knees to her chest, rocking back and forth with the same zombie-like thousand-yard stare her sister had. She was hiding, and crying—as quietly as she could.

I called up to her and told her to come down, but she wasn't budging. She was in shock and had no intention of coming back into the apartment. She just sat there barefoot in the fetal position, rocking, sobbing, and bleeding.

It seemed like the perfect time to give my feel-good speech again, so I told her we were the police and everything would be all right, but she wouldn't move. She was only ten feet away, but she wouldn't even acknowledge me. I was going to have to climb up and get her.

I moved the bed out of the way and climbed onto the fire escape. I was hoping if she saw me in uniform she would realize she was now safe and could come down, but no luck. Uniform or no uniform, she just sat there crying, refusing to move.

As I climbed the metal steps, I shined my light on her and I could see she was hacked up just as bad as the first woman. She had cuts and slash wounds all over her body. I kept shining my flashlight up and down, and into the alley below. I was looking for the maniac with the knife, making sure he didn't sneak up on me.

The last thing I wanted was to get into a knife fight on a fire escape in the dark.

After a few minutes of calm, soothing talk, I convinced her everything was over and she was safe. I put on a pair of rubber gloves, reached out, took her by the hand, and helped her down the steps and back into the window.

She wasn't too crazy about going back into the apartment, but I convinced her the perp was gone and everything was going to be all right. As I guided her through the kitchen I couldn't help but notice she kept her hands over her face and only looked straight ahead. She didn't want to look at all the blood. Or remember what happened here.

I walked her outside and reunited her with the sister. The two bloody women hugged for what seemed like a long time. They seemed really happy to see each other, and to be alive. I sat them on the front steps of the building, and I called for another ambulance.

At this point the dispatcher was getting a little confused. I had to explain to her, slowly, that I had a male shot on Twelfth Street, a pickup of a female stabbed on Twelfth Street but the place of occurrence was actually on Eleventh Street, and now I had *another* female stabbed inside a building on Eleventh Street.

A few minutes later another sector showed up, and after a couple of "Holy shit"s, they started scratching out the necessary paperwork. Luckily one of the cops spoke Spanish, and we got half a story from the victims before they went to the hospital.

They actually were sisters, and the first one's husband was the perp. Turns out it was a family dispute turned really, really ugly. The wife explained that she was having a heated argument with her beloved, and sisters being sisters—especially in the heat of battle—they stuck together. And when the second woman butted in, the husband went ape shit. He didn't like being double-teamed, so he grabbed a large kitchen knife from the sink and carved the two of them up.

During the struggle one ran out the front door and the other jumped out the window. The husband, realizing he fucked up big-time, fled into the night to parts unknown. Family disputes can get very ugly. I think next time, the sister is gonna know better than to throw her two cents in.

The wife finishes up by telling us they are Colombian, and she thinks her husband will try to flee back to Colombia on the first flight he can get. I make a mental note to tell the detectives. She also tells me he is a cop back there. Whatever the fuck that means. I'm sure "cop" in Colombia can be a very vague term.

I take a walk around the corner back to the shooting scene to talk to the detectives, and when I get there I'm a little surprised to see only two. Usually there are more at a crime scene. They explain to me they have two shootings uptown already, and both victims went "out of the picture" (DOA). Two detectives was all Night Watch could spare at this time.

When I tell them I have two stabbing victims from an unrelated incident around the corner, they just shrug and tell me to notify the Borough. They can only do one thing at a time.

In the police department, assault victims fall into one of three categories: DOA, "likely to die," or "not likely to die." And homicides are always a priority over victims who may or may not go out of the picture. Before I make a call I need to know what condition my victims are in, so I jump in the car and take a ride up to Bellevue emergency room.

When you walk into the ER on a busy night, you might think there's a war going on outside. People are laying around shot, stabbed, bludgeoned, sick, and crazy—all waiting to be treated in priority order.

I walked up to the desk and as politely as I could inquired on the condition of my victims. The nurses and doctors were as busy in the ER as I was out in the street and not too interested in a long conversation. Cops can be a little demanding when we want something, so I put on my happy face and asked real nice.

The nurse told me my shooting victim was up in the OR in critical condition, and that he was probably "likely." Next she went out on a limb and told me the stabbing victims were probably "Not Likely." Although they were a bloody mess, most of the cuts were slash wounds and nothing too deep. That one surprised me a little. I thanked her as we both exchanged smiles. Two professionals having a busy night.

I borrowed the phone behind her desk to make my notifications to the Borough and Night Watch, then I jumped into the car and headed back to the precinct. Just because I had one shot and two stabbed didn't mean the night was over. I had at least another hour before the sun came up, and the world would be normal again— and a little while after that, I could go home.

The night was buzzing along, and I hardly had a chance to catch my breath. It was almost 5:00 a.m., and finally the radio was starting to slow down a bit. My growling stomach reminded me I hadn't eaten anything all night. I looked down at the paper bag on the floor next to my feet and told my driver to pull over so I could have my now cold coffee and stale bagel.

We found a quiet corner to chill out, but just as I brought the cold coffee to my lips I got interrupted again. Central was trying to give me a job of a "man down."

At first it sounded like a bullshit job. Probably another drunk who fell and can't get up. Sergeants don't usually interrupt their cold, stale breakfast for a job like this, so I tell her to give it to the next available sector. But not this time. The dispatcher tells me there are additional calls coming in. The male either jumped or fell out a window.

I put the lid back on my coffee, wrap up my bagel, and off we go speeding through the night—*again.*

We pulled up to the scene, screeched to a halt, and jumped out. A few people had stopped and were gathered around a crumpled body lying on the ground. I marched up and threw my usual question out to the crowd. "Anybody see what happened?" I got the usual answer in return. A bunch of shrugs and blank uninterested stares.

The flashing red and white lights from my car lit up the area, and from a few feet away I could tell the guy was in bad shape. He was a young guy, early to mid-twenties, lying on his side curled up next to a fire hydrant. He wasn't moving, and the only sound coming from him was a very faint moan.

When I walked up to him I could tell he was still breathing, but the back of his head was a matted mess of blood, hair, and bone. I shined my flashlight on him and I could see he had a large hole in the back of his head. It appeared to be pushed in. It looked to me like just before he hit the ground he clipped the back of his head on the fire hydrant.

I looked up and saw the open fourth-floor window he fell out of. When we drove by earlier I had noticed a party going on. The windows were open and the loud music could be heard out in the street. Maybe if the night had not been so busy, I would have knocked on their door and told them to turn it down, and explained that maybe they should have a little consideration for the neighbors. But tonight was way too busy to stop for a bullshit noise complaint.

I knelt down next to the kid and instinctively gave him my usual feel-good speech. In calm, soothing tones I told him to relax, the ambulance was on the way, and he was going to be all right. But this time I had a feeling that I might be lying.

Just then it dawned on me. I was giving my usual feel-good speech a lot tonight.

I'm not sure the kid even heard me. He was pretty much out of it. He was moaning and gasping for breath at irregular intervals. I'm no surgeon, but I could tell he had a traumatic brain injury in addition to any other broken bones and internal injuries the fall might have caused. There was not much for me to do except radio Central and ask for a "rush on the bus."

As I hovered over the kid I could feel eyes peering over my shoulder. Heads moving in closer trying to get a better look. I turned and saw the crowd of about a half a dozen bystanders inching in. Just like at an accident on the highway, people want to slow down and gawk at other people's misery. I guess it makes them feel better about their own lives—things could always be worse for them.

Sometimes the public can really piss you off, and I snapped. I turned around and yelled, "Get the fuck away from me!" The crowd could tell from my tone of voice I wasn't kidding, so they jumped back and started walking. But not before turning to take one last look.

I turned back to the kid and inched in closer. I was on my hands and knees, hovering right over him to shield his face with my body from the nosy public. I was trying my best to give him some privacy and little dignity.

As the kid struggled for every breath, all I could do was talk to him in a calm reassuring voice. I told him to keep to breathing and "Don't give up." I grabbed his hand and told him to squeeze it if he could hear me. But I got nothing, his cold fingers hung limp in mine. When I asked him if he could hear me, his eyelids fluttered up and down. His eyeballs were rolling back and forth in his head, and he seemed to be looking up at something. Something only he could see.

I was feeling a little helpless. I knew for sure the kid couldn't see me, but maybe he was listening to me. There was nothing I could do except to talk and try to comfort him. I kept telling him to keep breathing, and that he was going to be okay. But right then, as I watched him struggle for every breath, I realized that my voice was probably the last thing he was ever going to hear on this earth.

I don't know if you've ever had the opportunity to kneel over a person lying in the street and talk to them while they die. It's something you don't forget—no matter how hard you try.

EMS got there pretty quick, but there was not much for them to do either. This kid needed a brain surgeon. They bandaged him up and loaded him into the back of the ambulance and raced off. At Bellevue this kid was going to the front of the line.

Turns out he was at the party, drinking and having a good time. It was a little hot in the apartment, so he sat straddling the windowsill—one foot inside, and the other dangling in the cool night air. There was no foul play. He was just drunk, lost his balance, and rolled out the window to the street below.

I told the sector to secure the crime scene and I would start making the necessary notifications. When I called the detectives they must have thought I was making this stuff up or breaking their balls. A male shot, two females stabbed, and now a guy out a window "likely to die." All in the last four hours!

When I told them I wasn't kidding, they wanted to know about the kid's condition. I told them he was in bad shape and was probably going out of the picture. I also told them we were holding a bunch of angry partygoers at the scene who wanted to leave. The party was now over, and they wanted to go home, or to some after-hours joint, not sit and talk to the cops. But tough shit, they weren't going anywhere till they got interviewed by the detectives.

I volunteered to take a run up to the hospital and check on the kid's condition and if he was "likely" they would have to dig up a couple of detectives to send to me. Seemed like everybody was busy tonight.

I grabbed my driver, jumped in the car, and headed for the emergency room. Red and white flashing lights swirled around us as we raced through traffic—*again*.

When I walked in, I checked the examination rooms, looking for my victim. I found him in the big room on the end, the one reserved for the serious cases. When I poked my head in, there were a couple of doctors and nurses working on him. One doctor had his hands in the kid's chest doing open-heart massage while the others were milling around the room. The look of non-urgency on their faces told me all I needed to know. The kid was probably dead a while ago, and they were just going through the motions because they have to.

The doctor with his hands inside the kid's chest saw me standing in the doorway and looked up. He knew what I was there for. As he squeezed the kid's heart a few last times he looked at me and shook his head "no."

The kid never even made it to the operating room. I wasn't surprised. I had a feeling I was lying when I told him he was going to be all right.

I took out my pad and pen and asked for a time and a name. I needed the time of death and the doctor who would pronounce him. Time of death was 5:49 a.m.

I looked at my watch and all I could think of was how busy it had been. All this carnage happened in the last four hours. A kid shot, two women stabbed, and a guy out a window, and the night wasn't over yet. Soon the sun would come up, and the world would be normal again, and I could go home. But not yet. I still had about two more hours to go before "end of tour."

I borrowed the phone behind the nurses' station and made my notifications. The detective promised to send me someone as soon as he could.

When I got back to the car, my driver slammed the gearshift into drive and got ready to race back to the precinct, but I told him, "Hold it!" I looked at the bag on the floor with my stale bagel and cold coffee, and decided I needed a minute to myself.

I unwrapped my bagel and took the lid off my coffee, but before I could take a sip, I looked down and saw blood on the front of my shirt. A shirt that was fresh from the dry cleaners only a few hours ago.

And as I sat there eating with one hand, and trying to wipe the red drops off with a napkin in the other hand, it dawned on me. I felt nothing! I was numb inside. I wanted to feel bad for these people. I should feel bad for these people. But I felt nothing. I especially wanted to feel bad for the kid out the window, but I was as cold inside as my coffee.

I'm not heartless or uncaring, it's just that I see a lot of misery in my line of work, and you have to be a survivor. Normal people don't live like this, but cops do. You don't only have to survive physically, but you have to survive mentally. You not only have to be careful not to get shot in the back, or get into a knife fight on a fire escape, but you also have to keep from losing your mind—and your humanity. And you do that by building a wall between you and the outside world. You do it by building a wall between you and your feelings.

I do it because I'll be back on patrol tomorrow night, and the night after that. The radio never stops and the misery never ends. And chances are I'll be kneeling next to some other kid soon, telling him he's going to be all right—and maybe lying again.

I have friends and relatives who have much better jobs than me. They work in a beautiful office, wear nice clothes, and make a hell of a lot more money than I do. And I can't help but smile when they tell me how busy it is at work, and how stressed out they are.

8

Stockbroker

I was hanging out behind the desk in the Ninth Precinct staring up at the clock. It was 1:50 a.m. and in ten more minutes I could sign out and call it a night. As hard as we tried, we came up empty. Me and my guys had been looking all night for a collar, but nothing worthwhile came our way. I was thinking it was time to switch to plan B—go have a beer.

Some nights it just turns out that way. My guys were good cops and the Ninth was a busy place but anti-crime cops are only allowed to make quality arrests, like robbery, burglary, grand larceny, grand larceny auto, assault, rape, and of course, gun collars. Sometimes we make a couple of collars a night and everybody gets on the "sheet." And sometimes no matter how hard we look we come up dry. Tonight was one of those nights.

Anti-crime cops are usually the best cops in the precinct—or, as we say, the most active. They're the cops that like to go out and do the job and don't mind rolling around on the ground once in a while with some bad guy and getting a little dirty. We're the cowboys in the precinct who go out in the street and come back with the best collars.

The only ones who will argue with that are the guys who tried to get into A/C and didn't make it. And for all that enthusiasm and good work, we get to ride around in unmarked cars and wear plainclothes while we cruise the streets looking for trouble.

We're not allowed to answer radio runs or take a collar from a sector car just because they don't want it. All our stuff is self-generated. Our job is to go out and hunt. And it is like hunting—very much so.

All night long we ride around searching for bad guys who are looking to commit a crime. Our job is to find them before they commit the act, and be there when the crime happens. There's nothing better than spotting a guy who you know is looking to do a stickup. You can almost see the lightbulb go on over his head— he has a great idea. It's in his eyes, he's on a mission, he's looking to make money. Then you follow him, sometimes for hours, while he looks for just the right victim, and then you jump him when he's in the middle of doing his deed.

If we're good at what we do, and we usually are, he never knew we were there. He never had a clue he was being followed. Then when he attacks—we attack. The predator suddenly becomes the prey.

I often equate it to a submarine. The only time anybody sees us is when we surface to attack. The perp only knows he was being followed after it's too late. Over time you become an expert at following people through crowds and busy streets, but it's not as easy as you might think. It takes patience, and I have the patience of a fisherman.

And when you go to court and tell the ADA (assistant district attorney) you followed the perp for a few hours and then watched him do the robbery, the guy almost always pleads out. He has no choice. He'll never win at trial.

Most of the time we ride around in a yellow taxicab that is actually a police car. We have other unmarked cars, but the cab is always my favorite. Most of the precinct anti-crime teams in Manhattan South use cabs because there are approximately thirteen thousand yellow cabs in New York City and ours is identical to the rest. Everywhere you look, you can see a yellow cab. You can look over your shoulder till your head falls off trying to figure out which cab is ours, trying to figure out if you're being followed.

I had just come down from the locker room after taking off my vest and switching to my little .38-caliber off-duty revolver. Hanging out behind the desk with me were two of my cops. They hadn't changed yet. I guess they were hoping someone might get robbed in front of the station house, which wasn't all that unusual in this neighborhood. So I nudged them along—"Come on, I'm thirsty, let's go get a beer."

The desk in every precinct is the center of all activity. This is where the desk officer runs his mighty ship, and everything that occurs in a precinct flows through this five-foot-high by fifteen-foot-wide wooden helm.

Behind me the wall was lined with several plaques bearing the faces of police officers followed by the words *Killed in the Line of Duty*. It's a constant reminder for everyone, cop or civilian, who stands before the desk of the sacrifices that have been made. It is a constant yet subtle reminder of how dangerous police work can be. All cops convince themselves, "It won't be me," myself included.

I was starting to get a little antsy and told my guys when they were done dicking around to meet me at the bar down the block. As I turned to leave, the cop on the telephone switchboard said, "Hey Sarge, I got a girl on the phone who says she was raped and she knows where the perp is. Do you want to talk to her?"

I looked over to my two cops and said, "You guys still looking?" Both heads enthusiastically nodded in the affirmative.

I took the phone, identified myself, and asked the girl what happened. From the tone of her voice she sounded upset, but she had it together enough to give me a brief story. I told her to stay where she was and we would be right over. It was now 2:00 a.m. The Detective Squad was already gone, and it was too late to call the Special Victims Unit, so this caper was ours to handle.

As I was interviewing the victim on the phone, she said the perp was a millionaire stockbroker and he would be leaving the country in the morning. She warned us if we didn't get him tonight she didn't know when he was coming back, so we had to grab him now. She also said he lived in some really expensive loft apartment on the Bowery. This was starting to sound like a breeze. Most guys we lock up are hard-core career criminals, savages who would do anything to keep from going back to jail. Locking up some Wall Street suit-and-tie type in his fancy apartment would be easy.

My plan was to meet the complainant, reinterview her in person, then hurry over to the perp's apartment and grab him before he had a chance to flee the country. If everything went good we could scoop this guy up, bang out some paperwork, and I might have enough time left over to grab a beer before the bar closed.

Nice and simple, so I skipped running back up to my locker to get my vest and my much larger duty gun.

We found the girl's apartment easy enough. She lived in a nice building not too far from Riverside Park. When we walked in we introduced ourselves and she did the same. She had a girlfriend with her and asked if she could stay while we talked. She wanted the female support and I had no problem with it.

As soon as I looked at these girls I knew they were not your ordinary run-of-the-mill secretaries or soccer moms. I would later find out my complainant had been a topless dancer in her not-too-distant past. Not that it makes a difference, topless dancers can get raped also. But it can throw some added bullshit into the mix that doesn't help the case. Making the collar is one thing, going to trial is another.

I went through the story with her one more time but in much more detail. There are elements of the crime that I want to satisfy myself about before I go and kick some guy's door down in the middle of the night and throw handcuffs on him.

After hearing the story again I was sure we had a collar. She was upset but also very articulate. She seemed like a savvy no-nonsense girl who could take care of herself, but it was obvious something very traumatic had happened to her.

She explained to me she met the perp not long ago and decided to go out on a date with him. He spared no expense to impress her and treat her right. She explained that he seemed like a "nice guy." During their first date he told her that he had recently separated from some supermodel he had been dating. At first I thought that was bullshit, but believe it or not, I later checked it out, and it was true. It was also true he was a millionaire stockbroker. The guy was fucking loaded. She thought she had a real catch on her hands.

The second time he asked her out she didn't hesitate. Why would she? The first date went very well. Again he spared no expense and sent a limo over to her apartment to pick her up and bring her over to his place. But instead of meeting her downstairs and going out to dinner like they had planned, he told the limo driver to send her up to his apartment and then leave.

When she got upstairs he wasn't wearing the nice clothes and expensive loafers he did on their last date. In fact he wasn't prepared to go out at all. The next thing she knows he throws her on the sofa and rapes and sodomizes her. She screamed for help, but the loft apartment, which was probably a factory fifty years ago, had thick cement walls, so the neighbors heard nothing.

The details were a little brutal. She found out the hard way rapists don't always hide in the shadows and drag you off the street into the bushes. Sometimes they're good-looking and have nice loft apartments.

After he was finished he threw her a twenty-dollar bill for cab money and that was it. That was her second date. Not even a limo ride home.

Rape is not always as black-and-white as you might think. There's several shades of gray in the middle. This is what we would classify as an "acquaintance rape" or what most people call a date rape. She knew her attacker, as opposed to a "stranger rape."

I'm sure that when I catch this guy he will have a different version of the events. In most he said/she said cases they do. He will most likely admit to having sex with her but insist it was consensual so there will be no DNA issues. He'll probably say she was drinking or smoking weed and her recollection shouldn't be trusted. Acquaintance rapes often boil down to who is more believable. But after hearing her story I was inclined to believe what she said.

The bottom line is, when a woman says no, that's it, it's over. If the act continues, that's when it becomes a crime, a very serious crime. And in this case, she repeatedly screamed NO.

I interviewed her for a few minutes until I had heard enough.

I was ready to go and lock this guy up. I asked her if she had his phone number and she said yes. I wanted her to call him and have him meet her outside of his building so they could "talk." I wanted to scoop him up off the street if possible and not have to deal with him locking himself inside the apartment and not letting us in. I figured we were dealing with some nerdy little stockbroker who might panic and barricade himself inside. I wanted this to be a nice, quick, easy collar. Plus I wanted to get a statement out of him before his team of high-priced lawyers marched into the station house.

I had her call him to try to arrange a meeting outside somewhere so they could talk, but he wasn't picking up. I had her call him several more times just to annoy him into answering the phone, and after a few more calls it worked. The problem was he was in no mood to talk, so meeting somewhere was out of the question.

He finished their brief, tense conversation by adding he was leaving the country for a while and didn't want to be bothered while he was trying to pack. I didn't like this little prick already.

I looked over to my two cops and said, "Come on, let's go get this guy." I looked over to my complainant next and said, "You're coming too." I don't think she expected this, but I needed her at the scene of the arrest to identify him once we grabbed him. She asked if her friend could come along. She still needed or wanted the female moral support, so I agreed. My guys didn't mind either, the girlfriend was very pretty. I'm not sure if the friend was a pole dancer also, but she definitely could have been.

I didn't want to waste any more time just in case we spooked this guy with the phone calls. I knew where he was and wanted to go and get him, now.

We jumped into the unmarked car and headed for the perp's apartment. I threw the flashing red light on the dashboard and stomped on the gas. As the engine roared and everybody was pushed back in their seats, I could see in the rearview mirror that my already stressed-out complainant was starting to tense up. The reality of the situation was sinking in. She was the victim of a serious crime, and the police were about to do something about it. The wheels of justice were now in motion.

It was almost 3:00 a.m. and the streets were quiet. We pulled over down the block from the perp's apartment and walked the rest of the way, just in case he was looking out the window.

The building was old and simple. A glass front door opening to a nonexistent lobby, with stairs and a small elevator leading up to several very expensive loft apartments. Even by New York standards, this was big bucks. By now I was figuring he wasn't bullshitting about being a millionaire stockbroker.

I still wanted to take him on the street if possible, it would make things a hell of a lot simpler, so I told our victim to ring his bell and ask him to come down. I told her to tell him that she needed to see him face-to-face so they could "talk."

My guys positioned themselves on one side of the glass door, and I was on the other while our victim rang the bell. She rang it several times but no answer. It was an expensive building so I was pretty sure the bell worked. I leaned over and whispered into her ear, "Keep ringing it till he can't stand it anymore."

While she leaned on the buzzer with gusto, we waited. Finally, after what seemed like a long time, a male voice came through the intercom. "Who is it? What do you want?" I whispered in her ear again telling her what to say, "Tell him to come down, you need to see him. You just want to talk." She pushed the transmit button and repeated what I had said. I was proud of her, she seemed good under pressure. I was sure she would make a solid witness if we ever had to put her on the stand.

She got him to answer again, but the guy's tone was cold and terse. "Go away, I don't have time for this shit right now."

I made a pushing motion with my index finger and smiled. She understood exactly what I wanted and leaned on the buzzer again with everything she had. I was hoping the volume on the speaker in his apartment was turned up loud and this was annoying the shit out of him.

My guys stood ready on the other side of the door. Shields hung from chains around their necks. Guns perched in unsnapped holsters stuck out from under their jackets. Something was going to happen soon, I could feel it. The excitement level was rising.

The gruff male voice answered again, "I told you go away, I don't have time for this shit." I whispered into her ear again, telling her what to say. "Tell him you only want to talk about what happened, but if he doesn't come down you are going to call the police." She repeated what I said and again she played her part well.

We waited, but no answer. I whispered to her again, "Keep ringing that buzzer till he can't stand it anymore." She leaned on the buzzer for a long time while we stayed ready and waited. I was starting to think I was going to have to come up with a plan B, and this time it didn't include going for a beer.

After what seemed like a long time, her eyes opened wide and a frightened look came over her face. As she looked into the tiny lobby she suddenly blurted out, "Here he comes."

My shield was hanging from a chain around my neck. I held it in my left hand and prepared to shove it in his face as soon as he opened the door. I knew we were going to startle him, so I wanted him to know we were the police and not some of the complainant's friends coming to beat him up.

I looked over to my guys, who were pressed up against the wall, knees bent, ready to pounce as soon as the door opened. The metallic click coming from the dead-bolt lock was thunderous. I thought, "Here we go—we got him."

As the door inched open I spun around and shoved it into his face. I wanted to get my foot inside before he had a chance to close it on us. As I did so I held up my gold NYPD sergeant's shield and yelled as loud as I could, "POLICE!"

He seemed shocked to see us, but not as shocked as I was to see him. The wimpy little stockbroker I was expecting to see was standing there wearing Kevlar body armor and holding a loaded .380 automatic pistol in his hand. He had no shirt on, just the vest, and he was pretty cut up. It was obvious this guy spent a lot of time in the gym.

For just the briefest moment, as I looked at his vest, then looked at the gun in his hand, I couldn't help but think what an asshole I was. He had his vest on and mine was hanging in my locker because I was too lazy to put it back on. At stressful times like this your mind goes into hyperdrive. You have the ability think full, complete thoughts in just a fraction of a second. Right now I was thinking, "I can't believe my vest is hanging in my locker." Goes to show you there is no such thing as a "ground-ball" collar.

I was charging forward as he was trying to back up. He was raising his pistol to take a shot as I reached for my holstered .38 revolver. Time seemed to stand still. My mind was still in hyperdrive and my body was trying to keep up. I remember my thumb just barely touching the snap on my holster, and all of a sudden what sounded like a loud, clear voice in my head said, "Forget it, you're never going to make it." I'm not sure if it was a voice or just a thought that was shouting in my head, but the message was clear—there was no time to go for my gun. And it was no time to start arguing with the little voice or the thought in my head so I just continued charging forward.

I pushed the door into his face, knocking him backward and slightly off balance. The only thing I could do was go for the gun so I reached out with both hands, grabbing his wrist, and shoved the gun into his chest. There's not much to talk about at a time like this and communication between partners is short and simple. I yelled, "GUN!"

It's times like this, when your whole world turns to shit, that you are glad you work with good cops, and my guys were great cops. You don't go out on patrol night after night and do the things we do unless you have one hundred percent confidence that the guys you're working with are going to have your back. And as soon as I yelled "GUN!" these guys had my back. They were right on my heels, and were literally climbing up my back to get at the perp. I love these guys.

We all tumbled to the floor of the tiny lobby, rolling around, kicking, punching, yelling, and fighting for our lives. I could hear the girls behind us screaming, which just added to the confusion. I don't think they felt sorry for the perp, it was just that most normal people are not used to witnessing real violence.

I held on to his gun hand, trying to twist the pistol from his grip, while my cops were all over him trying to subdue him. The guy had a good grip on the gun and I was having a hard time trying to twist it out of his hand. I thought about yelling, "Shoot him," but the lobby was so small chances were one of us might get hit.

Just when I was thinking how strong this guy was, a big meaty fist flew over my shoulder and landed with thud right in the perp's face, stunning him. The punch took a little of the wind out of his sails and I managed to rip the gun from his hand. I rolled over and away from him, clutching the gun in a two-hand hold like a football player who just recovered a fumble.

With me and the gun out of the way, my guys overpowered the perp and slapped handcuffs on him. It was over just as quick as it started. Things settled down and the girls finally stopped screaming and waking up the entire neighborhood.

People often ask me if I ever get afraid at times like this, and the answer is not really. It's not because I'm exceptionally brave but because in police work things happen fast. They start fast and they're over quickly. You don't usually get much time to think. You have a split second to react.

Most normal people go to the gym because they want to lose a few pounds and look good at the beach, but cops go to the gym because some day when you least expect it you may have to fight for your life.

We lifted the perp to his feet and gave the complainant a chance to "view" him before putting him in the car. After a quick "show up" she identified him as the person who raped her. We needed her to identify him to make sure we didn't just roll around with some nut who lived in the building and liked to answer the door in the middle of the night with a gun and a bulletproof vest on. That would have been pretty funny.

As we escorted him out of the lobby of his very expensive building and toward the backseat of the unmarked car, I watched the complainant give him a cold, icy stare that said, "You son of a bitch." The perp hung his head and just stared at the ground, trying to avoid eye contact. His sad, defeated look said, "I think I fucked up—big-time."

When we put him in the car he was rear cuffed behind his back and still had the vest on. It was one of those heavy military-type vests that could have easily stopped the bullets we were carrying. I couldn't help but think the headline in tomorrow's newspaper could have been "Cop Killed. Perp Had Vest, Asshole Cop Didn't."

I called for another car to transport my victim and brought the whole caper back to the station house for processing. We had paperwork to do plus he had to be fingerprinted and photographed and she had to be seen by a doctor for injuries and evidence collection.

While my guys did some paperwork and argued over who would get the collar, I went back to the holding cell to make sure our wimpy little stockbroker didn't hang himself or try to escape. It was slightly gratifying to see my millionaire rapist stockbroker sulk inside the dingy cell. I mused silently to myself, "And justice for all, motherfucker."

When he saw me walk into the room he peeked through the bars and asked if he could make his "one phone call." He obviously watched television.

You might think that I would be pretty pissed at him right now for trying to kill me. You might think that I would tell him to shut the fuck up or maybe open the cell door and beat the shit out of him with the phone. But it doesn't work that way. I realized a long time ago you can't take this stuff personal. If you do, it will just eat you up or worse, get you into trouble. He was not trying to kill *me*. He was not trying to kill *Steve Osborne*. He was trying to kill the cop that was coming to lock him up. I was actually more pissed that one of my guys almost got hurt.

I took him out of the cell and walked him over to the phone. I dialed the outside line and handed him the receiver, then stood next to him and listened to his conversation. In a low voice he

grumbled into the phone, "Hey, it's me. Listen, I got a little problem. I just got arrested and I need you to call my lawyer." After a
short pause he continued, "What's that stock going for?"

He waited for an answer, then replied, "A dollar a share. Sell two
hundred thousand, I'm going to need some cash for this."

Now I wanted to punch him in the face! He just made more
money from one phone call from jail than I made in more than
two years.

I escorted him back in the holding cell and slammed the door
shut. The boom from the closing door made the air around us
vibrate. Then I shoved the six-inch-long skeleton key in the lock,
securing it with a metallic click. I love those sounds. It sounds
like justice. And I wanted to remind him he wasn't on Wall Street
anymore.

People like to think cops are racists and only lock up minori-
ties. Nothing could be further from the truth. After being a cop
for a few years, you learn to dislike people equally. I enjoy locking
up some white millionaire stockbroker who raped a topless dancer
as much as some black crackhead who robbed a little old lady. To
keep from becoming too bitter and cynical about the world in general, occasionally I have to remind myself that I only deal with the
bad people of all races—and now religions.

Because he actually did date a supermodel and was featured in
the gossip page of the *New York Post* a week earlier, I called the
Deputy Commissioner of Public Information with the details of
the arrest. I was a little surprised when headquarters called me
back a short time later and said a television news crew was coming
to the station house to do a story. I was even more surprised when
they told me it was okay to give an on-camera interview.

A television news crew came to the precinct and interviewed me
on the front steps of the station house. My guys and some of the
other cops stood in the background behind the cameraman making
faces at me and giggling while I tried to sound professional and not
make an idiot out of myself.

The next day the story ran in three New York newspapers. One even printed a picture of the gun and the vest.

A few days later I went down to court to testify in the grand jury. I got the feeling bad news was coming when the ADA called me into her office and asked me to close the door.

First she explained to me we weren't going into the grand jury that day. Next she threw a name at me that I vaguely recognized from reading the newspapers.

Turns out the name she mentioned was a very high-priced attorney who was well known for representing some of the biggest organized crime figures in New York City, and now he was representing my perp. My first reaction was "So what? Who cares?"

She went on to explain that if our perp took a felony conviction he would lose his stockbroker's license and thus, in his mind, lose everything. He was willing to spend every penny he had to prevent this. And he had a lot of pennies.

I sat and listened as she continued. Looking at this objectively, she explained, if we went to trial most likely we would lose. She was afraid they would destroy our complainant on the stand. I tried to assure her our complainant seemed solid, good under pressure, and I thought she would hold up well on the stand. The ADA had already spoken to the complainant and agreed she seemed solid, but the topless dancer issue was too much of a problem to overcome.

The ADA was well known and well respected in the field of sex crimes. I had a case with her earlier and liked her. She was afraid the City of New York would invest a lot of time and money to prosecute this case only to lose. She pointed to a pile of other cases on her desk that needed to be prosecuted. Cases more vicious and violent than mine. I understood—with a limited amount of time and resources, you had to pick your battles.

It was time to pull the ace from my sleeve. What about the attempted murder on me? I asked. We had charged him with attempted murder for pointing the gun at me. The apologetic look on her face said more bad news was coming. She explained if he fired a shot at me we would have a great case, but just pointing it at me was not enough. I asked her if he pointed it at some ADA, would it be enough then. She failed to see my humor.

A little frustrated and disappointed I asked her, "So what now, do we buy him a martini and apologize for locking him up?" I was starting to regret not shooting this little prick. The wheels of justice just came to a screeching halt. Funny thing about the law is, one day you are completely justified killing a guy and the next day you can't even get him one day in jail.

In the end he took a plea to a misdemeanor gun charge and received a year's probation. This wasn't the first time a case of mine went down the crapper through no fault of my own, and it wouldn't be the last. I had to remind myself again, "Don't take this stuff personal—it's only business." I'm just one spoke in the wheel of justice and I did my job. I can't do everybody's.

About eight months later I strolled into a regular coffee spot of mine—a deli down the block from the perp's apartment. When I walked up to the counter and ordered, I felt an uncomfortable feeling over my shoulder. I felt the uneasiness of eyes on me, like someone was staring. I looked over my shoulder and it was him! It took a second for me to recognize him. Since his arrest we had slapped cuffs on a few hundred other guys, and they all start to become a sea of sad, defeated, angry faces. But it was obvious by the way he was eyeballing me he recognized my face right away.

This time I had my vest on, and a 9mm Glock tucked under my shirt. I really didn't expect him to pull a gun on me, but I didn't expect it last time either. And I had learned a big lesson.

There was an awkward silence as we both stared for a moment and sized each other up. It's always a thorny situation when you run into someone in the street who you locked up. Especially when you almost killed each other. I could feel my body tense up a bit and my right hand ball up into a fist. I thought, "If he tries something stupid I'm going to fuck him up big-time."

He broke the edgy silence by muttering an unexpectedly humble "What's up?"

My body and balled-up fist relaxed a bit when I saw he had no interest in fighting. But I growled back the first thing that came into my mind, "You got off pretty fucking easy, huh?"

He spoke slow and deliberately, like he was about to say something that he obviously gave a lot of thought to. "You know you ruined me."

He had me at "ruined." I was intrigued. I don't know what I expected him to say, but this definitely wasn't it. I had to know more.

"Oh yeah, how so?" I said, not trying to hide my impish glee. I was hoping he wouldn't disappoint me.

"That little press interview you did. As soon as my clients saw that they all dropped me within a week. I lost everything—millions. Then the company I worked for fired me, and no one else will touch me—I'm finished."

Even losing millions doesn't substitute for a little jail time, but I was starting to feel better. It had pissed me off thinking that the only punishment this guy got was a six-figure attorney's fee. But money to a guy like him was everything in life and he lost it. No more supermodels for him.

It wasn't the jail time I was hoping for, but it sounded pretty severe so I figured I would cheer him up—show him the bright side. I said, "You're lucky we didn't fucking kill you."

He pursed his lips and nodded his head, contemplating what I just said. He knew I was right. That little 3:00 a.m. run-in we had could have easily ended up with somebody getting shot—either him or me. He realized out of the other possible outcomes that could have happened in that lobby, he didn't do too bad.

He tried explaining to me that, at the time, he was afraid the victim might show up with a couple of her guy friends and try to beat him up. That's why he answered the door with the gun and the vest. He tried telling me that in those few seconds of excitement and confusion he never heard me yell "police" or saw the shiny gold shield hanging around my neck.

Maybe it's true, maybe it's not. But it wouldn't have made a bit of difference if he had got that shot off—I would still be dead. And most likely he would have been dead about one second after me. My guys would have lit him up!

During our conversation he must have sensed my disappointment at the fact he didn't receive any jail time. When I grabbed my coffee and turned to leave he tried to console me and said, "Don't worry—you got me good."

Before I left and, I hoped, never saw this guy again, I wanted to impart some wisdom I had learned along the way—maybe this little episode in his life could be a learning experience. The answer popped right into my head.

I said, "Don't take this stuff personal, it's only business."

9

A Different Path

I was in bed snuggled under the covers, in a deep REM sleep, when in the far reaches of my brain I heard the jarring, irritating sound of a ringing phone. I really didn't want to be bothered and tried to ignore it, but it was on the nightstand only two feet from my head and I couldn't make it go away.

I was beat. My team and I had collared up last night and worked overtime till five in the morning processing arrests and transporting prisoners. I needed to get some sleep because I was going back to work in a couple of hours—to do it all over again.

I was working in the Fugitive Division up in the Bronx, and we had done a warrant sweep over in the Hunt's Point Market area. The Point is an industrial area and the largest food distribution market in the city, and during the day the streets are lined with commercial vehicles either picking up or making a delivery. But at night, the streets are lined with crackhead whores in short skirts and high heels waving at passing cars while their boyfriends (pimps) watch from the nearby shadows, keeping a careful eye on business. From sunset to sunup cars from the surrounding suburbs, even some with baby seats in the back and "My Kid Is an Honor Student" bumper stickers, parade around the blocks, in a never-ending cycle of picking up and dropping off.

The precinct commanding officer had asked us for a little help cleaning up his prostitution problem, so we went over there and grabbed every hooker we could find and ran their names for active warrants. This is a little like shooting fish in a barrel. Most of the girls had active warrants under various names for failing to return to court on their open cases. When you have a crack hangover and after a long night of twenty-dollar blow jobs I guess it's easy to forget you have a court date in the morning. And even if you do remember, you probably just say fuck it. But when they don't show up the judge just issues a warrant for their arrest and the process starts all over again.

It only took about thirty minutes and we had eight pissed-off ladies of the night handcuffed in the back of the prisoner van on our way to the office.

You probably never had to deal with eight angry hookers crammed into the back of a van, but it can be a handful. If they're not fighting with us they're fighting with each other. It takes days of riding around with the windows open before the smell of cheap perfume dissipates out of the seats. Right off the bat two of them let me know they were PMSing and were in no mood for any bullshit out of me. The funny part was one of them was a transvestite.

As the phone continued to ring I willed one of my eyelids half open so I could check the clock on top of my dresser. It was 7:00 a.m., an unusual time for someone to be calling for no reason. It was either bad news or a wrong number.

I started to get concerned, thinking it was one of my guys calling from court telling me there's a problem with one of our prisoners. I started to imagine the worst, maybe one of our perps escaped, or they found a gun, or some other interesting foreign object, hidden up one of their vaginas when they went through the metal detector. It happens more often than you would think!

The ringing thankfully stopped and the answering machine finally picked up. Speaking was the familiar voice of a friend of mine I hadn't seen or heard from in a few years. Through the sleepy haze I could tell his sentences were short and a little broken up—like he was nervous and searching for the right words.

He said, "Hey Oz . . . uh, it's Dan. Uh, uh . . . you home? I was hoping. Uh . . . I got to talk to you about something."

I could tell by the sound of his voice something was wrong, so I picked up the phone and grumbled, "Hey, what's up?"

Danny apologized for waking me up so early, but he had to talk to me about something and said I was the only one who could help him. I started thinking maybe he got arrested—but no, Dan wasn't that kind of guy. Unlike some of my other friends he always stayed on the straight and narrow. He got married early, had kids, and found himself a decent job. But I could tell in his voice something was up.

When you're a cop your family and friends like to come to you with their "legal" problems. Usually that means someone got arrested. Or they were pulled over and got a ticket for something that wasn't their fault. Sometimes their car got stolen or their house was broken into and they want your help or need some advice.

I don't mind, but most of the time there's not much I can do, so advice is all I can give. Usually the advice is some inside "cop" information I might have. It makes people feel better, especially when it's coming from a friend or relative. For twenty-five years my father was the "neighborhood cop"—everybody came to him with their problems. But he had recently died, so the torch had been passed down to me.

I asked Dan if he was all right and he said yes. I asked about his wife—I knew her also, we all grew up together on the same block and went to the same schools. I asked about his kids, they were okay too. From the tone of his voice I knew something bad was up and my curiosity was getting the best of me, so I told him to hurry up and get to the point. He stumbled a little, searching for the right words again, then finally said, "Remember Jimmy?"

I said, "Yeah, what about him?"

And after a short dramatic pause he added, "He's dead."

I wasn't totally shocked. I hadn't seen Jimmy in quite a few years, but from what I remembered he lived life on the edge. And with Jimmy the edge meant drugs—hard-core drugs.

When I was a kid everybody drank beer and smoked a little weed, but after a few years Jimmy and some of the other guys in the neighborhood needed more and made that cavernous leap to the dark side—heroin.

Jimmy was a stocky, muscular kid and a pretty good ballplayer.

He and I played baseball together on the same Little League team. There wasn't much difference between us. We grew up in the same neighborhood and went to the same Catholic grammar school together. And if that wasn't enough of a righteous upbringing, we both went to Catholic high schools for four more years of religious brainwashing and higher education. But somehow, after all that, we ended up on very different paths.

He wasn't the only one, there were other guys I knew that made the jump, and they became their own little secret society. The heroin guys—and girls—soon hung out by themselves and stopped playing sports.

I'm ashamed to admit it, but at the time, the thought of it did intrigue me—going into the really seedy neighborhoods of Manhattan to score. Doing something dark and mysterious, living on the edge. But there was one thing that didn't intrigue me—sticking a needle in my arm. When I envisioned myself doing that it just seemed terribly wrong. Smoking weed and drinking beer was one thing, but sticking a needle in my vein didn't seem like a normal thing to do and it scared the hell out of me.

Once, when I told a good buddy of mine I was contemplating trying it just once to see what the big deal was, he looked in my eye with a seriousness I'll never forget and said, "You do and I'll kill you." He was normally a calm easygoing guy, so his straightforward reaction was a little startling and confirmed for me that it was probably a bad idea.

And it wasn't long before the members of the secret society became disheveled zombies going through life in perpetual slow motion with hollow eyes and thousand-yard stares.

I was nothing special growing up. I was no smarter or dumber than any other kid in the neighborhood, but later in life I realized it all comes down to choices. Some of us make good decisions, and for whatever reason some of us don't. And the choices we make determine our path in life.

Dan went on to tell me the cops had just been at Jimmy's mother's house in New Jersey and notified her that he was dead. When

I asked what the story was, he didn't know much, just that Jimmy was killed in a car accident in Manhattan down on Fifth Street and Avenue D. They told her his body was at the Bellevue morgue and his car was vouchered at the Ninth Precinct for safekeeping.

Right away it didn't seem to make much sense to me. I knew the Lower East Side neighborhood very well and couldn't figure out how a car could go fast enough on those narrow residential streets to cause a fatal accident.

I quizzed Dan about exactly what the police said. But from the story the cops gave, Jimmy was dead, his body was at the morgue, and his car was at the Ninth Precinct. The family just assumed it must be a car accident.

If the case wasn't deemed a homicide or suspicious and the victim lived out of state, it was routine for the detectives to ask the local cops to make the notification. Usually just the basic information was given; if the family wanted more info they had to contact the case detective.

As usual there was not too much for me to do. Dan just wanted to know if I could call the Ninth and get a few more details for Jimmy's mother.

This was my lucky day. I had recently been transferred to the Bronx, but I had just spent the last four years working in the Ninth Precinct and knew everybody there. I could probably make one quick phone call, get the details, and be back to sleep in no time.

Dan again apologized for waking me up so early but explained he was sitting in Jimmy's mother's kitchen trying to comfort her and thought I might be able to help. I told him not to worry about it and that I would make some calls and get right back to him.

I got up, walked over to the bathroom, threw some water on my face, then looked for a pen and paper. I dialed the number for the Ninth Precinct desk from memory and was glad to hear a familiar voice. The desk sergeant was a friend of mine. This was going to make things nice and simple.

After exchanging some pleasantries and catching up on what had been happening in the precinct since I left, we got to business.

I gave him what I had so far and asked him to check and tell me what he could find out. I told him about the car accident theory and we both agreed that didn't sound too likely. Besides, he hadn't heard of any fatal car accidents from the previous tour. In that neighborhood they're a little unusual.

On the other end of the phone I could hear him flipping through the pages of the Aided and Accident Index—a large folder used to record all DOAs, sick, injured, and accident victims. When he got back on the phone his tone was a little different, a little more subdued, and bit more cautious. He asked, "Was this guy a friend of yours?"

I explained that he was a guy I grew up with in my old neighborhood and played Little League baseball with, but I hadn't seen him in years. I told him I was calling as a favor for his mother and just wanted to get a few more details because the Jersey cops who made the notification were a little vague.

He said, "I got bad news for you, buddy, your friend didn't die from a car accident. He crapped out from an overdose." I wasn't surprised. I could hear more pages flipping as he scanned through other reports looking for more info.

He continued, "Looks like your pal was found unconscious in an abandoned building down on Five and D."

He was reading and talking at the same time. He said, "Looks like EMS found him unconscious—with a hypo sticking out of his arm. They tried to revive him but no luck. He was transported to Bellevue, where he was pronounced DOA."

There was an uncomfortable pause, then he added, "Sorry to give you the bad news, man."

I asked him about the car. More pages flipping, more reading. He said, "Looks like the car was double-parked outside the building—and running. The cops who had the job found it, ran the plate, and when it came back to your friend, they vouchered it for safekeeping."

It seemed pretty cut-and-dried to both of us: he double-parks outside, buys the shit from one of the dealers out front, goes in the building to shoot up, and overdoses. It happens. The call to 911 was made by an anonymous male, probably one of the dealers. They don't like dead junkies lying around—it's bad for business, and ruins the ambience for the other junkies trying to shoot up.

The one thing I couldn't figure out was why the car was left running. This was a bad block filled with junkies, dealers, and every other kind of shithead you could think of, and he was just asking for the car to get stolen. I guess he was in a hurry to get high and not thinking straight. When junkies need a fix they're all fucked up. They're physically ill—nauseous, with the shakes and chills, and all they can think about is getting right. When you're like that I guess it's easy to forget you left your car double-parked and running.

Over the years while on patrol I've passed thousands of junkies on their way to go get high. You can always tell when they are going to score. There's a purpose in their walk, it's almost like they're marching. They can't think about anything else. They look straight ahead and walk fast, with the exact amount of money they need clenched tightly in their fist. You have to have the exact denominations because dealers don't give change.

They go to the same spot day after day, even year after year, because junkies are brand loyal. They know who sells the good shit and who doesn't. They're educated consumers. You can see it in their eye, they're on a mission. They need to get high and they need it now.

I copied down the voucher number for the car, the complaint and aided numbers, and anything else Jimmy's mother might need to claim the body and get his car back. I thanked my buddy for the help and told him I would see him at the next precinct Christmas party.

I called Dan back eager to give him the info and get back to sleep. I had to be back to work in a few hours for another night of fun and games. I called the number and he picked up on the first ring. He must have been sitting next to the phone, waiting.

I told him, "Listen, I've got bad news for you. Jimmy didn't die in no car accident—he OD'd."

Danny wasn't completely surprised either, but obviously he felt obligated to protest a little, and said, "Are you sure? How do they know that? How can they be so sure?"

I shot right back at him, "Listen—they found him in an abandoned building in Alphabet City dead with a fucking hypo sticking out of his arm. Believe me, it was no car accident. I got it straight from the cops at the precinct. You don't have to be Columbo to figure this one out."

Dan knew I was right and didn't question me any further, but said, "I can't tell his mother that."

I said, "I don't care what you tell her. Tell her it was a car accident. Tell her he had a heart attack. Tell her whatever you want. I'm just telling *you* what the facts are." I could hear Danny breathing on the other end of the line. He was nervous and definitely stalling.

We both knew what the problem was—Jimmy's older brother had died a few years earlier of a "drug-related death." I had heard a few different stories out in the street about an overdose or AIDS. I hadn't seen him, but people told me he looked like shit before he died. Somebody tried floating the cancer story, but nobody bought it. Whatever the cause was, it was absolutely "drug related."

When I was a kid Jimmy's older brother and another guy stuck up a store at gunpoint. When the cops stopped him a few hours later, they found them stoned, with the gun, some cash from the store, and a few hundred dollars' worth of heroin on them. The first thing these two brain surgeons did was to go and get high. Somehow, through some good police work the detectives traced the robbery back to them, and Jimmy's brother did a couple of years in prison for it. I felt bad for Jimmy's mother, she seemed like a nice lady. She just had some fucked-up sons.

Dan was still stalling, contemplating what to say to Jimmy's mother, when he surprised me and blurted out, "You gotta tell her."

I couldn't believe what he just said, so I shot back, "Tell her what?"

He said, "Tell her what happened."

Again I shot right back, "No fucking way. You tell her."

He tried convincing me that because I was a cop, I must be used to dealing with this sort of stuff, and I would be better at it than him. He was probably right, but I still wasn't going to tell her. I hadn't seen Mrs. Murphy in almost twenty years and didn't want to get reacquainted under these circumstances.

I gave Dan all the numbers and information they would need to take care of things. I wished him good luck and told him if he needed anything else, don't hesitate to call. But as I was waiting for Dan to thank me for all my help and say good-bye, I could hear some muffled voices on the other end of the line. He was talking to someone with his hand over the receiver.

Then it happened—it was like a punch in the stomach and just as unexpected. Suddenly I heard the sweet voice of Mrs. Murphy saying, "Hello."

I couldn't believe it, that motherfucker handed her the phone. I swore to myself I was going to kill him the next time I saw him. Now I was stuck, there was no getting around it. I was going to have to be the one to tell a brokenhearted mom how the only son she had left met his inglorious demise. Maybe if the building Jimmy was in had been on fire, and he died rescuing a bunch of orphans, breaking the news would be easier, but I wasn't that lucky. And my baseball teammate and his mom weren't that lucky either.

There was nothing heroic in Jimmy's death. I guess the only good thing about dying from an overdose is, it's a painless exit. All the pain happens in the years prior.

I thought about telling her his heart stopped. Technically that wouldn't be a lie. But if I was going to have to be the one to break the news, then I was going to tell her the truth. I briefly thought about telling her that the cause of death had not yet been determined and they wouldn't know anything for sure until after the autopsy. But no, that would be the coward's way out. That's not the way my father would have handled this if he was still alive. She would have to hear the bad news sooner or later. I knew this was going to be difficult for the both of us, but I was not going to lie. She would hear the truth and she would hear it from a friend. It was the only right thing to do.

After I said hello we made some quick small talk. I asked about how she was feeling and then I offered my condolences. On the job I had only done this a few times, and even with people you didn't know, it was always difficult.

Even though she couldn't see me, I put on my cop face and got ready to get to business. But before I could start she cut me off and asked me how my family was doing. She asked me about my mother and father and even remembered my sisters' names.

She asked how I liked being a cop and added she was sure my father must have been very proud of me. She was sad to hear my father had passed away but happy to hear my sister had a baby and was thinking about having another. We chatted for a few minutes about the old neighborhood and what a great place it was to grow up in. How everybody knew everybody. She even remembered that Jimmy and I played Little League ball together.

After a few minutes of pleasant conversation we were both running out of things to talk about. There was some awkward silence as we remembered what the purpose of the call was. We were both stalling, trying to delay the inevitable, but sooner or later we were going to have to get down to business.

I wasn't sure exactly what I was going to say. Dan had just handed her the phone and I really wasn't prepared for this. I wanted to get it over as quick and as painlessly as possible.

I cleared my throat and started. "Mrs. Murphy . . . I made a call to the precinct and checked some things out for you, and I've got some bad news."

I waited for her to say something, but there was only silence on the other end. She was just listening. It was early in the morning and I just could picture her sitting at the kitchen table, probably in her robe and slippers with a tissue in one hand and the phone in the other waiting to hear what she most likely already knew.

Searching for the right words I continued, "Jimmy didn't die in a car crash. He died of what looks like it . . . might possibly . . . be a drug overdose." I spoke slowly and carefully, giving her the information as gently as I possibly could.

Still only silence on the other end. I was hoping she wouldn't protest and say I was wrong, or the cops were wrong. I was hoping to leave out the part about the abandoned building and the hypo sticking out of his arm. She was stoic and seemed not to be surprised. She told me that she was aware of Jimmy's drug problem. I guess she figured a call like this was going to come sooner or later. I hoped it made it a little easier hearing it from me.

I genuinely apologized for having to give her the bad news and again offered my condolences. I told her that I had given Dan all the information she would need, and if she needed anything else, please don't hesitate to call. In the kindest voice she thanked me for all my help. I really didn't do much, but I guess hearing it from me was better than hearing it from some detective she didn't know.

In a time of such great sorrow she was dignified and gracious. During our conversation she was kind to me, and sympathetic to the predicament I was placed in. Having just lost a second son in such an ignominious and untimely manner she seemed more concerned with my feelings. She took the news as well as could be expected, and I was grateful. This could have been a bad scene.

She thanked me for my help and told me to be sure and say hello to my family for her. When we were done I asked her to put Dan back on the phone.

As soon as I heard his voice I yelled, "You motherfucker. How could you do that to me? I haven't talked to her in twenty years and you make *me* tell her."

Dan was a nice guy. Even as a kid he was a nice guy, and I could tell he felt bad about what happened. I could never be mad at him because in my mind I felt that I owed him. When we were kids Dan was a few years older than I was and he always looked out for me. When we were choosing up sides for baseball or football he would always pick me for his team. As a kid I was a good ballplayer, but I hung out with a crew of older guys and had to struggle and do my best to keep up. When I was too young to have my own paper route, Dan let me help him with his—and paid me. It was my first paying job.

When I finished with Dan I hung up the phone and laid back down in bed. I wanted to go back to sleep, but I was wide awake, and just laid there staring up at the ceiling. I was thinking about Jimmy and the old neighborhood. I felt grateful but I also felt lucky. My life had gone all right. I wondered what Jimmy's life was like. I wondered how two kids could start out in the same middle-class neighborhood, go to the same Catholic school, and end up—years later and miles away—in the same shit, drug-infested neighborhood, one a cop and the other a dead junkie.

I wondered if I might have passed him on the street one dark night, me on patrol, him going to shoot up. I wondered if I would have even recognized him. Junkies always look old and decrepit. And I wondered how two kids from the same Little League baseball team ended up on such different paths.

10.

Mug Shot

I opened the lid on my coffee, unwrapped my bagel, and propped my feet up on my drab, government-issue, gray metal desk. I was ready to start my day. The clock above the door read 4:30 a.m. I hated waking up so early every day, but I did enjoy the work. I was a sergeant in the Fugitive Division assigned to the Bronx Warrant Squad, and our job was to hunt down the most wanted fugitives in the Bronx.

We call this work, but to me it really wasn't. I loved this shit. This wasn't work, it was fun. I had a sign hanging above my desk with a saying by Ernest Hemingway, THERE IS NO HUNTING LIKE THE HUNTING OF MAN. I'm sure going face-to-face with some lion in Africa is pretty exciting stuff, but going toe-to-toe with a desperate man willing to do anything to get away will also get your blood pumping.

Years of experience had taught us the best time to apprehend a fugitive was early in the morning, preferably 5:30 a.m. Not too many of these shitheads we were hunting had jobs, so we weren't worried about them getting up early and leaving for work. Usually they were out partying all night or doing something else they shouldn't be doing. By 5:30 they had found their way home and were lying in bed half comatose, less inclined to fight, pull a gun, or try something else stupid.

I took a long sip of coffee, hoping to get my motor running while I fingered through a stack of fresh bench warrants from the Bronx Supreme Court.

The warrants are all basically the same. Each one specifies the individual's name, date of birth, address, and the crime they were arrested for. The judge's signature at the bottom makes it a binding legal document.

This binding legal document commands any and all police officers in the state of New York to take the above-listed individual into custody and bring him or her before the court without delay. It authorizes me to use force if necessary. That includes breaking down the front door of the person's residence, if needed.

Attached to every warrant is a recent mug shot, and I don't care who you are, nobody takes a good mug shot. I don't think Pamela Anderson topless could take a good mug shot. Okay, maybe she could, but no one else.

And these guys sitting on my desk glaring up at me while I have my breakfast are mostly career criminals. They make a point of looking as mean as they can when the flashbulb goes off. So every morning I start my day with coffee, a bagel, and these pillars of society staring up at me with scowls on their faces, defying me to catch them.

The first person on today's stack to give me the evil eye was an individual by the name of Hector, aka "Flaco." At a young age he had been arrested numerous times, but it was the latest arrest that I was concerned with. The judge had released him at arraignment and gave him a return date thirty days later—which was now yesterday. Surprise, surprise, he failed to return.

Hector obviously led a very busy life doing things he shouldn't be doing, so he forgot to return to court on the date the judge set. Maybe next time he will buy himself a calendar and jot this stuff down. Unsurprisingly, the judge was annoyed at Hector's absence and total disregard for the law, so he issued a bench warrant for his arrest. The warrant was immediately processed through channels in the Fugitive Division, and as usual the next morning it found its way to my squad for execution.

Believe it or not we usually don't get that much background information on the guys we go after—just the basics. There's no time to learn every little detail about some perp's arrest history and what type of individual he or she might be. A defendant doesn't show up one morning and the next morning we are out looking for them. My squad is like an assembly line for warrants. At the time there were literally tens of thousands of active warrants in the Bronx, and we would normally hit seven or eight every day before we sat down to have lunch. Every morning they come in by the basketful, we execute them, then hopefully bring them back to jail. So we treat them all the same—like bad guys.

I had heard Hector got into a beef with somebody and there was some gunplay involved. I didn't know if it was true or not, I never had a chance to verify it, but it really didn't matter to me one way or the other. Even if you had a bullshit warrant for drug possession, I treated everybody I went after as a dangerous individual. It's called survival.

I had six very talented detectives in my squad, and each morning all contributed one or two warrants from their assigned caseloads to the morning pile. Hector was on top because we usually hit them in priority order.

As I finished my breakfast of champions, my phone rang and a familiar voice from the detectives' room downstairs said, "Ready when you are, boss."

It was time to get to work. I patted myself down, going through my checklist: gun, handcuffs, spare magazine, flashlight, mace, and backup gun tucked in an ankle holster. I threw my Kevlar vest on, grabbed my pile of warrants with the smiling faces, and headed for the stairs with a spring in my step that said, "I love this shit."

Downstairs my squad was going through their last-minute checklist also. Newspapers were closed, coffee cups, napkins, and paper bags found their way to the garbage can, and we headed for the door.

We jumped into three unmarked cars and quickly caravanned over to our first hit. Hector lived in a large apartment complex and I had been here several times before. These were some bad buildings and it seemed every time we came here there was a problem. Whether it was perps fighting with us or somebody throwing bottles or bricks off the roof at us, it was always a pain in the ass.

I looked at my watch—5:20 a.m. and the neighborhood was quiet. Maybe this one will go smoothly, I thought to myself. Get in and get out before anyone even knows we were here.

The lock on the front door had been kicked in so many times, only a slight push was needed to gain entrance. The lobby stunk of urine and the walls were decorated with graffiti and bullet holes. On the floor were empty crack vials and beer bottles. The barely decipherable bubble letters on the wall let us know there were gang members living in the building. The broken mailboxes made me wonder how anybody received their mail, or if they even cared.

The warrant we were executing was for apartment 4B. A quick look at the first-floor layout revealed all the B apartments faced the front of the building. I motioned for two of my detectives to cover the front of the building while the rest of us "hit" the apartment.

Four floors sounds pretty high for a guy to jump out of a window trying to escape, but desperate men do desperate things and I've had it happen to me before. A perp had scrambled down some cable wires that went from the roof to the ground floor. And if he did jump out the window and kill himself, the family would be on the evening news swearing that we threw him out, in an effort to sue the city for a couple of million. Two detectives covering the front might save us all a lot of grief.

At the end of the first-floor hallway was a Hispanic male in his fifties dressed in a beige uniform with a mop and a bucket. He was obviously the super. He took one look at us and knew exactly who we were, so there was no need for formal introductions. The uninterested look on his face told me the police were here often and he didn't really give a rat's ass about helping us.

Two of us walked over to him and without saying a word flashed him the mug shot. The look on his face changed from one of disinterest to one of disgust mixed with a little fear. He glanced up and down the empty hall making sure we were alone and just mumbled, "4B." I mumbled back in my best white-boy Spanish, *"Gracias."*

We took one look at the elevator with the half-open door and decided the stairs were a safer route. The stairwell was littered with more empty forty-ounce bottles of beer, urine, and graffiti. Being the super in this building was obviously a shit job.

To normal people graffiti looks like some nonsense written by a two-year-old child with a crayon, but to the trained eye it contains a wealth of knowledge. Gang signs decorated one wall, with a list of several nicknames underneath them. These individuals wanted everyone to know that this was their territory. I tapped the third name down, wanting my team to take notice: FLACO.

I huffed and puffed my way up the four flights of stairs, gun in one hand, flashlight in the other, and the stifling sting of piss filling my nostrils. I poked my head through the door leading into the fourth-floor hallway and all seemed quiet. As we tiptoed down the hall looking for the right apartment we passed apartment 4A. I pointed to a cluster of oval dents in the center of the door. The dents were the exact size and shape of the business end of a police battering ram. Obviously Narcotics came by to say hello.

We found apartment 4B, and without a word of instruction two of us positioned ourselves on each side of the metal door while another got down on all fours to peek underneath. We had done this hundreds of times before, it was almost choreographed. I never had to say a word. Every person on my team knew what had to be done. A few hand gestures from me would suffice.

We stayed perfectly still for a few moments with our ears to the door. We were listening for voices, dogs, a television, a radio, a baby crying, or footsteps. Anything that might give us a clue to who or what was inside and what we might be walking into.

Most times things go smooth. An overwhelming display of force does a lot to dissuade a desperate man from trying something stupid. Five cops with guns coming through your front door and two more outside your window will make you think twice. As dangerous as some of these guys are, at the moment of truth most are chickenshit little punks who don't want to die. A couple of nine millimeters pointed at some guy's head usually make his survival instinct kick in and he does what you tell him. Most of the time.

When we hit a warrant we usually don't knock the door down.

Most times it's not necessary. Besides if we did that for every warrant on every day, half the apartments in the Bronx wouldn't have front doors. Normally we knock first, and not the loud banging that says the police are coming to get you. We give it a nice easy knock that may say a friend or a relative is at the door.

I stepped away from the door, turned the volume on my radio down, keyed the mike, and said to the team out front, "You guys in position?" I put the radio to my ear and waited for the response. "Hit it," they said.

I turned back to my team and whispered, "Ready?" Four heads nodded back to me in the affirmative. Everybody was in position and ready to get the show started.

I pulled the mug shot from my pocket and studied the scowling face one last time, committing it to memory. I concentrated on the protruding cheekbones, bent nose, and scar under his right eye.

In a dimly lit apartment, a brother or cousin of the same age can look similar to your perpetrator and add to the confusion during a struggle. I passed the photo around and let everyone else memorize the face one last time also. Each detective studied the face for a few seconds, then passed the photo down the line.

With firm but friendly pressure we knocked on the door, hoping to lure someone into answering. At this point it's all just a mind game we're playing here. If the person inside the apartment knows it's the police outside, they might just roll over and go back to sleep, hoping we go away. But if we can get them to come to the door and answer, they know that we know they are inside. They then feel obliged to open up.

We waited and listened, but nothing. Battering rams and sledgehammers were down in the car if necessary. A second knock was given with a little more force to wake up whoever was inside. Not so loud as to announce the police are outside and coming to get you, but loud enough to say someone is at your door and has something very, very important to tell you. Now open up!

With two of us listening at each side of the door and a third peeking underneath, we waited. Almost a minute passed, then suddenly we heard it, two shuffling feet coming closer. I turned to my team and pointed down to the floor wiggling two of my fingers. That gesture meant I was hearing footsteps. It also meant it was showtime.

Just then I heard a female voice saying "Who is it?" in broken English. I quietly keyed the mike on the radio and alerted the team outside, "We've got movement inside the apartment."

The female voice sounded annoyed, cautious, and curious all at the same time. Remember this is the Bronx and you don't open the door to just anybody who knocks. So she was being just as cautious on her side as we were on our side. I could hear the footsteps inching closer to the door. We knocked again without saying a word. I was trying to draw the voice closer to the door. At the same time one of my guys was shining his flashlight into the peephole. If you look very carefully you can see light on the other side when someone peeks out. Suddenly, very quietly and carefully, someone slid the tiny metal latch on the other side of the peephole open, and again the voice asked, "Who is it? What do you want?"

An NYPD detective shield was thrust up in front of the peephole, followed by a very loud authoritative voice: "POLICE. OPEN THE DOOR."

It had worked. I got the person on the other side to answer. Now if they didn't open up I would politely explain to them that the door would be flying off the hinges in two more seconds. It hardly ever comes to that. Once the person on the other side realizes we know they're inside the apartment all the bullshit usually stops.

The sound of sliding dead bolts and locks clicking open on her side was met with the sound of holsters unsnapping on our side. We turned our flashlights on and got ready.

The door opened a few inches, and the weathered, tired face of a woman in her fifties peered out. As soon as the door opened I stuck my metal light into the doorjamb to keep the door from being slammed shut on us. Without waiting for an invitation we told her we had a warrant and were coming inside to take a look around. My voice was polite but firm. I wanted her to know she didn't have much of a choice in the matter.

I keyed the mike on the radio and told the team outside we were going in, and to watch the windows.

The woman spoke in Spanish and broken English and seemed quite perplexed as to why the police were pushing their way into her house so early in the morning. As we politely forced our way into the apartment, flashlight beams danced around the darkened interior like a disco ball at a party.

I felt bad for the woman as she held her robe closed with one hand and brushed her hair back with the other. In my firm but polite voice again I told her to relax, that everything was okay. We just wanted to talk to her son.

The apartment seemed clean and well cared for, and she wasn't cursing at me like a lot of mothers do when I come to take their sons away. She had a red velvet sofa and chairs that were covered in plastic to protect them. She was doing her best to keep the furniture clean in this shit-hole building she lived in. Right away I got the impression she was probably a decent lady who unfortunately had lost her son to the streets.

I asked her if Hector was at home and told her I had something very important to talk to him about. Suddenly her tone changed. In rapid-fire Spanish and broken English she said he didn't live here anymore. My tone changed and my first reaction was "Bullshit, don't lie to me."

It may seem like I was being cruel to the woman, but I've had sweet little old mothers with rosary beads or a Bible in hand swearing to me they haven't seen their little Johnnies in months. Meanwhile the prick was jumping out the back window or hiding behind the bedroom door with a butcher knife in his hand. I don't trust anyone, even sweet little old ladies.

I motioned to the team to get started. We fanned out through the apartment, checking closets, turning over beds, and searching every space or crevice where a desperate person can try to hide. In a rear bedroom was a teenage girl startled awake by the police looking for her brother—again. We asked her politely but firmly to go out to the living room with her mother while we searched her bedroom.

The next room to be searched was Hector's. I tapped the door with my foot, causing it to swing open. With my gun in one hand and a flashlight in the other, I stepped inside, shining the light left, right, up, and down—but nothing.

I was relieved to see the window was locked shut. I didn't want to have to look outside and see him—SPLAT!—on the sidewalk four floors down. That would have ruined my morning and my plans for getting breakfast in another hour.

I stepped over to the bed and bent down to touch the sheets. They were cold, no one had slept here recently. A quick check of the closets and still nothing. I looked under the bed just to be sure. You never know what you're going to find. Drugs, guns, you just never know. I once flipped over a bed looking for a guy and a duck flew out and attacked me. It wasn't a pit bull, but the quacking and flapping wings were loud and it scared the shit out of me.

We went back out to the living room to re-interview Mom and the sister, but before I could ask any questions Mom let go with some rat-a-tat-tat Spanish that I did not understand. The sister, realizing I didn't understand, jumped in to help. "My brother is dead," she said, pointing to a makeshift shrine on a small table in the corner.

In the ghetto it is customary to place candles and graffiti at the scene of a crime to create a memorial. At the house the family will usually make a small shrine with candles, a crucifix, paintings of Mary and Jesus, and a picture of the deceased. On this one I noticed the picture of the deceased was missing.

Because there was no picture and because everybody lies to the police, my reaction was still, bullshit, they're lying to me. The kid probably fled to Puerto Rico and they're covering for him. But just to make sure we were all talking about the same person and I had the right apartment, I pulled the mug shot from my jacket pocket. I showed it to Mom and asked, "Is this your son?"

Immediately Mom began to cry. Tears streamed down her cheeks while she reached out with a trembling hand and tried to caress the photo with her fingertips. Soft sobbing Spanish came from her quivering lips: "*Ay, Dios mío, mi hijo, mi hijo,*" she muttered. This much I understood. "Oh my God, my son, my son." The sixteen-year-old sister clung to her mother's arm and with her head resting on Mom's shoulder, she also cried at the sight of the picture.

I immediately lightened up. They were telling the truth. Most people can't act that good. People lie to me every day to try and protect their sons, brothers, boyfriends, and husbands from going back to jail, but this woman wasn't lying. I asked her what happened, but all she could give me were some sketchy details about how he was killed a week before.

The girl hustled over to the refrigerator and retrieved a business card from underneath a magnetic holder and said, "This detective is on the case. He knows everything." I took a look at the card, handed it to one of my detectives, and said, "Make a call." I was sure the woman wasn't lying, but before I closed our case I had to be certain.

We got lucky. It was 5:45 a.m., and the detective squads don't start work till 8:00 a.m., but they caught another shooting the night before and were working around the clock.

It all checked out, Hector was the victim of a homicide a week earlier. I wasn't in the Homicide Squad, but I figured if it was true that Hector was in some gun-related dispute in the recent past, it might have had something to do with his early demise.

After talking to the squad and interviewing the mother, I was satisfied that we conducted a thorough investigation, and Hector aka Flaco was dead. Case closed.

It was time to wrap this thing up, so I stuck my hand out, taking the mother's hand in mine and gently shaking it, and said, "I'm very sorry for your loss." I also apologized for waking her up so early but explained it had to be done this way. She was very sweet and understanding, which made me feel even worse for her. This was not the life, or death, she had envisioned for her son when she brought him into this world. But even the best parents can lose a child to the streets when you live in a neighborhood like this.

I shook the sister's hand and repeated my condolences, but as I turned to leave, the mother called out to me and pointed to my jacket pocket. She asked if she could see the mug shot one more time. It seemed like a strange request, but I complied. At this point I started to get a little worried. Was she going to tell me that it wasn't her son? That she made it all up? I didn't know where this was all going.

I reached into my pocket and handed her the picture. She reached out and ever so gently took the photo from my fingertips. I watched as she gazed at it lovingly for a few seconds, then closed her eyes and clutched it to her chest like she was hugging the kid. After hugging the photo for what seemed like a long time, she turned to her daughter and said something in Spanish. As I waited for the translation, Mom stared at me with pleading eyes. The daughter relayed the request, saying, "My mother would like to know if she could keep the picture."

I explained to them the photo is police department property and we don't give them out to the public. I could not imagine what she would want with a mug shot of her son. It was an unflattering representation of her son's antisocial, unproductive existence. Why would she want to be reminded of what he had become? I was a little confused.

The sister went on to tell me they had no recent photos of Hector and very few even when he was a child. When I searched the apartment earlier, I noticed in the living room a bookcase full of nicely framed family photos. There were lots of nice pictures framed in gold and silver, so it wasn't that they were that poor and couldn't afford a camera. More likely Hector spent most of his life running around the streets and didn't spend much quality time with the family. He was too busy wreaking havoc on society rather than spending time with his mother during birthday parties and holidays.

There was something about this woman that got to me. Maybe it was that she didn't curse me like a lot of other mothers did and blame the police because their sons had to be hauled off to jail. She realized her son was a bad egg and it was no one's fault but his own that he met a violent and tragic death so early in life.

I told her it was against police department regulations, but she could keep the photo. She thanked me profusely, then turned to walk away. At first she wanted to place the photo on the shrine they had built between Jesus and Mary, but then thought better of it. I watch her shuffle across the tacky shag carpet and over to the bookcase with the family photos. In her slippered feet, clutching her robe closed, she tenderly placed the mug shot between Grandpa's World War II picture of him in uniform and a graduation photo of some girl in a cap and gown.

Years of police work can make you a heartless son of a bitch at a young age, and I was no exception. Watching people die in the streets will definitely harden your heart and make you numb to other people's suffering, but this got to me.

When Mom placed that photo of Hector with the numbers across his chest, sneering at the world, next to Grandpa I was stunned. My team and I silently glanced at each other with raised eyebrows and broken hearts. I couldn't help but think that when I was having my morning coffee with snarling mug shots staring back at me, this woman would be doing the same.

She shuffled back over to us in her slippered feet and thanked me repeatedly. I expressed my condolences again and headed for the door. I looked at my watch. It was 5:50 a.m. and I had a few more Hectors to catch this morning before it got too late.

As we walked out of the piss-and-graffiti-filled lobby, hurrying to our next hit, somebody from my team blurted out what we all were thinking. "Do you think she's going to frame it?"

11

Last Fight

I was sitting in my office at the Bronx Warrant Squad trying to study for the upcoming lieutenant's exam, which was only days away. I hadn't been studying much for the past couple of weeks because much of my time and most of my thoughts had been occupied with my father. He was dying of cancer and the end was very near.

I had my head buried in the New York State Penal Law, trying to memorize the difference between Kidnapping and Unlawful Imprisonment, when my phone rang. It was the call I had been waiting for but didn't want to receive. My sister's voice was on the other end, and with a calm, almost business-like tone she said, "It's almost time, I think you better hurry up."

She didn't have to explain any further. This morning my mother and two sisters were taking him to the hospital for the last time. On this trip, instead of going to the regular patient rooms he had become accustomed to, he went to a special wing down the hall. These rooms were for hospice patients. It was quiet and without all the hustle and bustle of a normal hospital floor. This was where you went to die.

I hung up the phone and threw the books in my desk because studying was useless. I couldn't help but remind myself that the last lieutenant's test was seven years ago and if I didn't hit this one I would have to wait another seven years for the next one, and by that time my career would most likely be over. As the drawer slammed shut I thought, "Fuck it. Whatever happens, happens."

Promotion exams in the police department are very competitive. To even have a chance of passing you have to study for at least six months. You have to buy the books, attend the study classes, and commit at least two hours a day to memorizing a huge amount of very dry, boring material. It wasn't easy and only a small percentage pass.

The fact that the test was only days away bothered my father much more than it bothered me. With all the things he had going on he would call me every day and ask how the studying was going. And every day, like a good son, I would lie to him and tell him it was going great.

He would remind me I had a "big day" coming up, and I better not let this "little thing" he was going through screw me up. I couldn't help but think he had a "big day" coming up also, but he seemed more concerned about my test than he did about the cancer that was rapidly spreading through his lungs.

He had retired from the police department as a lieutenant in the Detective Bureau and always felt "the job" had been good to him, and he wanted it to be good to me also. Aside from his family, the thing he was most proud of was how he rose through the ranks. To understand his sense of pride you have to realize he was a high school dropout.

He would smile at me with that crooked-tooth grin and tell me how he jumped out the second-floor window of Lincoln High School in his sophomore year, joined the navy, and never looked back. He would tell me how he sailed around the world a couple of times and in the process got his GED. This explains the huge blowouts we had when I brought home those less-than-stellar report cards of mine.

In some softer moments, usually with a couple of beers in him, he would tell me how lonely he was in the navy because, looking back, he was just a kid. He regretted the fact his mother signed the papers that allowed him to go into the military at such a young age. But then that crooked smile would come back at the thought of how he beat all those college boys in taking the sergeant's and lieutenant's exams.

After I hung up with my sister I called my wife, told her it was time, and asked her to meet me at the hospital. I grabbed my coat and headed for the car.

I was in the Bronx and the hospital was down the Jersey Shore, so I had a little bit of a ride ahead of me, and as I drove over the George Washington Bridge my mind started to drift away. The trip gave me some time to think and reflect on my childhood and some of the not-so-*Father Knows Best* memories I had of my dad.

To say my father was a character is to put it mildly. Most people loved and respected him, but if you didn't love him you feared him. He was equally satisfied with either reaction. My father was a fighter and took great pride in it. As much pride as attaining the rank of lieutenant. He was not a boxer or wrestler or martial arts expert. Anyone who put on gloves or silly tights or flew through the air throwing kicks was "full of shit," as he would put it. He was a bare-knuckle barroom brawling street fighter and he was good at it.

This was not a chosen profession but was born out of necessity. I grew up in Jersey City, New Jersey, a tough blue-collar neighborhood where drinking beer and beating the crap out of each other were everyone's favorite pastimes. The measure of a man's masculinity was how much he could drink and how well he could use his fists. The weak were looked down upon, pitied, or even worse, picked on without mercy. Respect was not earned by how smart or successful you were, but by how tough you were. Pleasant talk, discussions, or spirited arguments meant nothing unless they could be backed up by being able to "take it outside." And the forum for this intellectual and physical stimulation was the neighborhood bar.

Every neighborhood had its own bar, a place where you could go at any time of the day or night and have a beer with your buddies. A place where "everybody knows your name." The place where you could throw a twenty-dollar bill on the bar and it would last most of the day or night, while you watched a ball game or played darts and discussed the problems of the world. The type of place where you could wind down after work or get out of the house for a while on the weekends. A place where fists would fly over the slightest insult. Our place was called Pete's Tavern.

My father was not a big guy, only about five foot ten, maybe two hundred pounds, but as tough as they come. He wasn't the toughest guy in the bar, but that was only because of his size. He took pride in the fact that the other tough guys would think long and hard before inviting him to "take it outside."

When I turned eighteen I became a regular at Pete's. Not that I wasn't a regular before. Growing up as a kid, when my dad would invite me to watch a baseball or football game with him I knew he wasn't taking me to Yankee or Giants Stadium. We were going to the bar and I loved it. I loved hanging out with the guys, drinking root beer and listening to their stories. Especially the cops.

I remember having to stand on a milk crate to shoot darts or play pool because I was so young. Nowadays I think five-year-olds hanging out in bars is looked down upon by our liberal, overprotective society. But I don't care what they say, I had a great childhood. Hanging out with the guys was where I learned to become a man, even if I did come home smelling like cigarette smoke.

I remember my mother yelling at my dad the first time she heard me say "Fuck." She figured I must have learned it in Pete's and she was probably right.

When I was about ten years old my father worked in the precinct where we lived. I loved it when he would come by the house in his police car. When he would go into the house to say hello, he would let me sit in the car so I could listen to the police radio. He would tell me what his call sign was so I could run and get him if the dispatcher called. I would ask him what all the codes meant so I could understand what they were saying. To me this was the coolest job in the world.

Sometimes when he was the desk sergeant my mother would make dinner and wrap it up so I could take it to him. I would ride my bike to the precinct and deliver his hot meal.

When he was working 4:00 p.m. to midnight, a week could

sometimes go by before we would see each other. In the morning I would be off to school before he got up and he would have gone to work before I got home. So when I would stop by to see him at the station house, he would let me hang out for a while.

I don't know what people would think when they came into the precinct to tell the desk sergeant their sad story and saw some little kid sitting behind the desk with him. Cops work mostly nights and finding time to be with your kids isn't always easy, so this was our idea of quality time!

I was only a kid, but I loved being around cops. Guns peeked out from under their jackets and they told the most incredible stories about what happened out on patrol the night before. To me all the characters hanging out in Pete's were tough and cool, but the cops were the ones I looked up to.

Maybe if my father had been a doctor living in a fancy neighborhood or suburb, I might be a heart surgeon hanging out in some country club talking about my mutual funds and stock options. But it didn't turn out that way. I was the son of a cop born in a tough neighborhood a couple of blocks from Pete's Tavern.

The day I turned eighteen was a proud day for me because now I could walk into Pete's, throw my own twenty-dollar bill on the bar, and be treated as an equal. I could sit down with my father and his buddies and buy them a drink.

This was an important time in my path to becoming a man, and my father, just as he had always done, was going to make sure I was raised right. He taught me the proper way to stand at a bar, put your money down, and order a drink. To him there was a right way and a wrong way to do everything, and ordering a drink the wrong way in a room full of tough guys was a sign of weakness. Improper bar manners had led to a lot of missing teeth and broken noses, and he was making sure I was raised right.

To drive his point home, one day he shoved me while I was sitting on a stool and caused me to almost go flying on my ass. I grabbed the bar as the stool went tumbling to the floor beneath me. This got a chuckle out of Butch, the bartender. As I regained my balance he explained to me that I should never sit with my feet tangled around the legs of the stool because a guy could come up and sucker punch me and there was nothing I could do about it. Always have one foot on the floor for balance.

After I became a regular at Pete's I was able to learn firsthand just how good a fighter my dad was. Before, as a kid, I would just see him show up at the house with a busted eye or a ripped shirt and bloodied knuckles, only to hear how good he did.

One Friday night I was sitting at the crowded bar listening to the one-man band Pete had hired for the weekends. The guy played the organ, a guitar, a harmonica, and a little drum and cymbal that he operated with his foot, all at the same time. The guy sucked! He played for a few bucks and all the beer he could drink, but Pete thought having some entertainment on the weekends added a little class to the place.

It was late and the joint was jumping. The bar was packed three deep and the one-man band was cranking. Butch, his brother Richie, and an old guy we called Uncle Joe were scrambling behind the bar trying to keep everybody's glass full, when all of a sudden I hear a loud boom behind me. It was so loud I thought my mother's prayers had been answered and lightning had struck the place. My father had slammed the side door with his fist, causing it to fly open, and at the same time he was pointing at Dusty Campbell and yelling, "Outside!"

Dusty was a scary-looking dude. He had this mean face that came from years of working construction and too much booze. He was a ditch digger for some construction company and he spent all day shoveling dirt and lifting boulders. The old man had warned me always to stay clear of him. I didn't like looking at him because he scared me and most everybody else.

My father stormed out the door and onto the sidewalk with Dusty following. I went next, with half the crowd right behind me, all wanting to see the excitement. I admit I was scared. Dusty had muscles on top of muscles from moving tons of earth every day for a living, and my dad never worked out a day in his life.

I later learned that Dusty and my father had a little bit of a history. They had gone at it in the past and it was ugly. They both had gotten hurt, and much to my surprise the fights were pretty even.

This time Dad was in a rage and ready to go. His fists were balled up and he was crouching at the knees in a boxer's stance, taunting Dusty, "Come on, let's go." I made a token effort to step in between them because everybody else was too afraid to get in the middle of this. Dad made a sweeping motion with his right arm and brushed me aside, sending me flying while still taunting Dusty, "Come on, put 'em up."

This was crazy! As much as Dusty scared me, this time Dad was even scarier. This was about to get real ugly. There were apparently some long-standing doubts about who was tougher, and this was about to be settled right here and right now for everybody to see.

Just as all hell was ready to break loose, I looked over at Dusty and saw this scared and confused look on his face. His hands were down by his sides—he was not accepting the challenge to "put 'em up." His voice sounded almost pleading, as he said, "Tommy, what did I do?" My father shot right back at him, "You insulted me in front of my son!"

Now, I had no idea what the hell he was talking about because I didn't see or hear any insults over the noise of the one-man band, but Dusty had done something to piss Dad off and you never ever insult a man in front of his son. And much to everyone's surprise, Dusty put his hands out in front of him in the surrender position and said, "I'm sorry, Tommy, lighten up. Okay, I'm sorry."

Apparently Dusty knew what he did was wrong. I had no idea what the insult was and when I asked my father what happened, all he would say was "He insulted me in front of my son." I never found out what the insult was, but Dusty realized that as tough as he was, he couldn't beat a guy fighting for his honor in front of his son.

The years weren't kind to Dad. He lived a hard life and he paid for it. By the time he was thirty-nine he had his first heart attack, and three more would follow before he would ultimately need a heart transplant. His body was failing. He looked old before his time and felt even older. But he was as tough as ever. He would always tell me he had one or two more good fights in him and I wasn't immune to getting one myself if I didn't stay on the "straight and narrow."

He wasn't kidding about having one or two more fights in him. One Sunday afternoon I walked into Pete's to have a beer and watch a football game, when I noticed the cigarette machine had the front glass broken and there was a little blood inside. I sat at the bar in our family's regular spot and ordered a beer just as I had been taught. When Butch brought my beer over I casually asked what happened to the cigarette machine. Butchie shook his head, smiling, and just said, "Your father again." The old man seemed to amuse Butch as much as he amused me.

Butch went on to tell me that the night before, Dad was hanging out having a couple of beers. Now I'm shaking my head because he shouldn't be drinking in the first place. The doctor told him to lay off because of all the heart medication he was on, but he wasn't a good listener. Anyway some young guy about twenty-five years old comes in and sits down next to him. Nobody knew the guy. He wasn't a regular. Probably just some construction worker who popped in for a beer after work.

The guy pulls out a pack of cigarettes and asks Dad for a light. My father replies he doesn't have a light because he doesn't smoke. He had quit years earlier, the only healthy thing he had ever done in his life. To this the guy replies, "What are you, a fag?"

Now this was uncalled for. To call an old guy sitting at the bar, just minding his own business, names and insult him is just not right. As you have read earlier, Dad had a short temper when it comes to things like insults. Plus he was feeling sorry for himself because his youth and health were slipping away. So he dealt with this the only way he knew how: he got up and decked the guy. One punch and he puts him on his ass.

The bar in Pete's is shaped like a big square, and they were sitting across from the front door. When the guy tries to get up, Dad beats him down the entire length of the bar, makes a right turn, beats him along the other side of the bar, puts his head through the cigarette machine, and throws him out the front door and into the street. Butch is laughing like hell while telling me this story. He thinks it's hysterical. He could give a fuck about the cigarette machine.

Later, when I get home, Dad is sitting in his easy chair watching television with a sad look on his face. I couldn't help it, I had to hear his version of the events, so I said, "I hear you had a little excitement in Pete's last night." He just shakes his head in disgust. I thought he was going to regret this juvenile behavior he engaged in, but no. Without looking at me, just staring straight ahead at the television and still shaking his head, he says, "You know, I'm starting to look soft. These young punks don't take me seriously anymore. They think I'm a . . . cupcake."

I can't help but laugh at the analogy. I try to assure him that he doesn't look like a "cupcake," but he's facing the facts, soon he's not going to be able to do stuff like that anymore. Soon he's going to have to learn to walk away and he doesn't like it. But he assures me he still has one more good fight left in him, and by the look in his eye and the scowl on his face, I believe it.

Dad could be described as old-fashioned and stubborn. At home there was no such thing as democracy. There was no open discussion or exchange of ideas. It was his way or the highway. But he loved his children more than anything in the world, so this presented him with quite a dilemma when my sister dropped a little bombshell on him one day. She was coming out of the closet!

This definitely went against his number one rule for dating, which simply stated, "If you have to explain 'em—don't bring 'em home!"

He was devastated and confused. He even thought about blaming himself. Maybe if he hadn't taught my sister how to shoot guns as a kid, this wouldn't have happened?

There were no gay people in our neighborhood that anybody knew of, and if there were they sure didn't hang out in Pete's, so

Dad had no experience dealing with this subject. So he dealt with this the only way he knew how: he ran away from home!

He packed his little red Honda Civic with as many of his belongings as it could hold and took off. My mother and sisters were pissed! Out of all the crazy stuff he had done in his life, this was the last straw. I, on the other hand, found it all quite amusing. I had always found the crazy stuff he did amusing.

Once or twice I had commented to my mother that people in the neighborhood thought I was just like him. The apple doesn't fall far from the tree, they would say. Hearing this, my mother would get mad and shoot right back, "Oh no, you're not!"

Three weeks had gone by and nobody knew where he was. I would call my mother daily and ask if she heard from him. To this she would reply, "Heard from who?" and then change the subject. She was getting madder by the day.

Finally my phone rang. It was him. My father had a hair-trigger temper. Just ask the guy in the bar who wanted a light. I didn't want to say anything that might set him off, so I kept the conversation light. How are you? How are you feeling? Do you have all your medication? Most of my questions were answered with a grunt or one- or two-word answers.

Finally, I couldn't take it anymore. I had to ask, "Where are you?" To this he replied, "Wyoming!"

I almost lost it. "WYOMING! What the hell are you doing in Wyoming?" And in a very casual, matter-of-fact tone he answered, "I went for a drive."

I couldn't believe it. When normal people want to go for a drive they go to Bear Mountain or out to Montauk. They don't drive two thousand miles to Wyoming. Dad was anything but normal.

I tried to keep the conversation going, but he wasn't ready to talk just yet. He called me because he was lonely. I was actually a little jealous, picturing him out west surrounded by snowcapped mountains and wide-open spaces, but when I asked him how he liked Wyoming, he said it sucked. Then he said he was busy and had to go. Click, the line went dead.

He called me because no one else would talk to him. My mother was fed up with all the crazy stuff he had done in the past, and this was the icing on the cake. My sister, who had bared her soul to him, was busy packing her bags and looking for a new place to live, and my other sister was siding with the women just on general principle. That left me.

I couldn't wait to call my mother and tell her he was okay, but all she said was, "That son of a bitch better not call me." I couldn't help but laugh. Life with him wasn't always easy, but it was an adventure.

The only one who seemed to be worried about him was my wife. She had developed a special relationship with him. She looked at him as a wise old father figure, asking his advice on everything, and he loved it.

Soon after meeting him for the first time, she witnessed him getting mad over something stupid. In response she walked over to him and flicked his ear with her thumb and forefinger, causing him to wince in pain. She followed this with a stern warning: "Be nice."

You would have thought she punched a grizzly bear in the nose by the shocked look on everyone's face, but he just crumbled. It was amazing. She had him wrapped around her little finger.

After the phone call my wife was yelling at me, "You better do something about this!"

Over the next two weeks his phone calls to me became more frequent. I could tell he was desperate to come home, but didn't know how or he was afraid to face the music. As big of a pain in the ass as he was to live with, his family was everything to him. Without us he would wilt away like a flower without water. He was a general without any troops.

Finally, during one of our conversations he agreed to meet me somewhere so we could talk this out. I opened a map and decided Las Vegas would be as good a place as any to meet. I figured we might as well have some fun while we talked.

I called my mother and gave her the good news. Her reply was "Don't do me any favors." My mother is an Italian from Brooklyn, and in her own way she was ten times tougher than he was.

When we met in the airport terminal I could see from a distance he was old, tired, and lonely. He looked better when he was in intensive care after his heart attacks, but not by much. His shirt and pants were baggy from his losing weight. He obviously hadn't been eating or sleeping right. Running away from home wasn't half as much fun as he thought it was going to be, but when he saw me he perked right up. He was glad to see me.

Him and I weren't the touchy-feely type, so we skipped the hugging and hand shaking and got to business. He had a great idea. We were going to start at one end of the strip and have one beer in every bar we found till we reached the other end. Considering the size of the Vegas strip I thought it sounded like an overly ambitious goal, but I figured what the fuck, it would be a good way to loosen him up so we could talk.

We were only at the third bar and halfway through our third beer when I popped the question. "Why don't you think about coming home?" His answer was simple and direct. "Okay."

I was pissed! I said, "Okay? You've got to be kidding me, you couldn't tell me that over the phone, you made me travel two thousand miles to tell me 'Okay'?"

I could tell by that sly grin he knew exactly what he was doing. He said, "I'll come home, but you have to drive with me. If you don't drive with me I'm not coming home."

I figured what the hell, this sounded like a bonding experience— him and me driving cross-country. And by the way he looked, I knew he probably only had a few good years left in him.

However, I had one stipulation: I wanted to see the Grand Canyon. He balked. "I've been there already." I put my hand up in protest. "If we don't go to the Grand Canyon, I'm not driving back." He gave me that crooked-tooth grin. "Okay." And with business taken care of we continued on our journey down the Strip.

This was my first trip to Vegas and it was exciting. Halfway down the strip we stopped in front of the Treasure Island hotel to watch their show. Out front every hour or so they had these two giant ships filled with guys dressed up like pirates, and they would swing from ropes, wave swords, and shoot cannons, pretending to board each other's vessels.

There were at least a thousand people standing out front watching the excitement, and just as the cannons were firing and pirates were flying through the air, my father nudges me with his elbow and says, "Get a load of this guy."

He's pointing to a guy standing in front of him blocking his view. When I look over I notice the man he is talking about. He's about six foot seven, wearing a giant cowboy hat, size thirteen cowboy boots, a plaid shirt, tight jeans, and a big shiny silver belt buckle. This dude is huge and he obviously takes his Western heritage very seriously.

I shrug my shoulders and mouth "So what?," wondering what he's talking about. Dad looks at me, looks at him, then looks at me again and says in a very loud voice, "The closest this guy has ever been to a horse is a fucking merry-go-round!"

The guy heard every word he said because Dad said it loud enough for everyone to hear, and now Roy Rogers looked pissed. A couple of other people standing nearby were laughing, which only made this guy even madder. The guy looked at Dad, then looked at me. Then he looked at Dad again, sizing us up. My father was not a very imposing figure at this point in his life, with his baggy shirt and pants topped by a goofy golf hat to protect him from the sun. But there was still something intimidating about him, so the Marlboro Man turned and walked away.

I looked at Dad and said, "Are you crazy, did you see the size of that guy? You're not what you used to be and don't forget it." He looked at me with that grin and said, "I've still got one more good fight in me. Don't you worry about it."

*   *   *

Reminiscing about Dad and my childhood made me laugh, brought a tear to my eye, and made the drive down to the Jersey Shore go faster. And before I realized it I was at the hospital.

I pulled into the parking lot of Jersey Shore Medical Center and took a moment to get myself together. I didn't know what to expect when I got upstairs, but I knew this wouldn't be easy. In a very short time I would be the only man in the family, and falling to pieces just would not do. So I put my game face on and headed into the lobby. With no time to stop and get a pass, I "tinned" (flashed my shield at) the security guard at the front desk and hustled over to the elevator.

When I walked into his room, he didn't even notice me. He was slumped over in a chair with half his ass sticking out of the baggy, pale blue hospital gown. There was a small oxygen tube clipped to his nose and an IV attached to his arm pumping him full of morphine. Sadness washed over me. The toughest guy I ever met, and the menace of Pete's Tavern could barely sit up straight anymore.

My mother, two sisters, and a nurse were getting his bed ready. Getting ready to make him comfortable for the last time. I kissed everyone hello and asked how he was doing. They said if I wanted to talk to him I would have to hurry up because the morphine was taking effect and he would soon be completely out of it.

I didn't even take off my jacket. I knelt down next to him and struggled for something to say. I knew this was the last opportunity I would ever have to speak to him and time was running out. I also knew there wouldn't be any hugging, kissing, or crying. We hadn't done any of that before and I was pretty sure it wouldn't start now. He knew I loved him and he loved me. There was no need to get mushy about it.

If I could have had just one wish, it would be to have one last beer with him in Pete's. That's where we got along the best. There was never any friction between us there. But those days were long gone.

I put my hand on his arm and shook it gently. I said, "How are you feeling? You okay?" The morphine apparently was doing its job. He was in La La Land. He slowly lifted his head and opened his eyes. His eyes were yellow and almost lifeless, but he perked up as soon as he recognized me. He tried to give me that crooked-tooth smile one more time, but it seemed like it was too much of an effort. His strength and consciousness were almost gone, but he forced himself to sit up straight.

There was little time for him to tell me how much he cared about me and he knew it, so he didn't waste words. With a sudden quickness he reached out, grabbed me by the jacket, and yanked me close to him. I couldn't believe how strong he was all of a sudden. Two seconds ago he was half dead, now I didn't know if he wanted to fight or what.

His strength was dwindling, but he had something important to say and he wanted to make his message loud and clear. With a surprisingly steady hand and tight grip he pulled me in closer and whispered, "You listen to me and you listen good. Don't you let this little thing that I'm going through here fuck you up. You've got a big day coming up on Saturday and you've got to keep your head screwed on straight."

I was stunned. This was not what I was expecting for our last conversation.

He had to pause for a moment to take a few deep breaths. He was trying to rally the last bit of strength he could find in that broken body of his. He continued, almost growling this time, "Don't let me mess you up . . . you got to promise me that."

I could not believe what I was hearing. He was about to die and the only thing on his mind was my lieutenant's test. This was unbelievable! I didn't expect this! With all the crazy stuff he had done in his life, he should be more worried about himself right now, but he wasn't. His last conscious thoughts on this earth were about my stupid lieutenant's test.

I shook my head yes and tried to assure him I would be okay. Actually I wasn't sure of anything right now. I hadn't been studying much in the last few weeks and right now the test was the last thing on my mind. At that moment I could not care less if I took the test or not. But I wasn't going to tell him that!

He tightened his grip on my jacket and growled again, "You've got to promise me that. And I'll promise you something."

I didn't know where he was going with this, but there was no stopping him now and the last thing I wanted to do was argue with him. In between sentences he had to take deep, deliberate breaths because his lungs were filling with fluid and breathing was becoming an extraordinary effort.

He was on a roll now. "You got to promise me you're going to hit this test good . . . and I promise you"—he paused, taking in a long, labored, deep breath, then continued—"I won't die till Sunday."

After another long, labored breath he continued, "I'll hold on till Sunday so I don't screw you up, but after that all bets are off. I can't take this shit much longer."

I couldn't believe what I was hearing. This was Thursday afternoon. He knew my test was on Saturday, and his plan was to wait till Sunday to die.

I wasn't sure either one of us was in any shape to keep this promise, especially him, but I agreed. And as soon as I did, he seemed relieved. He loosened his grip on my jacket, reached up, patted me on the cheek, and mumbled, "Good boy!"

Just then his hand dropped, limp, to his side and he closed his eyes and that was it. He was finished. And that was the last conversation we would ever have.

My mother, my sisters, the nurse, and I all lifted him to his feet and put him to bed for the last time. Mom tucked him in and fluffed his pillow as he drifted off to sleep, never to wake up again.

I asked the nurse, "What's next?" She told me there was nothing to do now but wait. Waiting seemed like an easy thing to do, compared to all the suffering he had gone through—the heart attacks, the transplant, and now the cancer. But it wasn't. After just a short period of time his breathing became more labored. He struggled and gurgled for every breath as his lungs filled with fluid and his major organs slowly shut down.

As a cop I had seen plenty of death in my life but this was different. Most of what I had seen were people who had been shot or stabbed or met some other type of violent, sudden death. But there were no heroic efforts to save a life here, only letting nature take its course, and nature would not be rushed. We sat around his bed and watched as the intervals between each breath became longer and more labored.

My aunt, uncle, and cousins, whom my family had always been close to, came to the hospital for support. The waiting room down the hall was filled with family members telling their favorite Tommy Osborne stories. I wasn't the only one with tales about my father. It seemed everyone in the family had their own. At times the laughter coming out of the waiting room would echo down the hall of the peaceful, dimly lit hospice wing. It may have seemed disrespectful to others who did not know our family, but it was really a testament to a man who was truly a character and to how much his family loved him.

Somewhere in the middle of all this, during a quiet moment, I made the suggestion that maybe we should get a priest. The response I received was a chorus of laughter and one of my sisters calling me an asshole. My father was not a religious person and had not been to church in fifty years except for the mandatory wedding or funeral.

The last time Dad had been in intensive care, hooked up to an array of monitors and IVs, a priest had come to visit. The man of God was appalled when Dad informed him that the last time he attended Mass was when he was an altar boy in St. John's grammar school. The fact that Dad was once an altar boy must have given the priest some hope, so he pressed on, "Son, at a time like this you should think about getting closer to God." Dad's response: "Padre, if I get any closer to God we're going to be shaking hands. Thanks but no thanks." The priest left and never returned.

Minutes had turned into hours and hours slowly turned into more than a day. Watching him struggle and fight for every breath was torture for us. He laid there with his yellow eyes half open and his chest gurgling with every shallow breath. He was in great distress, and I wondered how long this could continue. Often, after an exceptionally long pause, it would appear his breathing and suffering had finally ended, only to continue with another gasp for air.

The nurse assigned to our family was a wonderful person, compassionate and informative. She had witnessed this hundreds of times before and guided us through the dying process. Finally I had to ask her how much longer this could continue. She told me she thought he would have been gone by now considering the condition he was in, but she added she had seen patients hold on for a week or longer. She told me a patient's determination to live and not let go should not be underestimated.

She must have noticed the pained look on my face as I thought about him suffering like this for a week. She also said that it is believed coma patients can hear when you talk to them and added, "Tell him it is okay to let go."

Right then and there it hit me. I knew exactly what the old man was doing. He was hanging on till Sunday. He was determined to keep that stupid promise he made.

I walked over to my mother, who was standing by the window. Everyone had left the room except us and we were gazing outside. A heavy snowfall had begun hours earlier and the streets were filling up. The serenity of the snow blowing through the yellow rays of the streetlights below made the scene around us seem surreal. We both wanted this to end. He had suffered enough in his life and it was time to let go.

After some contemplation I looked at my mother and said, "Do you think he's holding on for me? Do you think he's trying to hold on till Sunday because of my test?" She looked at him lying there fighting for every breath and said, "You know your father, I wouldn't put anything past him."

A wave of guilt washed over me at the thought of him suffering like this just for me. And I knew it was the promise that was keeping him going. He always said he had one last fight left in him and I knew deep down inside this was it. Dusty Campbell had learned the hard way just how tough Dad could be when he was fighting for his son, and he was doing it again.

This was a special moment between my mother and me. He had been a pain in the ass for both of us during his life, but we both loved him very much and did not want to see him suffer anymore. As we stood shoulder to shoulder looking out the window watching the snow fall, I came up with an idea. I said, "How about I tell him that it's Sunday? That I took the test, I did good on it, and it is okay to let go."

As soon as I said it I felt guilty. It seemed wrong to lie to a guy on his deathbed, but I didn't know what else to do. I didn't want to see him suffer anymore.

We both thought about this for a moment and I was a little surprised when Mom said, "Do it." I half thought she was going to say no and tell me that lying to my father on his deathbed just wasn't right. But I trusted her instincts and with her blessing I knew it was the right thing to do.

I collected my thoughts for a moment and asked Mom if she would excuse me for a while, I wanted to do this alone. She hugged me, kissed me on the cheek, and wished me good luck before leaving the room and closing the door behind her.

I was a little afraid he was listening to our conversation and was now going to sit up and bark, "Don't bullshit me. Where are your books? Why aren't you studying? You have a big day coming up." But that wasn't possible. Dad was somewhere between here and a far-off place, probably telling the person in charge, "Don't rush me, I'll come when I'm good and ready."

I grabbed a chair from the corner, dragged it next to his bed, and sat down. I took his hand in mine, then looked down to make sure my feet weren't wrapped around the legs. He trained me well.

I fought back a couple of tears that were now running down my cheeks. I wanted to sound upbeat and encouraging. If this was going to work I needed him to believe me. It felt a little strange lying to him like this but it had to be done.

The room was quiet except for the sound of Dad's labored breathing. It was dark, except for the single fluorescent lamp on the wall over his head.

I didn't know how to begin so I just started. I said, "I hope you can hear me because I did it! I took the test and I think I hit it pretty good! I don't want to say I aced it, but the answers seemed like they were popping off the page at me. There were just a few I wasn't too sure of but not many. I walked out of the place feeling pretty good about the whole thing. I really think I hit it."

I moved the chair as close to the bed as it would go and paused for a moment. With firmness in my voice I continued, "Now this time you listen to me. It's Sunday and the test is over, so you don't have to stick around for me anymore. I want you to go wherever it is you have to go and do whatever it is you have to do. You don't have to worry about me anymore. I'm fine. You take care of yourself now."

Getting all mushy wasn't his style or mine so I wrapped it up. "Thanks for everything you did for me. I know I wouldn't be the man I am without you. Everybody in the neighborhood thinks I turned out a lot like you. I know it doesn't make Mommy happy to hear that, but it makes me happy. I hope the apple didn't fall too far from the tree."

I couldn't get myself to say the word *good-bye,* it was just too painful, so I kissed him on the forehead and said, "I'll see you around."

I went into the bathroom, washed my face, and got myself together before going back out to the hallway where Mom was waiting. I smiled at her and said, "You know he was never a good listener before, so I just hope he was paying attention this time."

She smiled, hugged me, and in an encouraging tone said, "I'm sure he was listening, sweetheart."

I'm not so sure she believed it would work but we both thought it was worth a try. I must have looked like crap and my mother was worried about me. She said, "You must be hungry by now, why don't you go down to the cafeteria and get something to eat?"

We were all exhausted at this point. We had been by his bedside for almost a day and a half, but I was neither sleepy nor hungry. Mom resumed her place in the chair by his bed and I continued my pacing up and down the hallway.

For a while I stayed with my aunt, uncle, and cousins in the lounge down the hall listening to more stories about my father. Occasionally we would look out the window to watch the snow piling up outside and wonder how we were going to get home when this was all over. I joked, "Don't worry, it might be springtime before he finally decides to give up."

I couldn't help but feel he was in the room with us. Whenever there was a party he was always the center of attention, the one with the funny stories. When I was growing up Dad would sit on the front porch to read a book or to keep an eye on the kids playing ball out in the street. It wouldn't be long before the neighbors joined in and the party was on. It wasn't unusual for these get-togethers to last late into the night with half the block on our front porch.

A few hours had passed since Dad and I had our heart-to-heart talk and I was beginning to wonder if he had paid any attention to me. Suddenly I saw my sister waving frantically for me to join them in his room. I ran down and saw Mom standing next to him, crying. The room was peaceful and silent except for Mom's gentle sobs. My sisters and I put our arms around her. His labored breathing and struggle for life had ended. It was over.

While I was down the hall with the rest of the family and while Mom and my younger sister dozed off in the room, Dad had finally let go. During the quietness just after midnight, with the snow falling outside and his family around him, Dad stopped fighting. He always said he had one good fight left in him, and he saved it for his son. He gave up the fight only because I told him it was okay to do so. Now I had one of my own. We made a promise to each other, and I was not going to let the last conversation I had with my father on this earth be a lie. I had a test to take and I was going to kick some ass.

Twenty-two months later I was promoted to the rank of lieutenant in the New York City Police Department. The day of my promotion I was standing in the auditorium of One Police Plaza wearing my dress uniform and waiting for the ceremony to begin. The room was filled with other police officers whose big day had come also. Everyone's proud families were there, eager to cheer us on. Mom made her way through the crowded room and called me over. The ceremony was about to begin, but the excitement on her face told me she had something important to tell me. She pointed to a far-off corner at the end of the stage and said, "You know your father is standing right over there, I can feel it." I looked but saw nothing. She went on to tell me that he was standing there with his hands clasped behind his back, rocking back and forth in the heel-to-toe motion he so often used. I desperately wanted to see or feel something, but nothing came. Like my father, my mother is not the type you want to argue with, so I just nodded my head and agreed with her. But as the dignitaries found their seats on the dais and the police commissioner prepared to speak, I got the feeling Mom was right. Her instincts were always right. He was here, up on the stage somewhere, because this was his big day also. And he fought for it just as hard as I did.

12

Cops Don't Cry

A few months back I had come home late from work again. This time my wife was at the door waiting for me. I had just finished working sixteen hours and was dead tired. I had responded to a shooting the night before, right at the end of my tour, and got stuck doing a double. This wasn't anything unusual, it happened all the time.

It was early the next morning when I finally made it home, and when I walked in she had that look on her face that said, "We gotta talk." I hated that look. That look was never good news for me, so I started to get nervous. What I hated more than anything was that the look was sometimes followed by "I was watching Oprah today and . . ."

I hated Oprah. I hated Dr. Phil. Sometimes they would have some cheating husband on. The guy would look normal enough, but it turned out that he was living a lie. He had a double life that went on for years. He would confess to the whole world that he had another family in another city, and his wife never had a clue. Or sometimes they would have some other maniac on who was doing something even crazier. My wife loved and trusted me, but sometimes because of my long absences, the eye of suspicion was cast upon me.

After recapping that day's episode, she would start peppering me with questions, trying to figure out what I was doing when I was gone so long. It's not that I could blame her, police work is not conducive to a normal lifestyle or a happy marriage. My getting stuck at work and doing sixteen or even twenty-four hours straight was a weekly occurrence. I couldn't blame her for being suspicious.

Whether it was talk-show related or not, these "we gotta talk" looks always meant trouble for me.

So when I came in and got met by The Look, it was nothing unusual. I was getting used to it. But this time The Look was followed by "I'm really tired of being alone—I can't take it anymore."

I felt myself starting to get nervous. The "I can't take it anymore" part was something new. Right then, I would have rather been chasing a guy with a gun down a dark alley instead of "having to talk."

I didn't waste any time. I countered with my usual tap dance, a flurry of hugs and kisses, and said, "I miss you too. I don't like having to work this much either, but it's my job."

This time, though, she meant business. She followed it up with an ultimatum. "I want a dog and I want one *now*!"

When the word *dog* came out, I was relieved. It was like a ton of weight was lifted off my shoulders. I felt the knot in my stomach instantly disappear. There was another word she could have thrown at me that would have been a lot tougher to deal with. I would not have been the first cop to get divorced because he was married to the job. I was a good provider, but I probably wasn't the best husband in the world.

My wife is an animal nut, or I should say animal lover. If she had her way she would buy a big farm and save all the stray and unloved dogs she could find. The sight of a dead deer on the side of the road would make her cry and ruin her whole day.

So a dog it would be! If that made her happy and relieved some of the loneliness, then I would get her whatever she wanted. And there was no way I was ever going to tell her no. From the first day I met her, I could never really say no to her about anything. She had me wrapped around her little finger, and talking me into things was easy for her. If she had asked me for a giraffe, I probably would have gotten her two.

It only took about two minutes for me to start getting really excited about the dog. I liked dogs, who doesn't? I pictured us playing fetch with a stick, wrestling, and going on long hikes in the mountains. Plus I thought it would be a great idea to have a dog around to protect her while I was working all night.

But my dreams of getting a real dog were shattered when I asked her what type she wanted. She stuck her hands out, holding them about twelve inches apart, and with a big smile said, "Oh, about this size."

At the time, I hadn't been married very long, but already I knew that to have a happy marriage, you have to compromise. I wanted a big dog. She wanted a little dog. So after a little discussion we compromised and decided to get a . . . little dog.

I didn't want or need a big scary pooch to walk through the neighborhood with. I didn't need to terrorize everything in my path. My penis is an adequate size, and I don't feel the need to overcompensate and show the world what a man I am by walking around with a four-legged killer. I just wanted a real dog. Something to fetch a stick, wrestle with, or maybe scare away a burglar.

After a long search my wife finally found the perfect dog. It was called a Brussels griffon. Actually, when you said it you were supposed to pronounce it Brussels griffooooon, purring the griffooooon part like you were trying to speak French or something. To say he was ugly was to be very kind. And to call him a dog was to be even kinder. I never saw anything like this in my life. The hair on top of his head stood straight up, and he probably only weighed five pounds soaking wet and with rocks in his pockets. If he'd had pockets.

After we picked him up, we drove home with the little guy cradled inside my wife's coat. His tiny face stuck out and his little black eyes stared at me while I drove. Occasionally I would reach over to let him sniff and lick my hand. He definitely wasn't what I had wanted, but for some reason the little bastard was hard to resist.

Meanwhile my wife was rambling on about all the things she needed to buy for him. This was getting crazier by the minute. We went to a pet store to buy him a bed and food and whatever else she could think of that he might need. Luckily I was able to talk her out of buying him the little yellow raincoat, but the red and white ski sweater with the pom-pom on the hood—she promised—was going to be his Christmas present. I swore to myself right then and there that he wouldn't be wearing anything with a pom-pom while I walked him.

This has to be a tough time for any puppy, not knowing where he's going or what kind of a life he's in for. He could be headed for a life of toys, treats, and sleeping on the sofa. Or living with some asshole who wants to raise him for fighting. My wife whispered to me, "Look, look." He was sound asleep in her arms. I guess he knew this was going to work out just fine. We named him Griffin.

When we brought him home, guess what happened? The first night he was in bed sleeping between us. He was so tiny my wife surrounded him with pillows so I wouldn't roll over and crush him.

It didn't take long for the little guy to grow on me. He was definitely a momma's boy, but for some reason at night he wanted to sleep right next to me. All day long he would follow my wife around the house wanting her to pick him up, but at bedtime, he wanted to sleep snuggled next to his dad. This irked his over-protective mother, who coddled and pampered him all day long.

This irked *me* because the little five-pound bulldozer would push me off the bed. He would snuggle in close, causing me to inch away so as not to roll over on him. The next thing I knew, in the middle of the night I was falling off the bed.

A couple of times I took him on walks in the mountains near our house, and surprisingly the little guy was a hiker. His little legs chugged away, as he did his best to keep up. He would march up the trail, going over, under, or around fallen logs. He would jump over or walk right through puddles. He rarely needed help. He was a big dog in a little dog's body. He was not what I had wanted, but I was very proud of him.

At work I told all the guys about my new dog. I told them he was small but didn't really explain how small. Then on one of my days off I brought him to the precinct. There were a few guys standing outside the station house when I came walking down the block. They couldn't stop laughing at me and my little man-eater, all five pounds of him. He was strutting down the block with his chest puffed out, not knowing he was a little dog, or that anyone was laughing at him.

When I walked up the front steps one of the cops went in ahead of me and announced to everyone in a serious voice to step back and clear the way because the lieutenant was coming in with his dog. Everyone looked up from what they were doing, expecting me to come in with some killer. They all cracked up when the little guy came strutting in like he owned the place.

He was a great walking companion. The only problem was, every once in a while something—usually a loud noise—would startle him, and he would try to bolt. A loud truck, a siren, or something similar could set him off, but curiously not every time. I was hoping he would mature and grow out of it.

My car was acting up, so I brought it to the mechanic's, which was about a mile away from my house. I dropped the car off in the morning and walked home. Whenever I have a choice between walking or taking the bus, I'll walk every time. Later in the day the mechanic called me to say the car was ready and I could pick it up that night. I had a mile to walk back to the garage, so I decided to take my little walking buddy with me for company. It was winter-time in New York, so the sun set early but the weather was mild, and it seemed like a nice night for a walk.

I had one of those retractable leashes that stretches out about ten feet, but after a few minutes of running ahead and lagging behind, sniffing everything we passed, he fell into rhythm right alongside me. He was matching me step for step and I hardly knew he was there. The leash hung comfortably in my hand as he stayed right at my side.

He had gotten the hang of things and that night, as usual, was the perfect walking partner. He knew how to pause when we reached an intersection and wait for me to go first. If I saw him get tired I could always pick him up—but he never did.

I would get mixed reviews from the people we passed on the street. Some thought he was cute and some thought he was ugly.

But it seemed almost everyone gave us a comment or at least a look. Luckily it was always the women who thought he was cute. He was better than a baby in the park for starting a conversation.

As for the ones, mostly guys, who said he was ugly, after they passed I would whisper to Griffin not to pay any attention to that asshole. Sometimes when we would pass an aggressive dog who would bark and growl, I would scoop Griff up, holding him in the crook of my arm like a running back holding a football, trying to protect him. I would rather get bit than let anything happen to him.

The guys we passed with the pit bulls probably questioned my sexuality when I scooped the little guy up in my arms. I didn't care, Griffin and I were secure in our manhood. They could go fuck themselves.

Everything was great that night, and we were enjoying our walk together like we always did. The little guy was right next to me, matching me stride for stride. When we approached a busy intersection he stopped and waited for me to let him know it was okay to cross. He was a quick learner and I was proud of him.

We were almost at the garage when all of a sudden, it happened. Behind us there was a very loud BANG. It sounded like a truck backfiring. It startled the hell out of me, but it really scared Griffin. Both of us must have jumped two feet in the air.

I still don't know how it happened, but in the split second when we both jumped, Griff somehow yanked the leash out of my hand. He was small, but he was quick, and he took off like a shot. As he sped off toward the busy street dragging the leash behind him, it retracted and smacked him in the side. This only scared him even more.

I panicked! Instantly my heart was in my throat. The only chance I had to catch him was to go for the leash dragging behind him. I dove for it—but missed. It was obvious he didn't know where he was running to or even why. He just got scared and felt the need to run.

It was dark and the intersection was busy. Cars were speeding in all directions. I could see the drivers staring straight ahead, listening to the radio or thinking about who knows what. Nobody was looking for a panicked little puppy running right toward them.

I could hear myself yelling "NO, NO, NO!" as I watched the distance between us grow larger. He could have run in any direction, but he didn't, he ran straight toward the oncoming cars. If he had run in another direction, I know I could have caught him, but for some reason, he ran right toward four lanes of speeding traffic.

I was hoping someone would see him, but it was dark and he was so small. I ran after him, yelling and waving my arms. The brisk breeze smacked me in the face as the cars whizzed past me. The blinding high beams being flashed at me should have been a warning to get out of the street before I got myself killed, but I didn't care. I was like an absolute lunatic running through the middle of rush-hour traffic. The drivers couldn't see him, but I was hoping they could see me.

I know this sounds crazy, but at that moment I just didn't care if I got hit by a car. I didn't care if a truck plowed over me! I had to save that little dog. I was never so determined in my entire life to save something as I was at that moment.

People were beeping their horns and flashing their lights, thinking I was some nut running into traffic. I was in the middle of a very busy intersection along Route 9W. It was the main thoroughfare for cars, trucks, and buses in our town, and I wouldn't be the first person to get run over and killed there.

It didn't take long, only a few seconds before a car was bearing down on him only a few feet away. I know I wasn't thinking straight, but for the briefest moment I envisioned myself putting my shoulder down and blocking the speeding car like a football player making a tackle. I believed I could stop that car in its tracks.

Even with the flashing high beams half blinding me, I could still see Griff getting sucked under the wheels—and popping out the side. He was so small I know the driver never saw him and probably never felt anything, but luckily he saw me. With the horn blaring and tires screeching, the car swerved and narrowly missed me. He just kept going, anxious to get away from the lunatic who tried to attack his car.

I ran up to Griff, who was now lying in the road, and fell to my knees. He was motionless, unable to move. His tiny body was crushed and broken, but he was still breathing. Other speeding cars were swerving around me, beeping their horns and flashing their lights. The drivers were yelling at me to get out of the road and threatening to call the police. I didn't care. I hovered over Griff, trying to protect him from any more harm, and refused to move.

He was still alive, but it was clear he was hurt bad. My hands were shaking and I was starting to cry. I was babbling something like "I'm sorry, buddy."

I tried to sound confident and reassuring, like I am with all my shooting and stabbing victims I deal with out in the street, and said, "You're going to be all right." But this was different. Out in the street it's all business with me, I'm the cop and they are the crime victim. This time it was my little buddy lying there dying. I was suddenly sick to my stomach with grief.

As a New York City cop I've seen more horror, misery, and blood than anyone other than a soldier at war could ever imagine. And I never let it get to me. I handled it like a professional. I could stand stone-faced watching mothers cry over their dead children and just focus on doing my job. Cops learn to build a wall between their feelings and the outside world. But now I was in the middle of traffic kneeling over a dying little puppy and going to pieces.

Over the years since then I've looked back and realized some things just happen. I don't know how or why he yanked that leash out of my hand—it just happened. I know it wasn't my fault, but at that moment I felt responsible. He wasn't just a funny-looking puppy anymore—he was my little boy.

As gently as I could, I scooped him up in my arms and got back on the sidewalk. I had to get him to a hospital, but I didn't know where it was. He didn't need just a vet, he needed an emergency room. I was frantic. I had no car, and in my town cabs don't just ride around looking for fares. I needed help.

Some woman who realized what had happened stopped and asked if she could help. I told her I needed to get my dog to a hospital in a hurry. She didn't know me but opened her passenger door and said, "Get in."

I jumped into her car, expecting her to speed off to the nearest animal hospital, but she just sat there looking at me and finally said, "Where's the hospital?" She didn't know either. I have never felt as helpless as I did at that moment. I felt bad for the woman. Tears were rolling down her face, she felt helpless too. I did not know where the hospital was, and my little pal was dying in my arms.

I don't know if someone called the cops on me or the patrol car just happened to be passing by, but I saw a police car stop in the middle of the intersection. The cop was turning his head, looking around in all directions. Thank God he was here. There is an unwritten rule in police work that cops always help other cops. It doesn't matter what the problem is, where you're at, or where you're from, you can always count on another cop to take care of you.

I jumped out of the woman's car and ran toward the police car. I cradled Griffin in one arm and reached for my shield with the other. I didn't know if he was responding to a call about a lunatic running into traffic, so the last thing I needed was for him to think that the lunatic was now attacking him.

As I got closer to the patrol car I started yelling, "I'm on the job!" He seemed a little alarmed, but as I got closer he saw the shiny gold shield dangling in my hand and the unconscious puppy cradled in the crook of my arm. As quickly as I could, I shoved my shield into the open driver's window and explained to him that I was a cop and my dog got hit by a car. I told him I needed to get Griff to a hospital as soon as possible. He took one look at the shield, the tiny puppy in my arms, and the frantic look on my face, and said, "Get in."

I jumped into the back and slammed the door shut while he made a U-turn and flipped on the red light and siren. When he hit the gas I was pushed back into the seat. Good, I thought, we're going to the hospital and we're moving fast. I held on to Griffin.

The cop was sharp. Without missing a beat, he was on the radio notifying the dispatcher what he had and telling her to call the animal hospital and have them standing by. Hearing that made me feel better. I wasn't standing helpless in the middle of traffic anymore. Things were happening.

The blaring siren and swirling red lights made me feel a little better because I was in my element. Being in the back of the police car helped a little bit—but not enough. I felt myself completely going to pieces. I looked down at Griff and saw blood and bubbles frothing out of his nose and mouth. I could hear a faint gurgling sound as he struggled and fought for every breath. This was bad, his lungs were punctured and were filling with blood. I had seen this in people and I knew he wouldn't last much longer.

I was a mess. Tears were running down my face, and I was babbling, "Hold on, buddy. You gotta hold on. Don't give up, we're almost there. Come on, you gotta stay with me. Don't give up."

I must have sounded like some schoolgirl who got dumped on her prom night. This is not how a hard-core New York City cop should behave in a crisis. This was definitely not me. I've been through a lot worse shit than this.

For a brief moment I felt a little self-conscious, weeping and carrying on the way I was in front of another cop. So I started to tell him that this was my wife's dog, and I was upset because I knew she was going to be very upset. I knew it didn't make any sense when I said it, but I was trying to man up. I was trying to come up with an excuse for why I was losing it.

But when I looked up, I saw this cop—who didn't even know me—wiping his eyes. He didn't look back, or say anything. He just kept staring straight ahead, driving as fast as he could. He kept his one hand on the steering wheel while he wiped his eyes with the other. I guess he didn't want me to see that he was getting weepy also. I'm sure he had seen his share of blood and guts and misery in his career—but this little puppy was getting to the both of us.

I looked back down at Griff to see how he was doing and at that moment—it happened. I heard a small puff of air exhale from his nose and mouth while his chest fell. I waited for it to rise again. I waited for what seemed like a long time, then I gently shook his tiny broken body, trying to coax him into taking another breath. Nothing. The little guy was a fighter, and I wanted him to fight for another breath just like he had been doing for the last few minutes—but he didn't. The fight was over. His injuries were too severe, and I watched him take his last breath.

Without warning the cop jerked the wheel to the left, jammed on the brakes, and suddenly we were in the parking lot of the animal hospital. The front door was propped open, and the doctor was standing there waving his arms, motioning for us to hurry inside. I jumped out of the car and with Griff cradled in my arms, I ran past the vet and into the building. The vet was running behind me yelling directions and pointing to a room in the back that was waiting for us.

There was a stainless-steel table in the middle of the room with a big surgical light shining on it from above. As gently as I could, I placed Griff on the table and backed away so the doctor could get to work. But he took one look at Griff, then turned to me and said as compassionately as he could, "I'm sorry, there's nothing I can do." He wasn't telling me anything I didn't already know. I knew he was dead. I saw him take his last breath and die in my arms only a minute or two before. I was just hoping for some kind of miracle.

I stood there staring at Griff lying on that cold steel table. The glaring surgical light shining down from above made everything around me seem dark and distant. I never felt so alone as I did at that moment. The cop turned and walked out of the room. Men don't like to cry in front of other men.

In another feeble attempt to regain my manhood, I babbled to the doctor the same lie I told the cop, that this was my wife's dog, and I was really upset for her. The doctor politely nodded his head—he knew I was full of shit. Then he took his cue from the cop, excused himself, and left the room so I could be alone, and say my good-byes.

I really can't explain it, I didn't get this emotional when my father died. A few years back I watched a three-year-old girl die in the emergency room. She had drowned in the bathtub while taking a bath. We got her to the emergency room within minutes, but it was too late. I remember standing there as they pronounced her dead. I willed myself not to feel anything. Before I let one ounce of emotion well up inside me, I crammed my mind with all the notifications and reports that had to be done. I left no room for any other thoughts. My demeanor was all business. I had a job to do. So why was this so different?

When the vet left us alone, I leaned on the table on one elbow, hovering over my little buddy. I was petting him and apologizing for letting this happen. I felt responsible. Deep down I knew it wasn't my fault, but I still felt terrible. My heart was broken.

My legs got wobbly and I actually felt weak. I was drained. There was a chair against the wall, so I sat, trying to get my head screwed back on straight. I was trying to figure out how I was going to tell my wife. How the fuck was I going to explain this?

After a little while the vet came back in, and when he felt the time was right asked me what I wanted to do with the remains. I still wasn't in any mood to make a decision, so I told the doctor I would be back in the morning to make the "arrangements." I'm glad he didn't ask me for money. I might have strangled him.

When I walked outside, the cop and I both had our game faces back on. Cops don't cry—remember that. I think it was an episode we would both rather put behind us. I shook his hand and thanked him, adding I knew I could always count on another cop for help.

When I looked around, I didn't know where the hell I was. This was some dingy little animal hospital tucked in the middle of nowhere. It was dark, and the hospital was surrounded by trees. I looked at the road in front of me and didn't know whether to go left or right. The cop, realizing I didn't know where I was, pointed to the patrol car and said, "Get in."

This time I sat in the front seat; the back is for perps and victims, and I was neither. In the front I felt more in control. I felt like I was a cop again.

On the ride back I gave him the same spiel I gave him before—about how Griffin was really my wife's, and that I was really upset for her and not just for that little dog. He knew I was full of shit but nodded his head and went along with it. I appreciated that as much as I appreciated the ride.

When we pulled into my driveway I shook his hand, thanking him profusely. I handed him my business card and told him if he ever needed anything down in Manhattan, don't hesitate to ask. That's the way it works.

My wife wasn't home yet, so the house was empty. It felt especially empty now without Griffin. I paced between the kitchen and the living room, wondering how I was going to break the news to Griffin's overprotective mother. The sight of his water and food bowls on the floor was getting to me, so I walked upstairs to try and think this through.

I paced up and down the hall, walking aimlessly in and out of each bedroom. Like Griffin, I didn't know where I was going, I just felt the need to move. I kept looking at the clock, not wanting my wife to come home just yet. I wasn't looking forward to telling her, but I didn't want to be alone anymore either. I really needed to be with her. It sounds mushy, but I needed a hug.

I stood in the bedroom staring aimlessly out the window. The image of that car bearing down on Griffin kept playing over and over in my head. The flashing high beams and honking horns wouldn't go away. As I thought about what happened, I suddenly became angry. I was angry at the world—but especially at myself. Rage welled up inside of me! I was furious about what happened to that innocent little dog.

I don't know if I wanted to punish myself or just hit something, but I hauled off and head-butted the closet door. It was like a move right out of WWE wrestling. But this wasn't fake, and the door was made out of some pretty hard wood. I hit it so hard I knocked myself senseless. I was literally seeing stars!

After a few seconds, when I finally got my eyes to focus again, I could see a perfectly round hole in the center of the door, the exact shape of my now throbbing forehead.

I know it was an incredibly dumb thing to do, but it worked. The shot to the head suddenly snapped me back into reality. I could almost hear the little voice in my head saying, "Get a hold of yourself, dude. This is getting ridiculous."

I walked over to the bathroom and looked into the mirror. There was blood trickling down my forehead. It was running in between my eyes, and a huge red lump was starting to form. I leaned in closer, staring at the bloody bulbous mound, and muttered to myself, "You idiot."

I sat on the edge of the bed holding some tissues on my head, trying to stop the bleeding, when suddenly I heard the front door open. At first I got nervous when my wife yelled out, "I'm home." But then I was actually glad and relieved, I didn't want to be alone anymore. Who knew what I would do next?

She must have gotten suspicious when I didn't answer. Also, there was no little barking Griffin to meet her. I could hear her feet shuffling on the wooden steps as she came upstairs looking for us. She called out our names a few more times. I didn't answer, and obviously Griffin didn't either.

When she walked into the bedroom, her eyes almost popped out of her head. I was standing there with a drained, exhausted look on my face and a bloody red lump in the middle of my forehead that was growing bigger by the minute. My wife's usually not very good in stressful situations, so I braced myself for the impending drama. This was going to be bad. She took one look at my bleeding forehead and started yelling, "What happened to you? What's going on? Where's Griffin?" I tried to think of just the right words but nothing was coming, so I blurted out something like "Griff got hit by a car."

I don't remember exactly what I said because I had half a concussion going on at the time. She heard what I said about Griff, though, and it shocked her, but she was also fixated on my bleeding forehead. And from the looks of me, she immediately assumed I got hit by the car also.

To her credit she took it well. She could tell I was a mess. We had known each other for several years, and she had never seen me like this. She was used to that hard cop exterior that's difficult to shake, even when I'm home. She knew something very bad had happened to me and wanted to help.

She ran downstairs and got me an ice pack for my head. Then we sat down on the bed and I told her the story. She was such an animal lover I didn't know what to expect, but luckily my bleeding lump and near-concussion gave her something else to worry about.

In hindsight, whacking my head on that door was a stroke of brilliance. It really helped defuse the situation.

She was relieved to hear that I wasn't hit by the car also. But I had to explain to her what a head-butt was. She was no wrestling fan. As big a softy as she is, in this crisis she rose to the occasion. It was clear how terrible I felt, and she took on the role as the strong one. I sat there, depressed like a little boy who just lost his best friend, while my mom hugged and comforted me, and held the ice pack on my throbbing noggin.

A week later my wife had another problem to deal with. She told me there was a surprise birthday party for my cousin Tony and we were invited. I told her I didn't want to go. I was still feeling crappy and in no mood for a party. What I did not know was, the party was actually for me. It was a surprise party that had been planned weeks earlier to celebrate my promotion to lieutenant. My family was in a panic. They had spent quite a few bucks renting a nice hall, and about ninety people said they were coming. My mother called to plead with me, explaining that Tony would be very disappointed if I didn't show up for his big party. My head had healed, but my heart was still broken. I was still in no mood to go to a party and have fun.

I like to think that I'm a sharp investigator, but I never caught on. My wife, mother, and sisters were taking turns begging me not to disappoint Tony. Luckily, right before it got to the point where they were going to have to tell me the party was for me, I agreed to go.

When I walked in, everybody yelled, "Surprise!" And it certainly was. Either I'm not as sharp as I thought or my wife's a better liar than I give her credit for. Maybe that knock on the head was even harder than I thought it was. I was totally and completely surprised.

As I looked around at all the people who came to celebrate my promotion, I realized life wasn't so bad. At the party I was surrounded by people who really cared about me, and it helped snap me out of my doldrums. One of my buddies gave me a golf club for a present, so when I grabbed the microphone to thank everyone for coming, I looked like Bob Hope at a USO show. I had a great time.

During my years of police work, I've seen people die in almost every way imaginable: hit by cars, trucks, buses, trains, and even a plane (an Airbus A300). I've seen them shot, stabbed, bludgeoned, hanged, and drowned, and seen them jump off buildings. But nothing ever got to me like that puppy dying in my arms. It was the one time that the wall I had built between my feelings and the outside world didn't help. Maybe cops don't cry, but daddies of little puppies do.

The week prior to the party, life had sucked big-time. It would continue to suck for a few more weeks until my wife had a great idea: we would get another funny-looking little Brussels griffon. And we did. His name was Spanky.

13

Big Day

The hot shower felt good on my aching, stressed-out muscles. I hadn't gotten much sleep the past couple of nights, and all the running around was starting to catch up with me. So I stayed in there, taking my time, letting the steamy water do its job while I enjoyed the last few minutes of solitude, before what was going to be a couple of really hectic days.

I had been working on a big case—a major narcotics investigation—and there had been a million tiny details to deal with before we finally shut it down. When we shut down a case we go out and lock up all our subjects at the same time. We call it "takedown day," and today was that day. This was going to be big for me and the Gang Squad, maybe not the biggest day of my career, but definitely one to remember.

The case was called Operation Gladiator. It was in the making for almost a year, and we had put a lot of work into it. After a period of time, cases reach a natural conclusion because you've taken it as far as it can go, and over the past twelve months we had taken it pretty far. Through some good police work we managed to infiltrate three separate crews of Bloods that were dealing drugs up in Harlem. My undercover detectives had bought drugs and guns from these guys, and in the process we identified fifty-two subjects. Today we were going to start "hitting" doors, and putting handcuffs on these assholes. The plan for today was to start scooping up our main subjects, then hit seventeen search warrants simultaneously. And I figured before this thing was over, we were probably going to have at least another seventeen to hit. It was too much for just my squad to execute, so every gang unit in the city was going to lend us a few teams so we could get most of it done in one day. It was going to be a big operation, and just the thought of it had all of us wound up.

My squad consisted of almost fifty cops, detectives, and sergeants, and anything gang-related on the island of Manhattan was our responsibility. It seemed like every other day we would get involved in some kind of caper that would cause you to pull your hair out. Maybe that's why mine is gone. I didn't mind giving my heart and soul to the job, but I would really like my curly hair back.

Before we started this investigation a couple of my detectives spoke to the commanding officer of the precinct, figuring it had some potential to be a good long-term major case. The CO was getting his nuts twisted about his crime stats, and the Detective Squad had a few unsolved homicides and nonfatal shootings that were going nowhere fast. The more I looked at it the more I liked it, but I had to pick my battles carefully.

The case centered around a housing project and the blocks that surrounded it. For a long time the neighborhood had been plagued with drug dealing, shootings, stabbings, robberies, and any other crime you can think of that occurs when junkies and drug dealers take over a neighborhood. Murder and mayhem were a daily occurrence, and most of the problems in the neighborhood seemed to have the same root cause, drugs—and the drug of choice around here was crack.

When you just look at pin maps, a neighborhood can look like a war zone. We had one color for homicides, another for nonfatal shootings, while other parts of the rainbow represented felony assaults, robberies, burglaries, and grand larcenies. Each pin indicated where a body dropped or a life-changing felony occurred. If one of those little pins was you, you might be dead, or in a wheelchair. Or maybe if you were lucky, you ended up with just a busted head, and a little PTSD that keeps you awake at night and afraid to leave the house.

It seems hard to believe that some really decent people live in these neighborhoods because we hardly ever get to see them. They wake up in the morning, send their kids to school, then go to work. When evening comes, they barricade themselves inside their apartments and lock the door, afraid to come out. When the sun goes down there's not too much hanging around, unless you want to get caught in the cross fire of two assholes shooting it out, and maybe end up as a colorful dot on the map. So at night, the only people out in the street were the gangsters, junkies, crackheads, prostitutes, and otherwise useless individuals who had nothing better to do with their lives. And us.

Locking up fifty-two really hard-core shitheads makes you feel good about yourself, and about being a cop. You learn early on that you can't save the whole world, but you can make an impact on one neighborhood at a time. And with some hard work and a little bit of luck you can make that pin map a little less colorful next month.

When a problem becomes so bad that it is necessary to start a major case, it gets a name. Just like when a storm gets big and bad enough to become a hurricane, it gets a name. Only we don't give it a sissy name, we think of something cool, and so we named this one Operation Gladiator. People often ask how we come up with these names. It's not that complicated. One night, after doing a gun buy from one of our main subjects, we were sitting in the office eating takeout and discussing the case. On the TV was the movie *Gladiator*, which we were watching for probably the tenth time. And as we sat there watching Russell Crowe whack some bad guy's head off with a sword, my lead detective on the case says, "Hey Lieutenant, what about Operation Gladiator?" All I could do was smile.

On TV there are always one or two heroes working the big case, trying to take down some drug crew. In reality it's not like that at all. None of us are heroes, and if anybody tells you he is, he's full of shit and has an ego problem. It's always a team effort, and I was lucky to have some genuinely talented and dedicated investigators working for me. Without them, none of this would have been possible and that neighborhood would continue to be a war zone.

When we started this case, I had no idea it was going to turn out to be as involved as it did, but these things tend to take on a life of their own and when they do, you give up your life. You start to eat, sleep, and breathe the case. The closer you are to takedown day, the more hectic things get: drug buys, gun buys, and surveillance operations at all hours of the day and night. You start to replace sleep with power naps in the office, and real food with cheeseburgers, pizza, and Chinese. I was going to be glad when this case was finally over. Then maybe I could get back to somewhat of a normal life, at least until we started another one.

I stepped out of the shower and toweled off. I was surprisingly wide awake, considering the amount of sleep I had been getting, but I think it was more nerves and adrenaline keeping me going than anything else. I checked my cell phone and had no missed calls. I had some of my guys doing late-night surveillance on our main subjects, so we could find them in the morning. We called it "putting them to bed," and if I had no early-morning calls, that meant no problems.

I sat down on the bed next to the clean clothes I had laid out and got ready to get dressed. Today there was going to be a lot of running around so the "uniform of the day" was going to be jeans and sneakers. I had the nice suit and tie in my locker for another big day, tomorrow—the press conference. I also told my lead guys to have a nice suit ready because I wanted them up there with me. Two days before, when I briefed my boss on the case, he said the Chief of Detectives liked it so much he wanted to make a big thing out of it in the media when it was over. That is, of course, if the takedown went well. If it didn't go well, there would be no press conference, no pats on the back, and my career would come to a grinding halt. If something went wrong, no matter whose fault it was, even if it was no one's fault, the big finger of blame would point at me. That just added to the stress I already have when taking down a case like this.

I turned on the TV and switched it to CNN while I got ready. I finished getting dressed, then patted myself down, going through my regular daily checklist: gun, spare magazine, shield, money, handcuffs, and cell phone. I was half paying attention to the TV when I noticed that CNN had switched to a live shot of the World Trade Center. There seemed to be a fire in the upper floors of one of the towers and smoke was pouring out the windows. I turned up the volume just as the reporter was saying a small plane had flown into the North Tower. The live shot they were showing was taken from a helicopter, and the first thing that struck me was how absolutely clear and blue the sky was. There was not a cloud anywhere in sight—it was a beautiful fall morning. It was Tuesday, September 11, 2001.

My wife grew up in Manhattan, and I knew she would want to see this, so I called her over and said, "Hey honey, check this out. There seems to be a pretty big fire going on at the Trade Center."

She came into the bedroom, and we both stood there watching the smoke pour out of the upper floors. "What happened?" she asked. I said, "I don't know, they're saying a small plane flew into the tower, but I don't know how that could happen, there is not a cloud in the sky."

Just then, as we stood there watching, a jetliner came into view and flew into the other tower, causing a large fireball to explode. Now both towers were on fire. I don't think I said a word, I was completely stunned, but my wife let out a scream I'll never forget for as long as I live—it went right through me. It was a harsh, guttural scream that came from deep inside her, like she was in pain. I reached out and grabbed her, pulling her close to me in a bear hug, and held on tight. She had her face buried in my chest, crying uncontrollably. I kept pulling her closer and tighter, telling her in a calm voice to relax, that everything was going to be okay, but that was bullshit. I knew nothing was gonna be okay. Right before my eyes the whole world had changed and nothing was going to be all right—ever again.

At the time most of us had never heard of Osama bin Laden or al Qaeda, but one thing was obvious: this was no accident, it was terrorism. And when I heard the reporter say that the United States was under attack, a cold chill went through me. What I saw was New York City being attacked, and I was a New York City cop. Now the big case I had been working on for almost a year and the fifty-two individuals I planned on arresting this morning were already forgotten.

I stood there holding my wife, while staring at the TV screen. On the outside I had to stay calm and reassuring, because she was flipping out. But on the inside my mind was going a hundred miles an hour. My voice was barely above a whisper as I kept telling her everything was going to be okay, but my brain was screaming, thinking of all the things I had to do, and the first thing I had to do was get to work.

My wife was holding on to me as tight as she could, as her fingers dug into my back. I could feel the front of my shirt was wet from her tears and hot, hyperventilating breath. I hadn't said anything, but she knew what was coming next, and it was going to be as painful and difficult to deal with as watching that plane hit the tower. She only looked up long enough to say, "Please don't leave me . . . not this time."

At a time like this, most wives who have a normal husband expect their spouse to race home and take care of them. But not us; being married to a cop is anything but normal. While most other women's husbands were heading home, I was heading for the door. Being a cop's wife is a tough life. I don't know how she put up with me all those years.

Whenever I could I would try to make it easier for her. Sometimes when I was working late I would call her—and lie. I would tell that I was having a quiet night, that I was in the office doing paperwork. I would convince her that I was fine, and she should go to bed and get some sleep. But in reality while I was talking to her I was about to enter a very dangerous situation, guns at the ready.

I stood there holding her, trying to calm her down while staring at the screen for what seemed like an eternity, but in truth it was probably only a minute or two. When I loosened my grip on her she knew exactly what that meant. I tried to step back away from her, but it wasn't that easy because she held on tight and wouldn't let go. When I finally got her to let go, she just stood there with her empty arms folded in front of her, staring at the floor, scared and lonely. It broke my heart to see her like that, so I reached down, held her wet, tear-soaked face in both my hands, and very softly said, "You understand, don't you?" She didn't say anything, she just gave me a halfhearted nod because I wasn't telling her anything she didn't already know. But that didn't mean she liked it.

Sometimes people ask how cops can see the things we see, and do the things we do, and not let it get to us. The answer is, very early in your career you learn how to build a wall between yourself and your feelings. It's not easy to leave your family like this, just like it's not easy to stand over some dead guy out in the street, or especially some dead kid. From day one, every time you have to deal with something that would give a normal person nightmares, it places another brick in the wall. And the wall protects you. It helps you detach and lets you do your job. It doesn't always save you from the nightmares later on, but it does help you do your job. If I feel the need to shake my fist at the world and ask God why, there will be plenty of time for that later. Right now, all I could think about was logistics: people, cars, equipment, and the fastest way possible to ground zero.

I darted over to the closet, grabbed my small gym bag, and threw in some clothes because I knew I wasn't going to be home for at least a couple of days. With my bag stuffed with whatever I could grab, I turned to my wife and said, "I'll try and call you later." But when I tried to leave, she reached out with both hands, grabbed me by the arm, and pleaded with me, "Just wait a second." It kind of shocked me back into the moment, back into that bedroom, and back to being a husband again. She said, "I know you have to go—but can you just wait a second?"

At that moment, the clock stopped ticking, the earth stopped rotating, and it was just my wife and me. For a very brief few seconds, everything around us melted away, and nothing in the world mattered but us. I dropped the bag on the floor, reached out, and took her in my arms. I held her so tight I thought I was going to hurt her. I placed a finger under her chin and tried to lift her head so I could look into her eyes, but she wouldn't budge. She just kept her face buried in my chest and held on tight. I asked if she was going to be okay, but she just shushed me. There was nothing to talk about and we both knew it, she just wanted a moment of my undivided attention—before maybe never seeing me again. The hell with the rest of the world—even if it lasted for just one brief moment, this was our time. And as we slowly let go of each other, she looked up at me with her soggy face and bloodshot eyes and very seriously warned me, "You better call me later—don't forget."

We walked downstairs together, letting the moment linger, but when I tried to leave, she called out to me and said, "Wait!" I was getting a little impatient, I needed to get moving, but I stopped dead in my tracks because it seemed like she had one last very important thing to say. And I wanted to hear it, just in case I never saw her again. We stood a few feet apart, me with one hand on the doorknob waiting to hear what was so important, and her trying to stop crying long enough to tell me what she had to say. And that's when she said, "I want to make you . . . a sandwich."

I didn't know whether to laugh or what, I was about to race into who knows what and maybe never come back, and she wanted to make me a snack before I left. She assured me it wouldn't take long, and if I wasn't hungry now, she could wrap it up, so I could take it with me. We both stood there, just looking at each other, and finally she stopped crying long enough to laugh a little.

I yanked open the front door, bolted down the steps, and jumped in the car. As I backed out of the driveway, I saw her standing on the front porch. The laughing had stopped and the crying started again as she waved good-bye. I rolled down the window and said quickly, "I'll call you—but if I don't, please don't worry. I'll be fine." The last thing I heard as my tires screeched out of the driveway was "Be careful!"

The next thing I know, I'm doing about ninety miles an hour down the Palisades Parkway with the red light flashing on the dashboard. I've got the police department radio on the first division listening to all the chaos, and the car radio on the all-news station announcing that there were more unaccounted planes in the air.

I flipped open my cell phone and hit the speed dial for Bobby. He's my administrative sergeant and right-hand man all rolled up into one. I freely admit that I'm administratively challenged. I would rather be out in the street making a collar than doing paperwork, so without Bobby covering my administrative ass, I would be lost. Besides, he was a good friend and I was really going to need him today.

As soon as he answered the phone I said, "You see the news?" I could sense his excitement on the other end of the line, and before I even finished the question he said, "Yeah I saw it. Un-fucking-believable. I guess the takedown is going to have to wait awhile."

I asked him where he was and how soon it would be before he got to the office. He told me he had his girlfriend with him. With Bobby that's not specific enough, so I asked him which one. He said he had the nurse with him and had to drop her off at the hospital first before going to the office. I figured I would most likely get there first, so it would be my job to get everybody squared away and ready to move while I waited for him.

I knew everybody would be in early, gearing up and getting ready for our takedown, so I was sure they would be ready to move out as soon as I got in. I told Bobby, "Hurry up, I'm not going anywhere without you—so don't leave me hanging!"

I could hear him laughing on the other end of the phone. "What the fuck is so funny?" I asked. "You *need* me," he replied, stressing the word *need*. Bobby liked to remind me that I counted on him to keep the squad running smooth, and he was right. And today I was going to need him a lot, so I said, "Yeah, yeah, just get your ass in here as soon as possible." Then I hung up.

Suddenly traffic stopped, so I jammed on the brakes. Up ahead in the distance I could see flashing red lights and a police roadblock. Nothing was moving, cars were at a standstill waiting to be detoured off to who knows where. I couldn't believe it, they had closed off the George Washington Bridge. They were shutting down the city! I had never seen anything like this in my life. I wasn't about to wait for anything, I had to get to work, so I jumped up onto the grass divider and drove around the stopped cars until I reached the barricade. A couple of cops with some really serious looks on their faces stared at me as I got closer. I flashed them my ID and told them I was on the job and needed to get to work. Immediately, no questions asked, they waved me through, and the next thing I knew I was on the bridge. It was an eerie feeling. Except for one or two cars going out of the city, I was the only one on the bridge. This frigging bridge has traffic jams at three in the morning, and here it was in the middle of rush hour and it was completely empty. The world had suddenly become a very different place.

Up until now, I had been flying, doing at least ninety, weaving through traffic with the red lights flashing, but suddenly I was alone, so I stopped for a moment, trying to take it all in. I looked down the river, and from ten miles away I could see the clouds of smoke pouring out of the towers. I could even see the tiny news helicopters buzzing all around, trying to capture the scene for the rest of the world to see. In the distance, I could hear sirens blaring everywhere as every cop and fireman in the city raced downtown, and that's when it hit me—in a few minutes I was going to be one of them. It was all too much to comprehend, and for the second time today, time seemed to stop, and the world stood still. When I woke up this morning I knew this was going to be a really big day, I just didn't know it was going to be like this.

*   *   *

When I got to the office, almost everybody was there gearing up and getting ready to go. I told them to grab everything out of the equipment locker: battering rams, sledgehammers, and pry bars just in case we needed them. My division was assigned to the Detective Bureau, and for some stupid reason I thought we were going to be hitting doors later and executing search warrants all over the city—but I could not have been more wrong. I thought there was going to be some kind of a terrorist watch list with hundreds of names on it, and we would be just one of the units going out to round up the usual suspects. Later in the day, in the middle of all the confusion, I would find out there was a list, but there were only a few names on it, and some were on there twice and most of them were out of the country. As far as police work as I knew it, there was nothing for us to do. My unit would end up being tasked to help set up a temporary morgue, and that's where I would be for the next few months, except for some days digging at the pile that was once the World Trade Center.

In the background the TV was on, and we could see that the first tower had just fallen. I'm sure we all had the "Holy shit" look on our faces, but that was it, there was no panic or hesitation about doing our job. I was kind of surprised by how calm everybody seemed to be, but every cop in that room was a professional and all they could think of was getting downtown, and I could not have been more proud of them. As I watched the chaos and confusion, I was determined to keep my people together as a unit. I was afraid once we got down to ground zero we would get separated, and then we wouldn't find each other for days. I kept stressing to them how we needed to stick together. In the past we had been through a lot of stuff, and I vowed that we were going to go through this together.

A few minutes later Bobby would come roaring up on his motorcycle. I threw him the keys, and we all piled into cars and started speeding down the West Side Highway—and that's when the second tower came down. Bobby remembers we were at Sixty-Second Street when the second plume of dust and smoke filled the sky, and over the radio we could hear the frantic voices of cops yelling that the second building was down. All the traffic was heading north in the opposite direction. There was nothing between us and the Trade Center, and I knew we would be there soon—real soon. Later we would figure out that we missed it by about ten minutes. Grabbing all our gear, getting everyone organized, and waiting for Bobby ended up being a blessing.

I didn't have much of a plan. I wasn't exactly sure where we were going, or what we were going to do once we got there, so we just headed for the smoke and dust. I kept thinking, I'll figure it out once we get there. Bobby and I were in the lead car, and the dust cloud was getting bigger and scarier the closer we got to it. You might be wondering what was going on in my head at a time like that, and the answer is—nothing but business. Not that I'm any braver than anybody else, but at the time my biggest concern was my cops in the cars behind me, They were my squad, my people, and I was responsible for them, and all I could think about was having us do our job, and somehow, at the same time, keeping all of us safe. At a time like this—especially at a time like this—you have to keep your head screwed on straight, and concentrate on doing your job. If you start thinking about anything else, that's how you get hurt.

We made it down to Chambers Street and stopped dead in our tracks because we hit what looked like a wall of dust and smoke. On the other side of that wall, it was dark and hard to see, and I'm not afraid to admit it, the thought of going in there scared the shit out of me. On the corner was a doctor dressed in scrubs, handing out surgical masks to anybody who dared go past the wall. I grabbed a couple, figuring we were going to need them. When I looked at the flimsy little paper mask, I knew this wasn't going to cut it. I figured if I went in there, I was going to choke to death in about two minutes.

We made a left on Chambers Street, stopping at every corner, trying to find an opening in the wall that we could enter, but there was nothing but darkness. I could see people staggering out, covered with this thick gray dust, unable to see or breathe. When I saw some fireman staggering out with these stunned looks on their faces, I knew it was bad in there. Firemen are ballsy guys, and if they needed to get the hell out of there, it had to be really bad.

It seems hard to believe, but I really don't remember much after that. It all seems like a big blur to me. I want to remember more, it was the Pearl Harbor of my generation, but for the most part, all I have are brief snapshots of some of the things we did and saw. Maybe it was just sensory overload—there was so much happening all around us, making it too difficult to absorb everything. Or maybe it's all buried deep in my memory, where it needs to stay—the mind's way of protecting you. I don't know, but I wish I could recall every second of it. When I talk to some of the guys I was with, everybody seems to have their own memories, their own snapshots and images. Some of these memories we shared—some we don't.

I've only told a handful of people what I saw and did down there, usually other cops. When a family member or a civilian friend asks me what it was like, the conversation usually stops when I tell them that most of the time I was assigned to the morgue. I can see it on their faces, they kind of zone out, not wanting to hear about it. Once I confided in my little sister about some of it. I don't know why I told her, I guess I figured if I got hit by a bus the next day, maybe one person in my family should know who I was, and what I did for a living. Her response to my story was "I think you should talk to someone—a professional." I shrugged her off because cops don't open up to anyone except another cop, and if medication is needed, we'll do it over a couple of beers.

The one image that really sticks in my mind is the next morning, September 12. I was standing right in the middle of everything on West Street, looking up at the pile, watching the smoke rise from the fires still smoldering inside. It had been dark for the past twenty hours or so, but now the dust was settling, the sun was rising, and for the first time the universe was shedding some light on what had happened. I was in a business where people die. I understood that and accepted it—but this was different. The only way I could describe it is that it looked like a small nuclear bomb had gone off. When I stood there looking around, surrounded by all that devastation and rubble, I was stunned, but more than anything I was numb. Maybe it was too much for me to comprehend, or maybe it was the wall, doing its best to protect me—just like it had done for the past nineteen years.

In those years I thought I had seen almost everything—nothing really shocked me anymore. Before 9/11 someone would ask me what was the worst thing I ever saw—people like to hear gory stuff—and I would always have a difficult time answering. Was it the guy who jumped off a tall building, or the person hit by a train, or maybe the abused five-year-old boy covered with fifty cigarette burns, courtesy of his crackhead bitch mother? But now the answer was simple.

The one feeling that seemed to overwhelm me in the months and years after was a feeling of inadequacy. When a cop sees something horrible, the way we find closure is to make an arrest, build a case, and see the guilty punished. But there was no police work to do—as I knew it. There were no doors for us to hit, or search warrants to execute, so instead, we would dig through the rubble and process human remains.

On my breaks at the morgue I would walk up to the corner on First Avenue to get some fresh air. I remember family members of the victims standing behind the barricades, waiting, hoping to hear some news that we found their relatives. They were hanging missing-person flyers everywhere, on walls, light poles, mailboxes, you name it. The flyers would always have a picture of a smiling face, usually taken at a party, a picnic, or a graduation, and underneath would be a phone number to call. I was usually dressed in scrubs, so they knew I was from the morgue, and they would give me their flyer and ask if I had found that person. I would take it, study the face carefully, and tell them, "Not yet." I tried to be helpful without giving any false hope. And as carefully as I could, I would fold the flyer and put it in my pocket, and promise if I saw their family member, I would call. I would end up with a pocket full of flyers, but there were never any calls. When I spoke to these people I was as kind and compassionate as I could possibly be, but inside I had to keep my distance. I had to keep that wall between me and them. I desperately wanted to help them but I couldn't, and it broke my heart, because in the months that I was there, there weren't too many faces, just tiny pieces of what used to be people.

A few days into it, we were down at ground zero digging through the rubble. A civilian engineer came over to me and said, "Hey Lieutenant, if I tell you to start running, grab all your people—and start running!" Cops don't normally like being told what to do by civilians, especially when they tell you to run away, but when he pointed to some giant steel beams on top of the pile not too far from us, I understood what he meant. They had bulldozers and cranes moving some of the debris, and he was afraid some of the beams were going to roll down on top of us.

That's when one of my detectives told me that McDonald's had set up a tent a few blocks away on Greenwich Street, and they were giving out free food. *Free* and *food* are every cop's two favorite words, so I rounded up a bunch of the guys and told them, let's go get something to eat. We hadn't had much food or sleep in the past few days, so I figured it was a good time to take a break.

When we got there, we found a small canopy with some tables underneath. There were bags of burgers and fries on one table and sodas on the other, nothing big, just a Happy Meal, but it meant a lot to me. After almost twenty years of police work, I wasn't used to the world being nice to me. Bricks and bottles being thrown off some roof at us was a more common occurrence. I grabbed a bag and a soda and looked for a place to sit, but there wasn't any, so I sat on the curb. I had grabbed a few napkins and tried to clean that gray dust off my hands and face. At the time I didn't know what exactly was in it, but it smelled bad, and I didn't want it on my burger.

I opened the bag and grabbed some fries. They were probably the best-smelling, best-tasting French fries I ever had in my life, because for the past few days, all I was smelling and tasting was the smoke and dust that hung in the air. Plus I was starving. When I reached into the bag to get my burger, I found a folded-up piece of construction paper buried on the bottom, the kind kids use to draw on. At first I didn't know what it was, but when I opened it I realized it was a homemade card done in crayon, by what was probably a five-year-old kid. I guess McDonald's was collecting these cards from kids all over the country, and putting them into the bags was an easy way to get them to the first responders.

Inside the card the kid had drawn two tall buildings with squiggly lines coming out the top—the World Trade Center, with smoke pouring out. Next to the buildings were two stick figures, one was wearing a policeman's hat and the other a fireman's hat. And on the bottom, first in big letters, and then progressively smaller as he tried to cram in everything he wanted to say, the kid wrote, "Thank you. You're my hero." Then he signed it, and after all these years I still remember his name: Alex.

For the past several days I had been numb, like I was made out of stone. All I would allow myself to think about was getting the job done. Everyone deals with an event like this in their own way, and I did it by shutting down emotionally. But when I read this kid's card, something happened inside me. Something deep inside began to bubble up, and I couldn't stop it. I wanted to stop it. I needed to stop it. I had no time for this—not here, not now, not out in the street. There were people out here searching for their lost loved ones, and I felt I didn't deserve the right to be emotional. Besides I was surrounded by my guys, a real hard-core bunch, and I would prefer for them to think of me as heartless. But whatever it was that was bubbling up inside me, I couldn't stop it, and I felt my eyes start to water a little. I covered my face with one hand while I shoved fries in my mouth with the other, hoping it just looked like I was tired. I certainly didn't feel like a hero, and neither did anyone with me, but the fact that some little kid, perhaps in another part of the country, was thinking about us—and looked up to us—hit me hard. For the first time in days, something was breaking through the wall, causing me to feel something. And I couldn't believe it, it was a Happy Meal, and a homemade card from some five-year-old kid that I never met, that broke through and made me feel like a human being again.

*   *   *

For the first two months we worked fourteen to fifteen hours a day, seven days a week, and in whatever free time we had, we went to cop funerals, sometimes two a day. Finally I got a weekend off, so I took my wife down to Ocean City, Maryland, just to get her away from the city for a little while. She needed to get away just as much as I did. I needed to smell some fresh air, and the ocean seemed like a good place to do it. When I got back it was Monday morning, November 12, and I was trying to restore some normalcy back into my squad's routine. I was only in the office for about an hour when we heard on the radio that a jetliner had crashed out in the Rockaways—it was American Airlines Flight 587. Within minutes I got everybody together, and the next thing I know we're racing, lights and siren—again—out to the crash site.

On the way out there all I could think of was terrorism, what the fuck else could it be? What are the chances it could be anything else? But it wasn't, it was an accident. And again, there was no police work to be done, except to process the remains. Because Bellevue morgue was geared up for a big event, all the bodies came to us, and in the next couple of days we processed what was left of the two hundred and sixty-five people who perished.

It might seem hard to believe, but for me, and a lot of the guys I was with, that time in the morgue was worse than 9/11. I didn't think anything could be worse than what we had just been through, but this was it. This time, most of the people I saw were intact—with faces to look into—and there were small children.

I remember the one night I was there, all night long we carried body bag after body bag into the morgue—the refrigerated truck was filled with them. Inside it was like an assembly line of death, everywhere you looked there were bodies lying on gurneys, waiting for their turn to be processed and then returned back outside to another refrigerated truck. I was dressed head to toe in scrubs with thick rubber gloves on, trying not to get the leaking body fluids on me, and again deep down inside, I was numb—just concentrating on keeping the line moving, and getting the job done. My trusty wall was doing its best to keep me a safe distance mentally from what I was doing, but in the middle of all this, something kicked me in the gut and snapped me back to reality. Outside, after unloading another bag from the refrigerated truck, I realized someone was standing behind me. When I turned around I saw there were two people, a man and a woman, and they had Bibles in their hands. They were from the Salvation Army, and they were silently praying over the bag I had just unceremoniously placed onto a gurney. I think maybe it was God's way of reminding me that there were people in those bags.

*　　*　　*

After about six months, the recovery was winding down—for us anyway—and it was time to get back to crime fighting. There were still fifty-two hard-core assholes out on the street who needed to be locked up, and we hadn't forgotten about them. Operation Gladiator was back on. It wasn't the big spectacular finale I had originally envisioned, everything seemed small and insignificant compared to what we had been through, but we got all of our subjects, and the case was a big success. Afterward crime dropped off dramatically in that neighborhood, and in the end that's all you can hope for. We don't do things for pats on the back, we do them because they need to be done. Because it's our job.

And not long after that, another feeling was bubbling up deep down inside me, and I couldn't stop it. It was telling me it was time to retire.

14

End of Tour

It was Saturday night, and I was halfway through a 6:00 p.m. to 2:00 a.m. tour. My plan for this evening was to do absolutely nothing—zero—and so far things were going according to plan. Most nights when I'm out with my squad, we're looking for collars, but not tonight. This was the last time I would ever strap on a gun, pin on a shield, and walk down the street as a New York City cop. That's because Tuesday morning I was going to walk into police headquarters, turn in my gun and shield, and walk out a civilian. I was retiring.

We had parked the car on the corner of West Forty-Sixth Street and Broadway—my favorite coffee spot. As usual we were in plainclothes driving a rental car, so to the thousands of people passing by, we were anonymous. Just like two shepherds, we were guarding the flock, and keeping an eye out for the wolves. I sat there quiet and empty inside, alone in my thoughts, watching the world go by, while I tried to figure out where I fit in the cosmos. It seems like a lot to contemplate, but at a time like this, a guy starts to think about where he's been, where he's going, and what the fuck it all means. I wasn't sad, but I wasn't happy either. I felt about this the way I felt about a lot of other things lately: numb.

The detective I had working with me tonight was my old anti-crime partner from fifteen years earlier, back at the Sixth Precinct. The thing about partners is, you become more than just friends. When you place your life in another man's hands, there is a bond that develops, and it never goes away. Over the years I've had several, and when I refer to them I hardly ever use the word *friend*, because *partner* has a deeper, more profound meaning. He was a big, thick, tough, football player type, and I always felt safe working with him. I always knew that no matter what happened, we could handle it, and I was going home in one piece, give or take a few bumps and bruises. It seemed appropriate to have him with me on my last night.

The only physical activity I wanted to engage in tonight was to shake a few hands and tell people, "If I never see you again, have a nice life." I had a couple of my guys out running around looking for collars, and I told them if they needed me, just call. They understood what that meant. I was looking for a nice, quiet, easy night. I wanted to enjoy my last few moments of police life.

Retiring from the police department is kind of like jumping off a diving board, there's no turning back. Not too many guys leave and then return, mostly because they don't want you back. At the time the NYPD had about thirty-eight thousand cops, and whether you liked it or not, you were just a number to them. There's an old saying, "You love the job—but the job doesn't love you." Somewhere out there was a young kid waiting and dreaming about going into the next academy class, just like I did, and just like it had since the NYPD first started, the cycle from old to new would continue. Since the Dutch first settled New York a few hundred years ago, and the first policeman, then called the night watchman, patrolled the streets, there has been a proud tradition that continues today. And I was honored to be part of it, because I felt like I belonged to something special. But my days as the night watchman were about to end.

I had some doubts about pulling the plug, everyone does, but the one thing I was sure about was that I was tired. My entire career I worked in busy squads, did all kinds of crazy hours, and was involved in more collars and capers than I could possibly count. Numerically I was still a young man, but when I looked in the mirror, I saw a beat-up old punching bag staring back at me. I wasn't a burnout, but I was numb, right down to the core. When I told people I was leaving they were kind of surprised. Some figured they would have had to put dynamite under my chair and blast me out.

I always enjoyed the job and wouldn't trade in a minute of it, but the past twenty years had taken its toll on me.

Everybody knows when it's time to go, when you realize you're finished, and for me, I remember the exact moment, right down to the very second. I was sitting in my office with my feet up on the desk, struggling to stay awake, and trying to convince myself that the four hours of sleep I got the previous night was plenty. That was when one of my detectives came in and told me he got a tip from a CI (confidential informant) that a guy we were looking for on a homicide might be hanging out up in Yonkers. We had been looking for this perp for months, but nothing. The guy was a Mexican immigrant with no roots or ties to anybody or anything, so he had just picked up and vanished on us. He supported himself as a day laborer, and the CI said we might find him hanging out on this one particular corner early in the morning looking for work. My detective wanted me to do a stakeout with him and see if we could scoop this guy up. The info wasn't rock solid, but it was something that would usually get my blood going. But when my adrenaline didn't start pumping and there was no tingle in my ball bag, I knew the time had come. This perp had stabbed a guy to death in front of his pregnant wife, and if I couldn't get excited about that anymore, I was finished. I was never the type of guy who would stick around and just take up space. Cop life had stopped being fun for me, and I needed to move on, and let someone else do the job.

I was never an "inside" kind of guy. I probably could have gotten myself a job pushing papers around, wearing a suit, and trying to act important, but that wasn't me. I was happiest out in the street making collars. I loved the sound handcuffs make when you click them on some bad guy's wrists. I loved putting him in the cell, and the sound the heavy steel door makes when you slam it shut. The sounds of justice in action. There's no better feeling than taking some robber, rapist, drug dealer, murderer—you name it—off the streets. And I loved the sleepy ride home in the wee hours of the morning after making a nice collar and working all night, knowing that I was doing something honorable in this world.

Leaving the police department wasn't easy, and I was taking a bit of a chance because I didn't have another job to go to. I only knew that I wanted, or maybe needed, a change. I wanted to see what else life had to offer. The world is a big place with a lot of opportunities, and just like Christopher Columbus, I knew I would never get to see the other shore if I didn't lose sight of this one. I had saved up some money, so I could take a little time off, recharge my batteries, and contemplate the universe. When people would ask me what I was planning on doing, the best I could come up with was I wanted to live life in the slow lane for a while. I was going to drink beer, go fishing, and maybe stare at a wall. My brain was a little fried, and that was the best answer I could come up with. Tomorrow was the Super Bowl, and the only thing on my "to do" list was hang out with some friends and watch the game. After that my schedule was wide open.

Normally I can sit in Times Square all night long. I enjoy watching the world go by, especially the girls, but tonight I was in a sort of melancholy haze, so we decided to go for a ride. I called my other teams and asked if they were okay. They told me they were fine, no collars yet, and if they needed me they would reach out. They told me to relax and enjoy my last night.

We drove around Midtown for a while, occasionally stopping so I could jump out to shake a few hands and say good-bye. I kept looking at the clock on the dashboard, watching the minutes tick down till I was EOT (end of tour) for the last time. It was like waiting for the ball to drop on New Year's Eve. As we turned another corner and cruised down another crowded street, my melancholy haze was suddenly interrupted by the sound of a woman screaming for help. We raced down the block toward the screams, and that's when I spotted two guys lying on the ground fighting. It was a brawl, with one dude on top of the other, throwing punches and doing his best to pound the shit out of the guy on the bottom. Hovering over them was the woman, waving her purse around in the air and screaming at the top of her lungs for someone to come and stop the madness. My first thought was this might be a robbery gone bad.

Maybe the guy on the bottom tried to steal the woman's purse, and the guy on top—possibly her husband or boyfriend—tried to stop him.

We jumped out of the car with shields hanging around our necks, yelling "police," and hoping that would settle things down, but they didn't. The punches kept flying and the screaming continued. I ran over and grabbed the guy on top, yanked him to his feet, and threw him on the wall while Les did the same with the other guy. And as soon as we did that, the woman stopped screaming for help, and instead started screaming, "They're brothers, they're brothers." That wasn't exactly the explanation I was expecting, and my robbery theory quickly went out the window.

After splitting them up and tossing them for weapons (there were none), I asked the woman what was going on. She seemed like the levelheaded one from this trio, so I figured I could get some straight answers out of her. She had finally stopped screaming long enough to tell me that the guy on top was her husband, and the one on the bottom was his brother. She tried convincing me that everything was okay, and there was no need for the police. Despite our first impression, they really were one big happy family. She explained to me that they were out drinking, having a good time, when the brothers got into a heated argument over who made the most money, and soon the verbal argument turned into a fistfight. She seemed reasonable enough, and it all made perfect sense, except for the happy family part. I figured there must be some deep-rooted childhood issues going on here that I didn't really give a rat's ass about. I just wanted them to take their stupidity off the street, so it wouldn't be my problem anymore.

The fight looked and sounded worse than it was, no more than some ripped shirts and scraped knuckles, nothing serious. I had only a few hours to go before going EOT, and I had no intention of making a collar, especially two drunken asshole brothers. Everything seemed to calm down. The screaming had stopped, the fighting ceased, so there was no reason to take this any further. I was anxious to get back to my melancholy haze and contemplation of my place in the cosmos, so in my best "don't fuck with me" tone of voice, I told them to knock the stupid shit off and start walking, or they were going to spend the night in jail. I was lying about the going-to-jail part, but nobody knew it but me.

The three of them started walking while me and my partner headed back to the car. Mission accomplished—or so I thought. As I got back in the car I watched the two brothers shuffle up the block, walking side by side, but before I had a chance to close the door, the guy who had been on top hauled off and sucker punched his brother right in the face. Here we go: round two.

Now I was pissed. All I wanted to do was be left alone and enjoy my last few minutes on the job in peace, but I can't keep these two overachieving idiots from beating the crap out of each other over who has the better job. I ran out of the car, grabbed the aggressor, threw him back on the wall, and yelled, "What the fuck did I tell you?"

When I got right up into his face, that's when I realized how much taller and bigger than me he was. Both brothers had more than a few inches on me and quite a few pounds. Plus they were about half my age. I was old enough to be their father.

Normally, out in the street, I don't give anyone more than one warning. If you're too stupid to take advantage of the one chance I gave you to leave, then you deserve to go to jail for the night. But tonight I really just wanted these two morons to go away. I stood there looking up at the guy with the anger management and childhood issues and yelled at him to stop his stupidity or he was going to jail. Again I was lying. That's when he looked down at me and screamed in this drunken crazy voice, "FUCK YOU!"

And with that, he hauled off and threw a big, drunken round-house punch at me. It happened pretty fast, and caught me by surprise, but I saw it coming and was able to duck a little, so the punch hit me on the top of my head. The force of it drove me back a little and I saw a few stars from the impact, but it was not enough to really hurt me.

Drunks do stupid things all the time—it's a big part of police work—but punching a cop in the head is a big no-no. Now it was my turn, and the little voice in my head was saying, "Fuck me? No, fuck you!" What happened next was a blur, so fast it was over in about one second. He was drunk, and his punch was slow and sloppy, but mine were fast and to the point. I threw a quick left jab, then I followed it up with a short right that caught him square on the chin. In twenty years of police work it was one of the best punches I ever threw. The next thing I knew his head snapped back, his eyes rolled, his knees buckled, and he hit the sidewalk like a sack of beer-soaked laundry. He was out cold. I don't remember hitting him that hard, but I caught him right on the sweet spot, and the lights went out before he even hit the ground.

The guy was a lot bigger than me, and when I saw him lying on the sidewalk, the first thought that entered my head was, I better get this guy cuffed, because when he wakes up, he's gonna be pissed. I jumped on him and managed to get a handcuff on one wrist, and that's when out of nowhere somebody jumped on my back and started clawing at me. It was the previously levelheaded wife, and now she's screaming again, this time wanting me to leave her poor hubby alone. Right then the husband wakes up and he starts fighting with me again. With one hand I have him by the throat trying to hold him on the ground, and with the other hand I have the wife by the throat trying to keep her off me. This is un-fucking-believable! All I want to do is go back to my melancholy haze, maybe plan a fishing trip, but no such luck.

I needed to get the husband cuffed, and I needed to do it quick. The guy had some muscle on him—he obviously spent some time in the gym—and if I had to start wrestling with him on the ground it was going to be a problem. I had surprised him with those two quick punches, but the second time around might not be so easy. Just then I saw this big meaty fist come out of nowhere and grab the wife by the back of the neck and yank her off me. The next thing she knew, she was flying through the air and ended up face-first against the wall. It was my partner. I had been busy mixing it up with the first guy and couldn't see him, but I knew Les was there covering my back. He always did. He had been holding the second guy on the wall, keeping him out of the fight, and now he had both him and the wife wrapped up in a bear hug, keeping them off me. With her off me I got back to business with the hubby. I got him cuffed, and the fight was over almost as quick as it started. But when I rolled him over I could see blood dripping out the back of his head. He had whacked it on the sidewalk when he hit the ground and now had a nasty gash. I couldn't fucking believe it. From a relaxing melancholy haze to trading punches with some drunken moron when you least expect it. But that's what police work is all about.

We brought the caper into the station house and had EMS respond so they could bandage up my perp. That's when I called my other teams and told them I needed somebody to take a collar. But before they took it, I warned them that I had given the perp a "Brooklyn party hat." That's what we call it when a guy gets his head wrapped up in gauze because he got it busted after a fun night on the town. I assured them that I was one hundred percent legit in doing what I did, and I wasn't dropping a bag of shit on their laps. They all got a good laugh out of me getting into a brawl on my last night.

In a real street fight there's no time to get ready and limber up, things happen fast. So in addition to the bump on my head, I pulled a muscle in my shoulder. I don't like going to the ER because of some bumps and bruises, but because we were charging the perp with assault on me, my injuries had to be documented. As Les and I were sitting in the emergency room at St. Vincent's Hospital, we too couldn't help but laugh. All I wanted for my last tour on patrol was a nice easy night, but police work is the most unpredictable job in the world. It's not over till it's over!

Later, when I signed out EOT for the last time, and walked out of the squad room never to return, I couldn't help but smile. Twenty years earlier, on my first day on patrol, I chased down a guy and collared him for an armed robbery. And now, on my last day on patrol, I was putting handcuffs on somebody again. Not too many cops can say they made a collar on their first and last days, but shit happens out in the street. God never wanted me to be an astronaut, or a doctor, or a lawyer. He put me on this earth to be a cop. And from the first day to the last, I did my job.

The next day was Super Bowl Sunday. The neighbors were having a party, and I promised I would come by. Because it was my first day of retirement, and because I had had a rough night, I got the big fluffy recliner right in front of the TV. By now my shoulder was starting to really stiffen up and hurt a bit. I had won that fight last night with a guy half my age with two quick, decisive punches, but the bumps and bruises made me realize I was getting too old for this stupid shit.

I wanted to enjoy the game, so I popped the painkiller and muscle relaxer the ER doctor had given me and washed them down with a sip of beer. The next thing I know, it's lights-out. They went out faster than they did for my perp when I popped him on the chin. When I woke up about five hours later, I was still sitting in that big fluffy recliner, with that first bottle of beer somehow still cradled in my limp, groggy fingers. When I looked around, everybody was mostly gone, and the party was over. I was surrounded by empty red plastic cups and half-eaten bowls of chips and pretzels. And just like that, in what seemed like the blink of an eye, the game was over. The party was over. And my life of adventure as a New York City cop was over.

Acknowledgments

To my circle of advisers, who took the time to read my stories and lovingly encouraged me to shut up and keep on writing: Maru, Karen, Elaine, Donna, Mariam, Gabriel, Katie, and Brian.

To my editor and agent: Gerald Howard and Jeff Silberman. Two guys who took a chance on some voice they heard on the radio.

To Kest, my buddy since the second grade. He would call at the most opportune times, usually when I was doubting myself, and quote Henry David Thoreau, "Go confidently in the direction of your dreams and live the life you have always imagined."

To the men and women of the NYPD who I worked with—there are too many to mention—thanks for the memories.

And to my mother-in-law, Susy, because if I don't mention her, I'll never hear the end of it!